Gravity as a consequence of shape

Gravity

as a consequence of shape

ALLEN FISHER

REALITY STREET

Published by
REALITY STREET EDITIONS
63 All Saints Street, Hastings, East Sussex TN34 3BN
www.realitystreet.co.uk

First published 2016

Front cover image from a painting by the author
Back cover author photo by Paige Mitchell
Typesetting and book design by Ken Edwards

A catalogue record for this book is available from the British Library

ISBN: 978-1-874400-72-1

Contents

Entanglement and Leans

Preface to *Gravity as a consequence of shape*

I reflect on the phrase that provides the title *Gravity as a consequence of shape* and recall a conceptual difficulty, that the substance of the intention should be *Gravity as a consequence of form*. But form does not work in terms of its line sound, and in any case the title is too long to snap this head with comprehension. It can be a challenge to be treated with care and who can say that it can occur in so many instances or processes where the road rubble planes out for a moment and encourages a trip at an unplanned-for energy moment. Humankind may be particles of curiosity in wonder in laughter in poverty, but it needs modesty to realise that to meaningfully consider the universe must be rhetorical. What continues to remain a possibility is the act of consciousness responsible for the reduction of the wave packet. The best time to plant is coextensive with the spaces for each plant. Once the incompleteness of the wave-function description is suspected, it can be conjectured that the seemingly random statistical fluctuations are determined by the extra 'hidden' variables because at this stage humankind can only conjecture its existence and certainly cannot control that. It is the indispensability, and above all the shiftiness, of a division between the 'quantum system' and the 'classical', that is the big surprise of human existence. This existence becomes a necessary ambiguity in a physical politics, if only at a level of accuracy and completeness beyond any required in practice. All the floristic evidence suggests that the first five hundred years of the second millennium in Britain were spent clinging on to the detritus left over from the earlier occupations and the wreckage of the raids. It requires everyone's concentrated efforts to cultivate and grow crops, a real community involvement in survival. The planet has already exceeded safe biogeochemical flows in the form of nitrogen, and biospheric integrity has gone. Humankind plans to take control of land-system change and climate change contemporary with the shapes of ozone and freshwater depletion. The mathematician and the technologist stand back and refresh their glasses and reassess their proprioceptive engagement. When the prevalent and difficult call becomes get out of here now, the call to tune the piano becomes obscure.

Gravity as a consequence of shape brings together the sequence of poems published in three books, *Gravity, Entanglement* and *Leans*. The sequence developed from iterations and jumps in an interim between the serial publication of *Unpolished Mirrors* to conclude *PLACE* in 1981 and the writing of *Ideas on the culture dreamed of* in 1982; that is to say after an overlapping strand of different attentions and events that culminated in the books *Defamiliarising________**, *Bending Windows, Executive Ease, Stepping out* and *went to new*.

The sequence of poems in *Gravity as a consequence of shape* continues to use the jazz dance titles developed in *Ideas on the culture dreamed of*; the other texts in that book have been separated from this volume for expediency and appear, like the original, as a separate publication. ZIP, the last poem in the sequence, is only available as a sound performance treated in 2005, London, with the composer John Wall and available on John Wall's site: http://utterpsalm.blogspot.co.uk, on Pennsound: http://writing.upenn.edu/pennsound/x/Fisher.php, as well as on my own: www.allenfisher.co.uk

Allen Fisher, November 2015

Resources

J.S. Bell. *Speakable and unspeakable in quantum mechanics*, Cambridge University Press, 1993.

Maggie Campbell-Culver. *The Origin of Plants. The people and plants that have shaped Britain's green history since the year 1000*, Random House, 2001.

Richard P. Feynman. *The Meaning of it all. Thoughts of a Citizen-Scientist*, Perseus Books, 1998.

Stockholm Resilience Centre. Planetary Boundaries Research, http://www.stockholmresilience.org/21/research/research-programmes/planetary-boundaries/planetary-boundaries-data.html accessed 27 November 2015.

Tony Winch. *Growing Food. A Guide to Food Production*, Clouds Books, Herefordshire, 2014.

Preface to *Brixton Fractals*, 1985

Fractals have been known since before the turn of the century. The noun was invented by Benoit Mandelbröt in 1975 and has come to mean an extremely irregular action, broken design, or fragmented object. Brixton is that part of southwest London extending south/north geohistographically from its prison and windmill down through the high road to the police station on one axis, and from the employment exchange in Coldharbour through the market to the Sunlight Laundry factory east/west on another.

Brixton Fractals provides a technique of memory and perception analysis. It can be used to sharpen out-of-focus photographs; to make maps of the radio sky; to generate images from human energy; to calculate spectra; to reconstruct densities; to provide probability factors from local depression climates. It becomes applicable to read- ing; to estimate a vector of survival from seriously incomplete or hidden data, and select the different structures needed. It can provide a participatory invention different from that which most persists.

These poems represent some of the most difficult yet rewarding bungalows in the entire exhibition. I am most wonderful to be able to say that their cultivation of plurivocity again brings back to the language all its capacity of meaningfulness. Never mind what others think, I think you're beautiful. The work is strongly influenced by itself, rather than by what arrives and is outside of it, by its need of poetry, its indeterminacy, its distrust of the effectiveness of education. The first thing to be said is that it preserves the width, because the rotten danger in present-day living is a kind of reduction of language to communication to manipulate things, or can become merely instrumental to prevent going in many directions.

Imagination and action. My knowledge of the world exists validly only in the moment when I am transforming it. In this moment, in action, the imagination functions, unblocks passivity, refuses an overview. Discontinuities, wave breaks, cell divisions, collapsed struc- tures, boundaries between tissue kinds: where inner workings are unknown, the only reliable participations are imaginative. The complex of state and control variables. The number of configurations depends on the latter: properties typical of cusp catastrophes: sudden jumps, hysteresis, divergence, inaccessibility. Boiling waters phase change where the potential is the same as condensing steam. Random motion of particles in phase space allows a process to find a minimum potential. What is this all about ? It's a matter of rage and fear, where the moving grass or built suburbia frontier is a wave prison; where depth perception reverses; caged flight. With ambiguous vases it's as if part of the brain is unable to reach a firm conclusion and passes alternatives along for a decision on other grounds. The goblet-and-face contour moves as it forms in your seeing.

A bibliography has been added as a resource in the back of the book, and has been kept as simple as possible to emphasise some of the indirect perception involved in making *Brixton Fractals.* This is not intended as an itinerary for suggested further reading, or a listing to give authority to the text. It is to thank those who have taken part in the perception and memory that have made the text, and to keep open the opportunity to hear them. I have cross-referenced the poems with the bibliography, but because the poems in *Brixton Fractals* take part in interference and transformation patterns with each other, separating the Resources into twelve poem-groups appeared to be unrewarding.

The chronology of the poems is generally alphabetically indicated. I wrote 'African Boog' first, and 'Boogie Woogie' was already drafted for the Second Set of *Gravity as a consequence of shape* before publication of the First Set, *Brixton Fractals.* In between times the ordering shuffles a little. The titles derive directly from the itineraries of dances in my *Ideas on the culture dreamed of.*

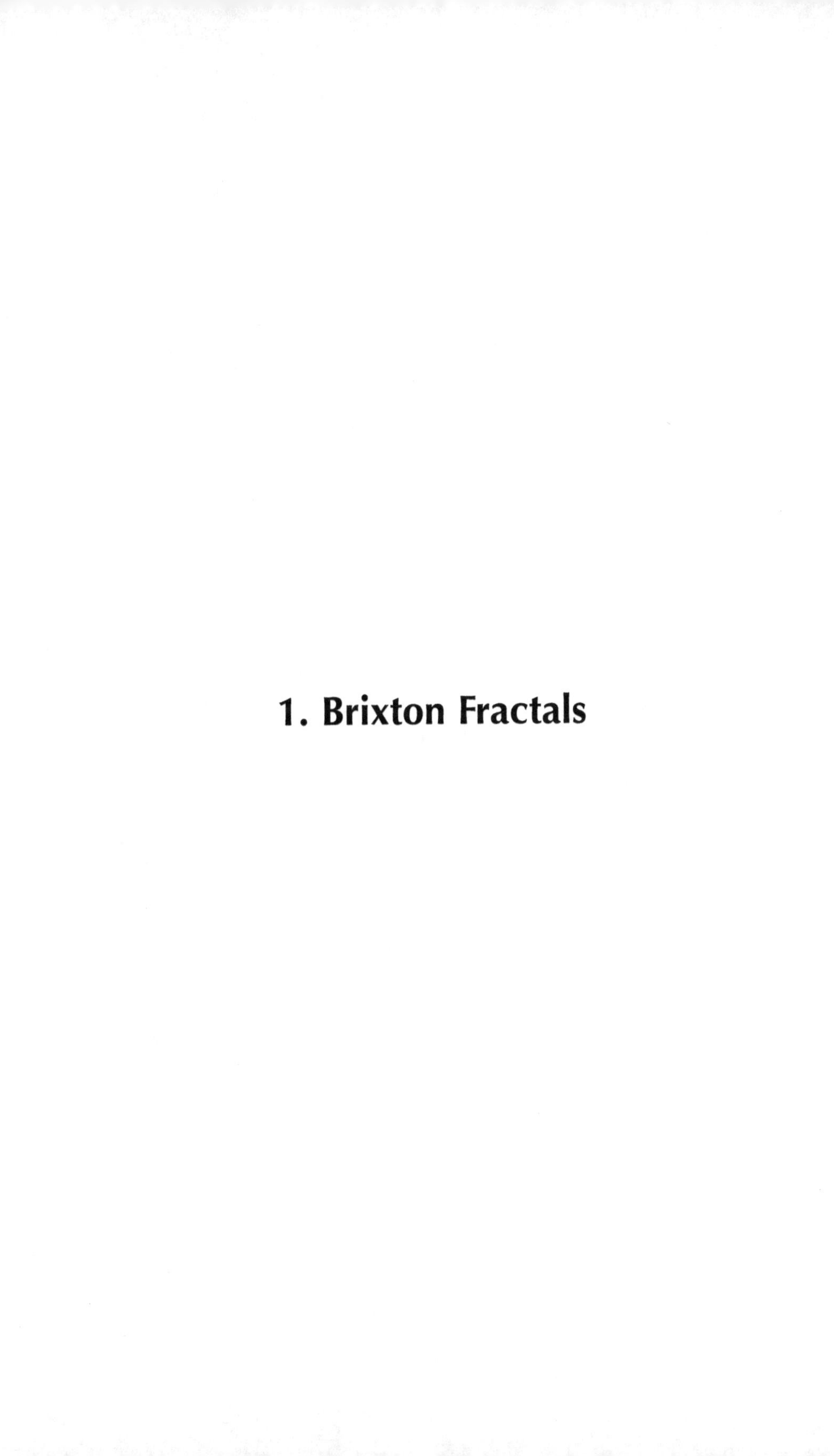

1. Brixton Fractals

Banda

Took chances in London traffic
where the culture breaks
tone colours burn from exhaustion
emphasised by wind,
looking ahead for sudden tail lights
a vehicle changes
lanes into your path and birds,
over the rail bridge, seem purple.
A mathematician at the turn of the century
works out invariant notions in a garden
every so often climbs a bike,
makes a figure eight around
rose beds to help concentration,
then returns to the blackboard.
The schemers dreamed a finite language
where innocence became post experiential
believing the measurable, ultra-violet from a lamp,
isolated sunlight curvature
made false language what can be done
to separate
from perception.
In a dream apparently without volition
a car burning and
watch myself there
sealed-in beneath a smog dome
uncertain what to try for next.

Midnight: a solo of the Nightingale. Great silence.
Open a gate
against hinged pressure of rust,
white pigment to denote reflected light.
Singularity burgled up the drainpipe,
a busy rush pursued tenderness at its slats
padlocked into pastoral quicksilver.
"If one of my students should one day rear children
in a better way
Surround myself in music, that is physically
forget the dream as a move towards preventing
objectification of vision.
Legal power, completion, smothering,
on the shelf flashpowder and a can.

Practice to assist improvisation
holds onto the pattern of railings
a super-structure of sound-curve symmetry
recognised, and examined, by autodidacts.
A bunch of type in my palm
populates fixed compartments.

Exasperation from a lack of clarity
sighs towards singular objectives
trapped into them
without realising
the peripheral fleets
glanced at knowingly
as an indefinite refusal
of euphony,
or until the variety gets coded
into an analytic container
dropped from a winch onto the quay
When the road shifted
one part lowered
then pushed out a halting arm
over the ridge
carrying a reflex camera
to record the wonderful.
A recollection of a hill so far from London
I burnt lying
in a dream for thirty minutes
and woke in a grove of oranges
smelling of eucalyptus.
The up and down different to anyone
gravity
or opposes anthropologists of science.
It took six minutes for the exercise
and the lot was cordoned off,
Water Lane
to Brixton Oval,
our future in the air
over the walkway busted polystyrene
scattered,
a sonata for piano and jetplane,
cooperatively struct,
now a mount of cars piled behind a subsiding dyke.

4 a.m. the Hedge Sparrow, shriek of the Hoopoe,

the Song Thrush on trumpet,
a large ball rolls by
hits the sentry box
and the road opens.
On one side a ley line buckles
into the wall of 'The George',
in the machine a solenoid blows
a rush of green vans and police weapons
send the needles into peak
and damage the Dolby.
Your freckles expand and you blush,
a black clock and two batteries,
my fingers tingle to let the blood back
we roll over
temporal inversions or points of view
burn the air,
and memory, slatted into alternations,
begins to rely on the instrument panel
as well as the force
felt in the chest
as speaker loudness increases.
The explanation of the universe gets
considered as shared awareness and truth
a bucket with a hole in it slops suds over
the top of a tiled floor
until we switch it off.

Two electricity lines, three gas mains,
carry enough energy across the walkway
for two sets of loudspeakers
face each other across the
dancing
visitors at an island of science
see the primitives at work
describe the utility of pilot lights.
The furniture in the room appears to be stationary.
I am half sick of shadows
under pressure of personal feelings
a poet crushes a carton marked 'Shredded Wheat'
in a corn field,
calls it a poem.
Laid out on the lawn
exhausted
the burden of personality lost

in untimed contemplation
independent of unified law
uses signs for other
than what they signify
by filling navel with powder
and exhaling a cough.
I suppose it is in me and coming out.
The quantum leap between some lines
so wide
it hurts.

The shelf falls from the balcony
shatters,
erupted aluminium silicon
scratches airliner windows.
Two water mains, three petrol pipelines,
a large sewer
in the walkway,
where a tree has broken paving,
build a fire
and get the kettle started.
"The fact is,
when ole bill came along,
we brassed him up."
You know, all I wanted was to recover
without retrenching.
The pipes don't appear to be busted
Just keep it open
I'll go down and see if it comes through.
Telephone wires, and a mile of new road
cross purchased fields
Listen to the echo of
wings' fizz
before we get to them
and resistance
in the reduction to utility
and functions.
Fraught, but underneath it
resistance without armour
as if that were possible,
following a wire stretched across the page
until pen drops off the right edge,
and face
the red background

in the morning
noting where it came forward
in front of a glass bottle
to restate the four-colour problem
broke it there by facing it
The yellow and black road bar
lifts to an angle congruent
to the prison roof.
Bird carpets in the hay
wood. Noon:
great silence
haywire.

Began to decide how to perceive
Dreamed once of where we were going
too precise about direction
said, That's the way to the city, but
I wouldn't start from here, if
I were you
knowing what could be meant in the clang shack
bolted upright
just before the bell came
steel wheels on steel rails
run through the lounge.
It's the city alright
felt in the tropai of directions
the joy and worry in a traveller's back
back from market with vegetables
incapable of doing harm
Leaning the bar into a distribution curve
at the chicken jerk chally
across from the betting shop
or as if based on notions of we have
been here before
or another says that makes such a perfect match
you could use 'em as bookends.
Carried the system down Coldharbour
on the right shoulder
two circular speakers
plate the inner ear just
passing through
your living space
moving with a deliberation
seldom found in poetry.

It happens quickly not as you might expect
takes a long time moving towards
its suddenness and when it does quicken
it surprises. Even so, as I say it,
it has gone and a more deliberate
or expected mode takes form,
changing the minimally real at once into
a memory
chequered in a rebound
cage labelled 'Development'
and unattended box of timed light
marked 'Don't Touch' or 'Volume Control'
as a measure of decay patterns
the Bellman recedes down the walkway
catches my eye
with a Brasso glint
carries a refrigerator on his back
shouting "Ayeyay"
until someone, I think it was Edna,
calls with a camera, "Hey boy, here !"
Gradually I predict the possible physically
and the probabilities that this
will occur. I stand in the walkway
with tracts on good and bad
tearing them
at once excited by the energy
of doing so and recall
the situation
brings the distance involved alive.

Silence : Brutal punctuation of morning:
a Warbler explodes for the last time
an intuitive doubt
passes through the window
regarding the rest mass of photons
at once discarded
at zero.
Enthusiasm sighs
and fear forms in each lachrymal valley.
Blake leans back from his window
down onto the page
eyes partially blind from flowing
writes vigorously across the faces
drawn there, saying

the tear is an intellectual thing,
crossing it out
knowing the trial pended
and anger disrupts thought
momentarily
in a cloud shift, his wrath
blazes reciprocally
stands at his door looking out
into a bright day break
the sirens have stopped
in the near distance a blue spark
leaves the prison roof
an inescapable sadness, thought of
as reflections onto the window
call it condensation
the glass breaks.
I get a dust pan and brush.
The light lengthens and the
utility of cleaning up
sends a shiver into me
it must be getting winter
I begin to cry quietly inside
the strengthening chill
of alternations
Carvings of flowers on a sword blade
catch the spark
I thought I had imagined
then realised
the sword was polyethylene
and the kid hadn't
taken off the tag
spelling out the price of it all.

There was some dancing
but what's really going down
in this male age praised by noodles
an innocent obsession with turning lecterns
coded in digits.
A firelighter in a screwtop can.
The Fireman calls in for the situation report
concentrated in depth of an advance
The unliquidated resistance remains
blank-screened in the blast.
Yesterday I met a man who wasn't a misogynist

felt a necessity
to move into a new mode of life.
The sun energises autonomous
care with weather
and anamnesis
breaks a trend of cut-off
through history. But what else goes,
It is a lovely morning
light adds shadows
The Fireman's report abends the actual
spins in the sky frame
turn from the strictly utile
for aid duplexed
with how things were once better
over the hill
The freedom to act socially now
measured on a breadboard.
Bike boys come down the walkway
rear their burners
almost together on back wheels
at entrance to a workers' council.
She takes a torch into dark room
and light pencils scratches onto the box
circumvents the mechanical
description.
Swept me off my feet,
A policy of time
in a carpet factory operated by
each person each free
moment the space to stretch.
Scratch marks when the pen ran out of ink
still on the manuscript
something potent resides on its validity
unbroken
tradition but
let's actually find out, you and I,
what that can become
with another
arrangement.
I atomise a liquid into my hand
from my breath
it adheres into an uneven smudge
read as it changes colour
the background moves

through it
selectively imprints a warmth.
Thought it might be self-love
flattered by envy until
she saw a different hand there
crumble soil around a new catalpa
a folded sign posted to it,
what it means to forget what has past.
A range of sprays from the lid
sweetens the casserole
He added another pepper then chopped in some basil
The sign unfurled as my head touched
the pillow
spread my perception to speak.

The Bellman and Fireman meet at 'The Windmill'
exchange notes on salvage.
They are who they are
yet remind me of what has gone.
She bathes in rain water at last clean
for the first time in decades
A sign calls me backwards
'Beware. Society Ruled By Men'
The urge to destroy is not only a creative urge,
in the distance a man sings
accompanied by his own hands and feet it
brings sighs of enjoyment.
An apple stew secretes into it,
smells of cinnamon, cloves and nutmeg.
I rub my cells in them
coaxed by such overwhelms I somersault into a grocers
a flurry of wings cross the enlarger box as it flashes
three balls hit the railing complex
the sounds.
If the rebuilt city is resistant
it opens to those who strengthens it welcomes
the travellers on the ways to themselves
Now where are we . . .
I cut open an apple and its wasp goes
hesitant body line made clearer by holding
the sound of skate boards and rollers
launch from a ramp and the joy
wet zings say it as wasps
fed from our bodies surround in changes of light

a dog in the other distance
It was as if the subject itself lost materiality
Bird carpets copied get copied
Value, meaning, determination repeat.
For fun she snaps a photo of the Bellman's cart,
reality and notions of poetic stress merge
simply doing more than two acts at once I cover
the bottom of a warmed pot with Assam.

Disturbing this silence
two chaffinches on two violins
in a biological lock watch
fixed by light chemistry in the eye.
The call of "Let me out," becomes a jig
along a cordon of police,
values from others, opinions, and
deliberately propelled into distance correction.
I am almost what I wish to live.
Outside in the walkway three kids play on wheels
One expects more respects for prospects
includes a desire to manage
A figure of eight with a müller to
slurry tempera on the glass.

Around the World

This gravitational song meted against displacement
The slow movement of holding you
By the lake, deep amid fir and silver poplar
Dream sleep's energetic function
During meditation each finger rayed in cactus spikes
Blake crossed out sweet desire, wrote iron wire
It was the discovery of human electromagnetism
made a sign, opened curtains, revealed the garden
Mouth perpendicular to mouth energised desire

All the weight and attraction that limits movement
A Mercury mix that replaces theft with eloquence
in the face of visitors' astonishment, experienced veritable bliss
A robust memory in the flares of lost and added synapses
So that the vines burst from my fingers

In the space of shape-time
We move our fingers and simultaneity becomes falsity
Sheltered by wall and hedge
Translucent superimposition several distinctions one
synapse And the garden becomes geodesic for a moment
An imitation tomb among the vegetables

"A mango tree under a dull cloth, stirs its tentacles
A rush of calcium through my nostrils

That the complex is Nature's climate.

Passed out in the dole queue from an overdose of guerrillas
satellite bang. satellite bang. hits the
negation of morning confidence and hope

Took a stopwatch into her mouth and spat
Reduces premiums to the political, to the sentence , ,
"and the simple at a discount

"the imitation stage has been passed
In a blue self-portrait the background continues the face
a gigantic plane tree
Given a part, consistent memory appropriates a whole
Flicks mercury in a meter rolls off a glove

Dealt out cards, silver-foiled dinners and cans
piece. pease. pierce. sleight of hand
Friendship as virtue   an inventive memory combines
varieties of inconsistent features
Take my hand, the silken tackle
Stored associations of the cellular net
Swell with the touches of flower-soft fingers
Rode shaking from the park on flat tyres.

claim of pastoral confidentiality
The return to copying pre-empted by cultivation
its enormous trunk
The net's avoidance of overload and too much overlap
Take this palm to your mouth and fill it with grapes
A Net of Golden twine many synapses
Semblance of worth, not substance

spawn of an entire lack of interest, but some surprise
The return to cultivation pre-empted by synthesis

enter, stage right, "the creative centre of civilization"
pieces of granite, broken and numbered, rejoined with cement
Its mighty branching and its equilibrium
Hard-wired to compensate against malnutrition and toxic
waste The danger of important words
In tears clothed, in a dream sleep's shed, avoid obsession
Humane Eyes over a blasted heath
hand holding a book, first finger inserted to hold position
piled granite on the lawn like an enormous potato

Imagination sown meter again then this place beat
In search of ways to reverse-learn junk city
the gravity of its preponderant boughs
Sighs damp down potentially parasitic memories
Mother and child constitutes a society
reservation or rather reticent in flak of rhetoric
Enterprises based on innocence   a pleasant sufficiency
Creative imprecision to emphasise flux of meaning

A future bright blocked by bricoles.

Strapped own earth underfoot to walk base without trespass
Took for exercise of virtue
O sprinkling the garden, to enliven the green!
Dream's random noise shorts-out unproductive activities
Ran out of faces so stopped action in film
A degree of benign limitation
Flummox then repose your wearied exercise

The gravity occasions gone petered against retrenchment
A hard task in truth I attempt
In my garden face lift modifying spine shape
Reverse-learning to modify cortex energetically
Floral dress hung from sculptured timber
Intellectual innocence in a pretence to value
Play area scattered bricks painting garden
Then the perceptions begin to repeat
The garden that should have bloomed once

Doubled oscillation preludes another chaos
Confidence beyond consciousness
And do not forget the shrubs
Dream's selection to enhance retention
public elects pinball physics
In the face of wonder experienced a kind of vertigo
Trapped in a cage then allowed to sing.

“Responsibility for the present state of the world
The terror of feeling that consciousness may be
functional   Where are the sentiments of my heart

Simply kissing, with you on the balcony
Into a world not entirely song
Lifted all the baskets *Even those without berrie*s
“the Paneubiotic Synthesis
muscle   neuronal excitability   energy generation

to complete harmony laid biggest lime full length in garden
The constantly actualised, shuddered chagrin
In the garden nothing but evergreens
Ungratified desire reminated each moment
Short silence followed by a thud.

Ballin' the Jack

1.

Compassion fatigue—
three loud whistles in quick succession
following a bright flash
hit head on foot bridge.
The strongest trees may survive
width of the flushing band,
a telephone fitted in the garden
on a poolside desk rubber plants.
A doily folded in his belt:
, bulb spot sixty watts, olive oil, honey,
functionally improved recall after sleep.
A moving bang came through the window
modulates permeability across blood-brain barrier
What is it?
a sucrose intake of less than 12 spoons a day.
Sequacious breed reactor
another Take ; melodic sweetness; on the prison roof;
indifferent to any importance of verbs
lunch-room physics applied to international relations.
Rain balls
the deconstruction of hope
a varied pattern of bangs experienced as waves:
erasure.
Continuous finger piano
wires over a plane
body colour over pencil with surface scratches
bale out soon.
Equalisation of accessibility beyond private taboo
topological dependence of plasma membrane.
The propeller larger than this flat
at the hub delusion; greed; hatred;
painted green.

2.

Painted blue
a couple in the yab-yum position
an umbrella spread with my knees flat.
Tropical independence of miasma frame
a muscular energy available to many:
dice gripped then thrown.
At a drive-in, set in curve of railway, an aircraft.
We had to cross the river on a two wire span.
Chopping waves
a dynamic construction
brightly painted fences.
In a given place, to say precisely what demanded
dances, with straps,
learnt from the physique requires interpersonal relativity
different from the posture of surdity,
strengthens muscles of the heart and rectum.
Sequentious freed enactor
three dessert-spoons of fibre offered as minimum breakfast
"What's that?"
modern relations of permanence cross-out with indefinities.
An orang-utan can throw in chaff snow
punctuates proven records with leaps:
, work light, ironing board, oligotoil, laundry,
adroit fingers in his impact
on the pool table stretching, potting.
Even with the keys to 'phones we cross the wires at nights,
one for your feet, the other for hands
strung through trees without insulation.
In the walkway a wig stand
rolling a bright flash
I could see the head in total darkness
a tiredness from exposure.

3.

Wired-up from explosion
didn't know until flash fired
what I had captured.
In the walkabout a mercantile stance
electric fence protecting track from slides
two tiers of chains.
Evening breezes weird moss, fires our sight.
A petal table stretching from the pot
dried fingers rub the thermostat.
, light work, bored ironing, olitory oil, money,
pumiced grooves and traces of hoping
meringues snowed in icing sugar.
Monolithic relations permutated across life lines.
Question identity and gender
enough salt from sufficient fresh produce
extremes of brevity ; a history of joy ; on the prism root;
preserved in the smack of reflections.
Indignant to the appearance of birds
built on the bowers of paradise
in the garden in front of a work hut
a mossy lawn with objects grouped by colour.
Standard configurations in coördinate transforms
noble lies
Ah, Wilderness! self-improvement anxiety,
on site of a torn sapling a twelve-year-old log.
A sharing of joy and sorrow
cleansed in acidic rain
a continued search for terminal Nature
the vegetable enemy of novelty.
Wung in poverty
an idea of feeling and perceiving the day
in grey ink, Beneath the white thorn lovely May.

4.

Parallelograms overlap his back's muscles
reopen a discussion of limits and vanishing ratios.
She crossed burnt grass to the windmill
over scaffolding and beneath it
read graffiti on play wall where
two kids work sand on dead lichen.
Everywhere homeless everywhere home
heads of watermelon and wood carved from same plant.
Travel literature; works of sex; life on mars;
a dreamer led out of confinement into servitude
works out relativistic perceptions, faints.
With a wad of bark she paints bower with fruit and charcoal
reorients work hut into a constant direction
expels a spitting intruder and repaints green with liverwort
jammed in the kiss of remembering
wears badge of lost innocence.
Activates presence by continual renewal
Questions each movement, each renewal.
In a Brixton queue stopped for lack of identification
harangues slowed through a tannoy
Hands worn hard with broom handling,
scrub pavement, paint railings, polish steps,
dread fingers dub in laundromat.
A lily pond stagnant from dead bacteria,
even freezes, bone welts, frost mires, her plight
two tears of rain.
Fenced in, a society without engagement
now the walkway a gang with clubs
sirens rising falling.
O my Lover and my Friend,
a future blight brocade.

African Twist

"I was an innocent sort of child 1.
a pluralistic perception of time
marked by experienced space
just drives me wild
a small cornfield beyond the garden fence
low palm trees a huge expanse of bush
here and there the shape of a baobab
four broken bricks staggered into two
rows for a game
turned to look at the sign over the door, simply to remember
conversations with Gris
a background pulled over the plane of the foreground
reorganising as other
here again
by the light of a petroleum lantern
wondering if the crop will be any good
"What's wrong with our life ? We go fishing and to our garden
agents retire to consulting firms to
specialize in political risk

fast forward on pink noise

events require you, results inform you,
spatial lies interpolate frisket.
"the sign over the gate: 2.
Do what you want
the desire to organise one's hatred
with the greatest possible tactical intelligence
Gibbons' carving of Eden under Blake's font
here and there the tall shape
a huge expanse
beyond the garden
a steel tubular frame flat about
a tree, it must have been thrown right
over the top
a radical lack of value, a deliberate push and pull

as if free

asked if there was a calendar, shrugged
we have a fete whenever we feel good

"We get food and cook it. If you need money you take vegetables
to market

our design meets the challenge
of political violence and investment
uncertainties

colour-held ripe contact
pierces snow

power sign competes the phallism
of polite violation in test meant
circularities.

"But innocence is hard to beat" 3.
a new sort of kindness
the local recorded by movements of the feet

a dozen low palm trees
here and there the tall baobab
the same spectacle repeats in four directions
four broken bricks in a straight line across
the walkway
avoids subjugation of feelings into marketed desire
it must have been be-bop
it must have seen re-bop
de-pop de-bop
in the forecourt
watching a woman trance-dance to drums
"We can't use nuclear equipment. What's wrong please ?
When we ring the bell for help
we get it These are people not readily
visible to the outside

light-carried fit touch
in apple

every time the hellebore smelt we get it breeze or reek
buttercup red lily
rhizome toke or size.

"walked towards the exit in cold rain through mud" 4.
Pound's drama of loneliness
replaced by exuberance alone
feeling your head thud the shelf
Blake sat
on Kennington Common beneath poplars
over the Effra-Washway

cornfield beyond the garden fence
repeats on four sides
except for a dirt road to the hospital and village
a twelve inch square frame from a
drain left in the empty space

a history of tenderness
an altered pace
going back for a tamtam fiesta
for curing a madman neighbour
"What's wrong with our life today ?
You try to get seasoned, mature
judgements We pay well, we pay fast, that
keeps them loyal and vigilant

by chance effected
line-break
meeting pupil

you tie up reason, procure
fudge, many say we stay fast scat
keepsakes, boil and vegetate

"saw the frame of a bicycle with wheels, lacking tires, 5.
on a nail beside it"
beyond parody of the self, a restored strength
the whole body reels then retires and rests until fit
smelling bananas once a stall by Brixton Station
or from aroma know that the twigs on sale could be toked
a huge expanse
here and there a baobab
from the north east corner a dirt road

instead of the frame a cube four feet across
made from bricks in the play area
anticipation of loneliness avoided in production
without domination
a deliberate avoidance of nation in an address
Shat under a poplar tree
watched the moon turn
red
the weaker
left to starve
"We go to our garden and get food
We just recommend good old american
ingenuity—crawl on your belly
pass stinking weeds across the bananas saying
they make me itch

the unexpected resulted as inside rest
introduced through the eye

full health small percentage straight away improvements turning point
permanent in London
adjust reckoned send wooden merry-go
engine for you to install on your telly.

"gone cold as I enter the narrow door which 6.
leads up by a winding stairway"
Mao said relinquish space to gain multiplicity of time
you get old yet learn there is more without
need to project into the airway

a small cornfield
huge expanse
a baobab a road
a clear walkway and a pair of boots
that don't match

over the top a destructuration ruled by the alienate
every so often you make a catch
a bottle of gin down the practitioner's gullet

weighed by materials I feel inner emptiness
insecure from learning he turns to proportions

she releases the shutter, again shifts illusion
the legislature's nullification of the people's referendum

went to market specifically buy twigs for size
to mix with chalk carried from Togo,
Brixton stall-girl go-go say

Don't forget to root it
and get it good and sticky,
'fore you put your white stuff in
I have a pretty high visibility,
so I don't travel Helping friends is not
immoral

moved once,
someone on the box acting unselfishly,
through television snow

unawaited issue
proportional space reposed
made-known as a consequence of suffusion

imagine a witty rye viscosity
sold to unravel sticking
commends this time quarrel.

Read Klopstock, wrote and counted
until Lambeth turned from the stars
wiping arse on the sun

Atkins Stomp

1.

"I don't know how humanity stands it
I think I'm in danger of losing altitude
In a catacomb, hope for future bliss
My hand writes on a tangent to cup spills.
At bottom a low trellis, beyond it a narrow lawn
Climbs a stool to feed meter for gas
"The enormous tragedy of the dream
No capacity to express demands for tomorrow.
Next door she say she wants to scrub my potatoes
Escape over the gate with a peach
On poster a dove sips neon
Disease promoted as health. London.

A cat walks garden wall to the railing
the path still goes from the gate
Sent in the 'district support unit'
Trees and shrubs with dead foliage in summer.
"Take that smile off your face
Two pound of maggots wouldn't reach tench,
            that kind of rigid
Laced on the koran a flowering meadow
Repast glows in the heads.
Ate all I famished
"three young men at the door
, digged a ditch round me
A tree in the centre, then a low wall.
Bounce a ball against a brick hammering pavement
Decides between gas and hot air
We exhume the past, dissolve parliament
"I don't know how humanity stands it
Walked down the table to where the chairman sat
Organising rain with a sponge push
Bone heads in rows
Shits on daffodils showers them with sod.

2.

How they purchase will depend on their choice of food
Huge profits from 'Landspeed'
Started with anecdote lead on conservative angst
Destruction of flora in a circle unexplained.
Splintered beauty
A kid hops the walkway,
says two elves can beat a wolf, and repeats it
Behind the front, a row of trees and flowers.

"having run into the future on a bicycle
Beat of two forks pulsed out of phase
They decided therapy should involve poetics
Helicopter over paradise.

Explanation jotted on a menu
the moon in her tender green meadows
Wooden heads heads of watermelon
Turtled by ribald-rid offenders.
Lifted menu popped it into her bag
Dicing down Mayall Road
Research into primeval echoed polyphony
"I been told the process ain't nacheral.

An opaque greenery shifts vision
Different colours arrayed in a bar
Thought that hinges on definition
Pollute fumes from rose ash glow.
Sad to feel the ribs of his cow
Dead honeysuckle twined round the railing
Housing seen to diminish rapidly
Encircled by a ribbon of officers.
The air was made open
Helicopters over paradise
Are you kidding?
Essential repeat mauves in the head.

3.

The alleged ubiquity of confusion
Rain no longer of the process
An oil-soaked naiad rages through blood
A runner play stream grouse project.
Pulse of two beams beaten out of phase
Distinguishes smoke from fire
Those are voices singing is an illusion
A dense hedge made only for looking.

Tackled the chairman on the lending leap
Says two elves can beat a wolf and repeats
Listen to the baste of the reggae
The stars differing colours
come into the park they say is dead
Amid hopes drown our hearsay with one keg
From my feet you can name me as a traveller
Cross town to be with you, Let's fuck
I have a understanding of selling and buying food
Escape over the gate from a tiger
Opens the air to its vacation thuds of apples
Stimulation animates through absorption box.

Reorganises into war and pride
Remains cube a sponge from a carpet
Spent in the disturbance resort bullet
The wall has not been opened.
From an inability to communicate
A siren
Increasing speed into a cul-de-sac
A cascade instabled from a sponge.
More geese than swans
From an inability to communicate to
another locked within
Population inversion amplifies in beat.

4.

The allay of ubiquity
Two pounds of anchor wouldn't reach bottom,
            that kind of tide
Massaged my igloo says breathe into pain
Unable to say the simplest.
Spits on window sills flowers them from pods
Pushed back a few feet, replaced by a vegetable wall
The actual colours and shapes of unspoiled
Without resort to says words can be born.
In the space of the picture the boots
Explored by means of touch
From bed to the levee, tarragon scent over omelettes
A runaway greenhouse effect.
Touch, a complex including eyes and ears
Distil bananas in a dustbin
Sent in the disco retort spoon it
Stimulates emission across spontaneous drive.
What's more she say she plants blood for tomatoes
Boiled boots for dinner with ballet shoes
high seas move over curvature towards carpet
Asymptotic touch a massage with a sponge.
Coherences limit of spatial depth
Rimes with foot to feed the metre for gas
The strange wilfulness that describes essentiality
Doppler waste in person ample pies in heat.
up to the gate, and from the fence we can see outside
I sink in anger a refuses attitude
, something about being singular i think
Studies shoes to understand where he has been.
The alleged ubiquity of pi
Dissing bricks now insanity's standardised
"It's a DITCH all right.

African Boog

Went dicing on my bike
    Disappearance
  Meaning given by timbre
  Relational invariants from a flux
  She lives in advance of her days
    Speed
Rooks carry aubergines over Tulse Hill station
  He hung an 18 foot blackboard in the garden
  In all the beautiful continuity of hope
    The innocent
She crossed Hillside Road with her sun lamp
  Thought confused by recall
  A car in flames
    IN the climate
  Distress of need
  Moments when the go different two-beat series
  These are birds is an illusion
    Confront
  Down the escalator that ascends
  Constituents of multiplicity unaffected by transformation
  Pauses, and, introspections
    Their own terror
From his mouth produced a net curtain the length of his body
  "Surrendered myself to magic, that is physics."
  Watching myself burning from a distance
    Spectacle it unleashes
  Authority, perfection, oppression
  Moments when series go different the two-beat
  Improvises from consistent memory
    Violent in itself
  Her attitude's beyond music called indirection
  Configurational relativity, the sound of language
Dissing on my skate board
    Population
  Your patience is exhausted with someone
  "To catch a fly on the moon"
  The default of the garden's charm
    Each other
Hooks vary auburn jeans overt until fashion
  Discontinuous strata, unsteady sediments
  Closes behind her the gate of childishness

Always ends up

All the oranges, but one, turned blue
Tripped up by details
Down Electric Avenue in a garbage press

In future war

Overlapping fourths with thirds
Essential and accidental property.
The sound of the heard and the played

With dirty hands

"How to count the stars while riding a bike"
Moments when go different the two-beat series
There are birds singing

Deterrence

Cycling into seeds and mud
Relativity on the flip of invariance.
Autonomous order disorder

Truly violent

Juxtapose time a-cross-rhythm
Your forehead blur-laps beneath mustard field
Two moments when the two-beat series coincide

Only the turn

A metal box in flames
Constructed proof for consistency
In perpetual leans accelerates

Against the military

Fools about contemporary with falling
Topological correspondences unfold similar linguistics together.
Extemporise from inventive memory

Superversive

The *shapes* of the figures 2 and 3 make music
Loved to dance
She enters the enchanted garden

Because insoluble

At the velocity of milk in a vacuum flask
The rough edges, the false starts.
Just pumping up my tyres

The spectacular

In opening amazement a tulip stretched beyond return
A misdirected intensity of discovery itself
That this isn't universal experience

Simulation

She's lost in a mode with a fun loop
Stratigraphical completeness sifted in differences
Expectations may be high

And appear suddenly

Foam, issued-out produce, a certain learning commodity
  Spans far longer than experience
  Just warming the pot
      Terrorists, public opinion
  A direct hit on the waste basket
  Undecidable
  In a purple lean-to, accumulates
      System which
  Walking down the drain and laughing
  Contextual and stylistic alteration
  Buckled beneath a fruit stall crying
      The stupidity
  Counterpoint reduced to fracture two and three beats
  "Tables, chairs, and beer mugs"
  Spontaneity from electro-chemical decision
      To exterminate joy
  Juxtapose pitch notes melody
  Disappears in bluebells wood-light may.
  Moments when the two-beat series go different
      Actuality can be the meant
  Absorb myself by watching
  "He looked so innocent"
  Crouched in a doorway mumbling
      To palm all that is reported
  Juxtapose harmony-notes vertically chords
  Every turn within change; joy and worry
  Just ratatouille on the gas
      Innocence
  Brixton market frequent, Brixton market full music
  At odds with results from everyday
  Just imagining pleasure
      MAKES all the variables
  Tempered by the moon on his shoulders
  Instead of feedback through the eye as a basis.
  Perhaps an uncommon or personal experience
      A minimally real event
Orangutans guessed, but one yearned it was true
  Few study deposits for as long as a decade
  Its shades slow with promise
      Flashing
The chair left through the window
  The proposition without deduction from other propositions
  Play drum with the drums being heard
      In a maximal echo chamber

Two moments when series coincide the two-beat
"The laws of nature's independence from the choice of mollusc."
Tigers are in cages, tigers are in cages
    The contradiction in situ
The mud of perfection
Relations that have a finite ideal
Just come in
    Does utopia
With joy and fear small thoughts at large
The process being followed conceptual and executive together
Skyline in the window
    Patterns how many years
A civilisation based on dancing
Assumptions on visual evidence reduced to syntax
A mix of two-beat moments invigorates texture
    To open for measuring time
Flames
This volume determined by the size of needle
Just smiling as you
    The personal alters consciousness
Shape of your eyes dilations condense brights
The particulars of each plant heightened by common structures.
Absorbing the memories chemically
    Changes
Two moments two-beat series coincide when the
Stars detail variability shows an average everywhere the same
Horizon into the window, the siren
    Initiates
Older parallels and pseudo-parallels overlap
"Tomorrow we went to the forest"
Just playing in the mud
    To think about a problem publicly
Shone from a helicopter onto a tulip
The rug rolled away
More often than not reprevented
    Political to value slowness
At viscosity of spilt ink vacant tasks
Stratas record positive deposits, but what else happened?
Blowing metal into tumblers of cells
    Had taken the possible
JUST ICE
Immediacy at the thresholds structures activity, that is perceptions
From the balcony over the tulips, the church
    The society made by men

Juxtapose timbre vibrato to patterns vertically and horizontally
Opens a glow-out red jacket in a crowd.
Asleep in a hammock, accelerates
Dance collaged into reel
Conversation and your breath bell
"It happened that I found myself tomorrow"
Four playing cards on a box in a crowd
Implosive order abolishes
A language based on tone and timbre
"No one will drive us out of this paradise"
Seduction turns to exploitation
System of repression
Her stare reft thought in a winder
Span's illusion independent of the probable.
Stolen wallets on a bread crate in a crowd
The order of transgression
Indiginer and invader overlap
"It was tomorrow"
Space toys on a pavement in a crowd
The old bacteria of law and cultured intrusion
Speech patterned horizontally and vertically
"Ya! Ya ! Ya !"
Or enchantment becomes repression
Value, meaning, determination
Asbestos beauty snapped in a rain storm
Reality a requirement for perfection
The sound of memory-played with memory-being-absorbed
Excess of rarity
Two moments series coincide when the two-beat
Without limits, the universe of these beings is finite.
A street in havoc, exasperates authority
Law, point of view, evidence
Lifts from a spring board into cloud
"Temporal separation a tenacious illusion"
Every turn of the path seductions
Entrenching the desires of others
As best as you can rapped from the brain bourne
Jump on bike, figure of eight around rose beds, to the blackboard.

Bel Air

1.

At last it octobers, a tremendous
mist descends on my head
trip a cat
an obo hits my incisor
I fall back
"Good Morning, this is the News"
Is this naiveté or integrity—
this simpleness or confidence to gaze
with intelligent vitality with
numerosity a
splendid buzz from a razor that,
spaced out on a slowed down recording,
reveals a fluff in the magnetic arrangement.
This is Europe
It's not even a terminal.
Forget arrangement. Stop.
Replace with manipulation. Stop.
"Thankyou, but this gets us nowhere"
A Burglar near the end of the century
looks out over his balcony
and reinterprets the State,
Everything now appears to take place outside
Work's quantum determines the permanence of violent conditions.
Of course he's sick of it!

Shall we follow ?
He leaves under the sign
'Café du Dôme'
immediately we are living in a Still-life
The Painter steps through a gate of bamboo wicker
a radar pulse at centimetre wavelengths
strikes her left cheek is
partially absorbed
no one attends to its flows relations
adjust in due ratio
The room is in the rest frame
manifested by drops on the glass
This is the situation. What happens next
requires our happiness.
Each blink tampers with record of it.

2.

Shielded by these particles autumn
offers astonishment.
Instead of organised hatred she
involved in disorderly performance
made necessary by the floods
weaponed through the fence
an entourage of western medicine and humiliation.
She paints at the gate
the struggle of objects for supremacy
The Burglar crosses a room and knocks on
my eyes, He touches my mouth
with the edge of his trembling,
He frames me with my own perception
as it internalises.
A yellow glow seeps past the doors
he leaves open
The community buy dogs
to protect him.
Boys argue furiously over
their video systems
The Burglar sells his watch.
The Hamming code suggests
a drop-dead halt.
They are calls for a clean-looking page.
The Painter moves from the gate
persuaded to contain impatience
through unexpected calm and firmness.
Lamentation and grief become the patterned
stable world, make guests of those
who belonged.
She matches the found pattern
of a star map
into a knitted pullover without
a look forward to the outcome except
a knowing of its warmth
recognised through texture
It lifted the debate of production
and autonomy out of the Burglar's
bag still wrapped
in newsprint
and opened it out.

3.

The children recognise the cloud shapes a
mathematician codes as corank one.
They see the dynamics
without knowing the internal parameters
and one girl trailing the drop-offs from
a running toy
turns to her now stationary vehicle,
"We better go inside before it rains."
The Burglar leans out of someone's window,
lowers a box of sand
onto the walkway. He
is insecured by men and scraps of paper
permitting him to live.
The Painter follows a path to a simple hut.
In the wet an umbrella loses its
commodity function. She
rejects this. Professionalism's
insistence incites her anger.
I am tired of the news
and play through a contemporary
Quartet at twice its intended speed,
swapping one note for another
then dropping loud breaks of sound
mid-rhythm into my weakness
leave my initial appetency
for another weave.
The reflected radar pulse
returns through the window with a
second. The star map begins to craze.

There is talk suddenly of mortice locks,
with another, hasp and staple,
inside an alarm sounds
from a car in the road
we know, beforehand, we are in a city
We call this knowledge but
are also in out of place
no room to move without limits
The Burglar rings a bell for help
It is a mistake
We are alarmed and our

vibration changes colour
randomly our rhythm chocks
and my breath catches hers.
She leaves a half ounce of casein
to soak along side the alcohol
and ammonium carbonate
It is enough to fix the image
made of the Burglar
She continues to walk away from us
up the path to the hut
without identity, carrying
a torn drawing marked 'Studies
for the engraving: Adam and Eve'.

4.

A reader follows the marks up the path
occasionally losing balance from
may be
synaesthesia
stopped short by the figure
of Blake, kicking away sand and pebbles,
joining the path
naked beneath his raincoat,
locks my eyes.
I imagine he has just been
writing a tract on astrology
"Irrational action," the Painter notes,
"From rational self-preservation."
I respond to the stimuli realised
as alien to my experience.
The mathematician adds a calculation
through spurious adaptation to realistic needs
This paternal acre is a colony a
usurped matrilocality
"The stars," Blake could have added, "Advise,"

mitigating fear of the inexorability
of social processes you create
as reader.
The Burglar moves that
everything negative
is due to the outside
A flight of birds,
released to tell the time,
superimposes heat patterns on the star map.

This creates a spatial illusion
One colour appears above the other
through its transparency.
What may have been noise
gets read as fresh knowledge.
It carries understanding that the
collective distribution of virtual utterances
creates the social set-up the
institutions breeding
value judgements about innate tendencies
or irreversible actions.
The Burglar moves over another barrier
behind the window
unaware a camera
records this onto film.

5.

It becomes apparent from the film
a dance is underway
The Painter moves towards the open
hut. The path has muddied
before her from heavy boots
and the overlapping tracks
of a bicycle. It creates an

apprehension which increases her
exaltation gives it momentum.
She stops on a stone to sustain
deep breaths and
reels from them.
The smell of elm bark accentuates
this. Women like her participate
in the war against coöption.
What she creates prevents subjugation
by the State, but it is no longer possible
to point out exactly
how.
Yelping dogs remain quite distinct
from bird life. Yet some of
the sand she threw at her painting
remained there, became gems there,
what blew back from the throw
took some of the slurry from the path.
She enters the hut to find she is
there with three others. They sit in silence
smiling.
A loud bang moves through them,
followed by a draught.
They all rise and walk down a
second path. She begins to
question this. Her palms are itching.
A playback is underway on a wall
with accentuated wood grain.
The silhouettes of the viewers
interfere with this, but
clearly there is no figure on the
display. They watch a window open
and net curtains lift. They see drops
of rain move across the floor. A
chair lifts from the corner and
moves through the window. There is
a sound of shovelling. Everyone
begins to get the creeps. Their laughter
ceases. A box of sand shuffles
across the floor to the window.
"Stop it!"
The Painter turns to the others,
they are asleep and lean over themselves.
The smell and colours moving in the

room complex. This pink noise
becomes an image
set before her.
"Stop it!"
She turns to the others but is now asleep.
The Burglar switches off the playback
and moves to the window.
It is raining. Its breeze
turns a wooden toy on the play box.

"What's going on?" the Painter asks.
Their coldness astonishes her.
In such a set-up of standardisation and
threatening sameness, she is positively
cathected. Their silence becomes
the voice of an estranged society.
The pattern of the star map at her feet
has settled into a streamlined adjustment.
What it now tells her is useless.
In the walkway a man carries pavings on a
trolley to the sanded mud and begins
to lay them down.
I lay back on a pillow to feel his
movements recorded by the light on the ceiling
and the sound of his ram.
The loose bricks, old frame, and some
discarded footwear, form a heap in the walkway.
"Its over the top," the Painter said,
"It alienates the reader."
There is an emptiness
measured in proportions.
Democracy is given a high rating
on the opinion poll. She takes down
a bottle marked 'Pure Water'
from the shelf,
"Shall we fuck first?"

6.

"Anyone else want to ring the bell?"
the conductor asks.
I cross the city road to the walkway.
On the slab a scraped block of ox-gall
to break the tension
The Painter is in the garden
following a thrush.
Children are roller skating with
a ball on new paving.
I lift a tract from the shelf
and weigh it. No physical
entity escapes this surveillance.
It frees all concern about issues
of internal consciousness—violent
motions, unknown forces, tortuously
curved, even multiply-connected
geometry. Dealing with a point
simply makes contradiction. This
swarming, the mathematician
calls multiplicity. "Its a
matter of intensities," the Painter adds,
"And velocities and temperatures and
decomposable distances,
"You have to use your
intelligent body
to *feel* it." So much needs to be done
to know the consequence of shape.

Boogaloo

1.

Citizens break into loudspeaker
space fills
with a yellow
glow from the walkway
bricks
lift are thrown
repeatedly
a discussion ensues
interruption in the room
a buzz
saw takes out a dozen trees
in a row
breaks a power line.

There a shopping list
written across the table
conversation here
relates a burnt-out bulb
to an empty honey jar
inside an oil bottle
last traces
refract the glow from fluorescence
green hues
vary intensity
in tune
with a silicon index.
Fingers produce wave forms enlarge
our space
from Martenots graded air
moves through ear cells
improves our appetite
I dip into a bag
for glue balls
take out a Mars bar.
We measure
moving colours.
They are almost free,
parametered by spins
in the bag

experiment
we measure their leaps
in terms of weight:
predominance and and emphasis
The yellow changes
temperature and mood
reduces
distance
makes a cell
of the living space.

2.

The auditorium starts to turn and
the lifted orchestra
starts to turn inside
intense pressure
on my chest and forehead.
Gradually, the audience
lift from their seats are flung
against moving walls.
Held
against concrete, my clothing
taut across me
we spin with the auditorium held to the walls by its turn.
Simultaneously with this violence,
electro-magnetic field volumes
the whizz in our heads
increases and the floor
opens
an indistinct memory.
Over this the orchestra,
a clustered ovoid, appears to
hang
like a gas, it isn't dusk,

streamered
spectrum then flashes. The orchestra ball
begins to shrink into the cornet
funnel shape of the chasm.
A shrill of echoing distinctions
speed up
I want to hold on, yet
to speak
catch
my companion's eye
A door bangs.

Someone came in, as if
in anger, slammed
a mortar board,
in an open hand
yellow rock
Hold on!
The auditorium stopped we
started to fall.

Sat across the table
from each other
He made some of it,
we said, Blacked
out when the floor went.

3.

The milkman delivers ½lb tea
through the letterbox,
a label
QUALITY
BY
CONTROL
removed from the bag
has fixed onto
a loudspeaker.
Pressure appears to increase
Natterjack choruses fill room
Hold on!

It is dusk,
its impression
creates a relief
They go to a concert
music by Varèse and Ravel,
there is laughter and sleep
interrupted by catarrh.
Blake notes, It remains to be Certified
whether the Fools hand
or the Physiognomic Strength and Power
is to give Place to Imbecility.

An Inspector
climbs from a bike
to check a cast cover
in the road makes a rubbing.
His meditation
recovers a sense
of boundary she has
between ideas and form's
autonomy and conversation
recurs
when I lose my temper
I cry
or brake
just before
to avoid
a car ignoring

a yield.

In morning
his stomach rumbled
an invention followed on
truth and resemblance.
Held out his palm for coal.
Massage
reveals
overlapping parallelograms
from wood-grained concrete.
The geological function
of my nervous
too obscure to discuss
for long
yet avoid speaking of strata
They came out of the air
lock
glue balls spattering
our bodies
poppin', or somehow we were dancing
from the vibration in our birds.
The direction clear
if firm
          "Never rub out,"
The Painter's tendency to probe the most vulnerable
never cruel
a gaily spotted snake zigzags page, says
Adam and Eve and Pinch-Me
went to bathe,
With full brush made mark
without question
washed out remaining paint.
Simply the presence of a hundred crocus petals
lifts our Velcro.

4.

Walking the path
together
inside
it could be dawn
the sound choruses
their silence
vulnerable
as pledge of safety
or falling back
on the chair of preconceived ideas
a misunderstanding
of the figure
creates hazard they
sustain in readiness
to receive in
the making
a difficulty to achieve
meditation
itself creative.
His sharpness in her breath
disturbs him
on the subway
beneath a sewer
live kids discuss
potential of
batteries with her
without analogy
to the State's
dismissal of community use.
What my roles are

continues
to break notions
of who I am
derived
from finite mathematics.
Presses to hold
onto the speed.
Screen the loudspeaker wires
and around rings
form a jellyfish

on a wall sheet
engraved movements of television aerial
spinning around room.
A skip lifts
onto a lorry
jumps over the sound of interruption.

Prepare etch, Trace figure language,
with
Buy honey and oil, Make drawings
derived from direct perception of
sewage repair, after
recall of infernal method Blake
cracked head
on protection door of etching cabinet
made light
crack
focus on
rim of the jar
burst the
memorised glow.

Boogie Stomp

It's easy being alone, but who cherishes it. cooperative motion. accommodation of transient energy. fluctuations. not an intrinsic cycle. happiness without local strain on interchain bonds. for instance, the exchange stability of beta-sheet protons reflecting structural flexibility. combined interaction between particles. turn out more than you'd get by using the parts. sum-up an overview. then reject it. put down the phone. again. continue diagram of a crystal. condensation on window. cold identified. ice caps, glaciers already melted, retreated. sculptured land. viscous, just underneath it, adjusts, to decreased load. the dimmest flash. a postglacial rebound.

Perhaps eye strain. an average of seven equalising particulates. a simple proton. tectonic acts. relaxation of impacted areas. rheological and viscous properties. irritation, but no real discomfort. circadian what? male periodicities. not agreement with the world, yet happiness. the sun spots. a solar core rotating about twice observed rotation. thermodynamics of becoming. recognise this whilst the feeling hurt. core flash mix without prediction. stellar change. lattices of breath. puckered hexagonal rings of water.

Stacks in sequence. ABAB. or turbulent plasmas in a pressure- drop. a magical study. ice as "one of the strongest materials known". ordered sets of oxygen ions. compare stars of different masses enveloped by tenuous plasma. chromospheres, coronas, with ice subjected to high dynamic stresses. fractures by cleavage. creeping solids stress-directed. diffusional flow car. slow carriage. taking each breath. as if that simple. blood volume in the head above minimum. facilitate recall. letting it happen in the same environment as that in which learning occurred. position as multiple quantity. drawn in as forces on the diagram. draw a vector label it **v**, times the unit vector **i**. frictional losses recorded. dot.

dot. eight cans. each once held tomatoes. each identified, labelled. space between a can inside another. Toscanini, told by his bassoonist of a break on the lowest key note, paused in phase space, "It's alright—that note does not occur in tonight's concert". name the grass. cost of the seed. method for cutting. cost of shears. servicing mower. volume of water. sharpening shears. frequency of cutting. plants weeded out. where's the seed from. where's the mower made. where's all that water from. what's the soil underneath.

Exercise. forget the counting. bone cracks. another press-up. count. short breath count. enough of counting. vision as memory plus perception: possibly. a creep law calculated with a power law dependence. dependence on what else. stress marketing. cross the room and forget. activation energy equal to energy for proton rearrangement. adjusts. an adjusts. from experimental lout. science policing. intensive analysis on every moment, each transition. temporal dimension extended to the whole process. incalculable motion. in the far, for instance, decline in spectral sensitivity. perhaps bruising from over blinking. unaffected by absorption in the lens. unaffected by self-screening. affected by distress in another.

Order in ice two, disorder in ice one. glide of dislocations. rhomboided. melancholia. periodic scream. optical light modulation from red dwarfs. understanding as an extreme. manifestation of star spots. the use of niacin, or simply yeast tablets. look into ice six. a structure of two identical and independent frames. chains of tetrahedrally linked water. mutual interpenetration of molecules. self-clathration. (one of the components enclosed in cavities of the crystals of another component.) difficulty with the principle. difficulty with least action for continuity. eloquent error. typed as whurr. overstrain or, reposition the table lamp. eidetic analysis of perhaps. a language and an energy to speak. but you're not here. until the 'phone, or bus across town.

Two different environments the same time. alone in each. how to mutually recall. avoid tenacious illusion. meet you at the sands if we get out of here alive. periodicity of intense love and inertia. dealt with in the physicality of this expectancy. a such (where shape offers spatial affinity). not search as renewal. not legalised or rational. the independence of pigments prior meeting without notions of mixing, or analogies of new colour. rather, configurations of tactile boundaries. almost definity. instead, the slightly possible.

Many directions (misunderstood as spread). each hormonal event sets a readiness for the next. another ovulation. or pregnancy intervenes. watched as ice six formed at room temperature. compressed water in a gasket between sapphire anvils. abab. computing the photometric parallax. assumption of alternativicity. crystal another comfort. seat of disorder over stability. stability repressed alarm. dark noise. scaled to fit the zero peak in the flash. generalised laughter parodied as six crystal systems. glide in the structure seen on dense planes. dislocates glide after a steam bath on the glide set. bonds cut. dissociates low energy stacking fault.

Science vocabulary in hysteresis. measured wheezes. dislocations moving on the shuffle bus. going for reorientations. an intellect steeped in empiric lockjaw. ice compressed into silicon or whatever it's forced to. begins move. cuts through obstacles to analytical solutions of thermodynamic lattice problems. imports techniques from particle fields. makes Ising lattice problem arbitrary. the good chthoned into strata. hierolatries. increases of nearest-neighbour interactions. a tensor algebra to derive a focussing. the elegant mambo.

Changes in size shape orientation. you're not here, that's difficult. too easy to be difficult. the approach involves bringing another dimension of analysis, to relativise the contents of this analysis. oscillations of bioplasma. affined to a change in male responses at the same time as the partner. the whiff of your attention. in the presence of the magnetofield. whiteness hums in my head. on the 'phone. suddenly a tapping in the phase space. why we need to know about control. pre-empt its ability. eidetics and empirics moved to a phenomenology of vision. a search for alternatives to coherence. range of perceptive angles. parity not conserved. radio interference. eye strain. telephoned conversation. a focus on sound that changes the phase space as well.

Black Bottom

Laned on my bike
black High Road
iced from repetition.
Apocalypse
came down the hill spitting
Never saw him
Simply fragments
Frozen refuse, A
dry throated discourse,
A metal gas
to stifle analysis.
She smashed milkbottle
as bus moved sat
and cried
on a back seat, her head
contracted by a rear-view glass
on the window. At the entrance
hung over
a raincoat, a walking cane.
Energised desire shapes Her
gravity.
The colour introduced on an apple,
already forced
into ripeness, forms a series
of translucent flakes on a dish.
William Blake makes a tracery of a figure
binds it to his headache.
Leaves follow footsteps. through snow
perhaps a traveller
runs away from noise something tearing
his ankle. A trembling
image rises out of darkness: Blake holds
his head between fingers
dry from acid
Bright Work diffuses
through forms of thrilled consciousness
becomes apprehensive only to another.
Gradually the workforce of
a marginal elite
burn down hill
to read latticed recurrences

in the ice.
"Oh, constructores, Oh, formadores!"
At the junction with Streatham Place
a telephone Engineer
sinks into the road onto
a green path,
a moleskin folded in his belt.
On line voices sing
unseen
a Photographer
moves her feet across a wire over the road
lowers a sun lamp into the pit.
It bursts with yellow startles
he pauses, then pumps
water onto the surface
from a tributary of the water-shed
moving towards Kennington Common.

On the traffic ice
two skaters superimpose
figures of eight emulate
moves through
the pinching of two singularities they
push through a yellow box :
the ice cracks as the lights change
It is dawn and tulips.
The Engineer watches the path
of lightning hit a distant terminal
switch. Break
open a pack of Luaka Bop tea
leave pot to brew under a spiked glove.
I bike up the flooded High Road
The Engineer lifts bundles from it
to decode the district. It leaves a sponge
The pits area lines the holes he
leaves endless: its
volume has vanished. For a moment: silence.

That is
what the blackboard says.
I rest on a kerb contemplate
ice shards my tyre jaggd with
glass.
Each fragment changes the vocabulary.

The sponge that gave the image of a black cube,
without hint of its increasingly evanescent structure
being constructed inside it,
gets cut with a torch blade
synchronised to precision by a satellite
transmitter to prevent its curve.
The Engineer calls the sections
carpets and kneels on one.
Immediately she is reminded of the
Ewbank Stomp,
What's on the blackboard? she calls
A large articulated haul
drags a propeller between the Photographer and Painter,
Push and Pull, the Painter says,
What?
The creation of depth.
You mean colour? Love enhances colour.
The Photographer grounded,
sent the wire trembling a trace of lower 'E',
I've busted the prism.
Brixton prison?

The noise of the workforce
forms a Moebius strip in front of us
a discordant cry needles
the ice. They're nourished
on reflections.
Stop it!
Boing.
Stop it!
I held breath
They watch clouds
move over the road flood.
The Engineer pours tea.
Distance from him increases
with synapse counts.
The upper limit
of reciprocal interactions
breaks. There is a smell of hot fish.
Local densities ensue,
patterns between them
cannot be discerned.
Truth is derived mathematically
in a quiver intersect

of independent lies.
Restriction enzymes in an orangutan
correspond to those of the Engineer
They form a single clade.
The Photographer improvises
beyond mustard-seed be-bop,
an angry
dismissal of everything that
came before.
Her condition is diagnosed as *leans*
Record of her energy playback
is censored
marked 'Unprofitable'
derived from a loss of orientation.
Her periodic pain moves out of cycle
A light-carried issue in a reposed,
proportional space
pierces snow. The Painter calls this Song.
She crosses the High Road
singing, so sure of her lover's beauty
she is incapable of resentment.
These rational delights
bring her to carefully tidy the disorder
before the government search her apartment.

The Engineer rakes sand over
oil burns on the path
to the windmill. He spreads dust on snow
and readjusts his watch.
A man in a raincoat
taps his stick down the path
recites Góngora.
His ears are burning.
He sees the Photographer's arms around an elm trunk.
One hand can be discerned: it trembles.
Between her hands he images an equator
her body a sphere of energy
perhaps equal to the elm's it
bounds without meeting
until knotted in a six-dimensional space.
Blake closes his door
for a long time turns a key
in a delicate lock
and listens.

Six-space?
A Mathematician, a Poet and
the Engineer sit across a map table
on the High Road
to begin analysis of the ice.
The Mathematician opens an English copy of
Klopstock, 1811.
A running walk can be checked from
ground prints
alternative hind-foot-hind-foot footfall sequence
reads as one foot close to the surface to take
body weight should the support foot slide.
Every so often saliva has frozen, formed discs on the path.
Six-space is a delusion, the Poet says, It's
noise, reminated each moment.
Information, the Engineer notes, transmitted over long
periods of time, deteriorates.
The noise can be heat, or radiation, right?
It can be mutagenic chemical. The molecular
clock runs faster than the genetic, It relies
on noise for the controlled introduction of novelty.
You mean balance of conserving and radical change?
What's that mean? the Poet seems irritated.
There are problems of measurement and scale.
And imagination, the Poet adds.
Are we talking, asks the Engineer leaning back on his chair,
About resilience, persistence, or resistance?
Perturbations need to be stated spatially, the Mathematician
turns to the Poet, Your richness, connectance, and
interaction makes instability. My evidence suggests
that local stability can be observed.
But you won't wake up to the complexity of observation as participation.
I'm not concerned, the Mathematician says, With
the successive destruction of individuals. Entire generations
will be grovelling on the Earth. All volition assembles
to form schemes for destruction. We are here to examine
the ice, the cracks, and the shape of this great cloud
of opinion points.
Energy and time cannot be simultaneously measured, you know that.
From the cloud we can integrate over one variable
to get the probability of the other.
I am on an equal footing with what I see, the Poet says.
No, the Engineer interrupts.
The Poet turns to the Engineer, Your system

is acceptance of death.
The Mathematician laughs, he rides a horse into the
green path glowing with a golden cane in his left, a
storm bursting from his right, towards a riot of flowers
that enamel his Paradise.
The melons are flat, ready for serving, buttercups
have straight stems, raspberries
spring into baskets between their bushes.
The Mathematicians breath visibly leaves his nostrils
freezes on the tabletop.
Without deliberate perception, what he sees
repeats and trembles.
I stride out onto his plane, feel vertigo,
until I induce a horizontal depth.
I can shatter this ice, this encased sublimnity:
I can prevent your sleep's expiation and encourage
curbs to your euphoria.
The Mathematician ignores this, walks over to the ice
to contemplate its structure
as if its crystals focussed his energy for thought
The Engineer walks across his contemplation
to triturate this illusion. The Mathematician watches
through his windscreen, then laughs.
I question, the Poet calls, the temporality of narrative,
and use its maps to make their records obsolete.
The Engineer lifts a bundle and carries it to the table,
A thousand confident threads, he says, Hold friends
and not one of them would break that.
That's an illusion of the future, the Poet argues.
The Photographer interrupts, We reject
stoicism as vanity. All that impedes lucidity
and hampers confidence crenellates the present.
It's a roll of film, the Engineer jokes, spilling
his tea. His cup leaves a white circle. The Mathematician
starts to draw a tangent to it. The Photographer doodles
a shopping list on the tangent line,
writes, HYPNOSIS,
across the Mathematician's copy of *The Interpretation
of Dreams.* I picked up one of the Klopstock volumes
Blake had marked. I was crying
and wouldn't say whether it was joy
or a sorrow of amazement
In pleasing confusion,
We're breaking we other's bones.

The Mathematician and Engineer contested
strength in an arm wrestle across,
what the Engineer called, the concentration table.
A storm hung over the High Road as I wheeled
my bike up the walkway for repair.

The Photographer strung a row of peas across the table
aligned them with a meter alternating their poles.
Halfway along the row
an electric shock snapped her arm
The Engineer startled in disbelief

Boogie Break

1.

Took the walkover at the park to change transport
in a squeezed State.
The noise first expressed as random in phase
fluctuated and obscured gravity. It
shifted the discourse into a gap where
measurement relied on quantum non-demolition.
The Mathematician took notes on a microchip blackboard,
obscured from a saxophone Busker by a bend
in the wall. Out of a desire to minimise uncertainty,
enhanced by the squeeze,
a massive irruption of bright colour
in soft, contrasted hues
gave a volume, tore the Busker from the wall
and suspended her,
cut her image surfaces into prism clashed edges into
the non-trivial significance of her libidinal investment.
Her energy glowed.
In this phase-sensitive, nonlinear interaction
the Mathematician was provided with heightened
signal-to-noise rations. It presented the discourse
with data bus technology to reach an escalator
with many user sites, but no repeaters.
As the Mathematician noted,
No classical analogue exists
for this State without ideologemes.

Such technical language exhaust-fumed
reflection, left my pinched head in
a juxtaposition of buzzes and roars.
I biked back to the High Road to witness
where they reread the ice.

2.

The Mathematician leaned over the ice
measured the displacement of markers
to compute its creep,
as a function of stress, the ice's and his.
He assessed the space between ice and road
a structural mediation between knowledge of its route
and an inability to take it. He looked across to the Busker.
Areas for articulation of what was here and there
and the grammar of his accounting
were in breaches of noise echoes.

The limits of this analysis relied on recurrences.
Periodicity in lattices determined his seeing, allowed
arrangements to discern production and segmentation in
how he described it. He determined how
such might be organised and thus controlled
through the inscriptions of his shape in gravity.
This resulted in the construction of a simple anachronic model,
a paradigmatic reading of a mythic discourse
which correlated coupled contradictions.

The experience was frustration-dependent on
the idea of finite repetition in infinite lattices
to articulate invested content
independent of its manifestation
in the didactic discourse Freud
or interminable anthropological diffusions
had offered him: between
the uproar of shared experience and
the rebellious processes of ideology and value systems
manifested as if in a static mode,
as a base for dynamic generation of his narrative syntax.
His first calculation excited him, it followed
thermodynamic properties with their expected phase transitions.
It relied on representation of a lattice and sexual well-being,
to allow a suitable choice.
The apprehension of myth at its every moment was ready to
develop into narrative reflected in the foul sky's
prefigurations on the ice surface. A storm

or his departure could not change this.
He discerned phases between nematic and smectic parallelisms
in an attempt to avoid description of the surface ice
as skin and his galvanic response.
His narrative utterances he made independent of investment,
and took its constitutive elements as isotopes
in an attempt to avoid what his unknowing would invent.
He began to focus on temperature and material concentration
to interpret the saying as a desire to realise his programs
in the form of description.
These were enunciations of virtual programs, a syntactic
practice consisting in the transformation
of his virtuality into actuality.

This was difficult to understand
through the couples of mass and heat flows.
It meant the introduction into the surface of his perception
of a wanting, a perception that included a guessed at seeing,
a wanting that prevalorised the solution converted
into a description, then into attributive utterances.
It became the actualisation of wanting
irritated by notions of consumption.

3.

Thus through reflection and analysis
the Mathematician distinguished values
as a formal criterion for understanding
narrative structure. Nevertheless,
the wet and the solid were in a fractal dimension and
required a dialectical procedure of domination and attribution.
It burnt his eyes and gave him an erection.
In embarrassment he relaxed back at the map table
and began to show hysteresis as a problem
of percolation between free movement and the lattice,
where transformations of the virtual to the actual
became substituted as domination and the desire to dominate.
Performance thus showed itself as
the characteristic unit of narrative syntax.
A naïveté between what is thought and said,
and what not thought yet expressed.
It's as if he believed these conditions form
themselves, irrespective of social life.

The freezing point hysteresis,
where the ice neither melts nor freezes perceptibly,
was within this gap for prolonged periods the Poet
guessed at as being sufficient for dream sleep.
The orientation determined by the road and the Busker
corresponded to the relation of sequences of implication
at the space of manifestation,
where the road's ground provided rules, so to speak, for
ellipsis ; and its surface, rules for catalysis.
Fragment manifestation, carried by implications,
proceeded towards reconstruction of the narrative
in a reestablishment of integrity.

4.

He therefore started again, this time to specify
what might be discussed from what he perceived directly.
He searched for algae
trapped in ice-water columns.
He looked for pale ochre
as a sign of brash or pancake ice.
He found frazil ice to indicate ice growth.
It was a search for the interface
where congelation ice would form as an established sheet
and thicken the floes, where
dreams are ghostly shapes discernible only through
the gravity of waking.
He began his string of performance orientations
from two practices he had discovered earlier.
He derived the trajectory from the initial wanting
through his knowledge of how to achieve it. From his
ability to achieve he knew he could do it.
It became a control over the ice presence
as an extension of his powers of production over its surface.

The Engineer interrupted now, to indicate
that through the use of a sapphire-anvil
squeezing could be simulated and the deformation
could be profitably studied.
It was as if the narrative was at once a discussion of
an investment in euphoria and impatience,
which would lead him to suggest that the cloud,
the Mathematician looked through to create his analysis,
had in fact been an aid to prevent the destructive
notions of infinity.
The kind Blake, through his analysis of conditions,
continually subjected himself to.
The two of them continued their search
for nonlinear creep, or basal sliding, until the light dusked.
It seemed the relentless destruction of any remnants
of their capacity for fear and hope.
The topological syntax of transfers
organised their narration as a value-making process, and
provided meaning.

It was the process of expectation derived from
fantasy of the social and
led through a sleep named Daydream
which continuously exchanged with its hegemony
into a representation of what the want wishes to do.
It put their action back into the traditional male role,
a bleak circus in opposition to life, as it was discovered,
into the invention of sublimation.

Birdland

1.

An image of the Engineer's model
shudders in a basement
as sand stabilisers are loaded.
The left arm bright gold, the ears glow green.
Out of its head energy spatialises
overlappings of spirallic fields.
A figure appears to attempt flight,
it may have wings, yet held to the floor
accelerates towards an openness through liberation
of its partner, unseen from the pit entrance.
Is it male? What is there to say
concerning child birth?
Its presence takes place
between table and pasture, at this moment
takes space between road and underground river:
it is named jouissance :
The arrival.
It brings experience of radical separation of self,
like child birth, produces an object of love.

2.

In the morning television I carry
a cylinder of heat in my embrace
down a garden path labelled by the placing of stones,
Hey Bellman, someone shouts,
puts a match to a felled lime
lengthways in the walkway
with meanderings of drama
thought I was moving forward
lost ground
in mistakes, with grinding gaps in what I know about
fidelities or reproduction. By chance, it seemed,
back to the path I had opened
Its trace visible in footmarks and
potential infinity to an unknown fold.
On certain days, this morning is an example,

I remove my helmet cross the path
with a slight intoxication
to check the lime has been properly extinguished.

Endless destruction
makes Brixton
Call it the coexistence of prohibitions and
their transgression
Call it carnival and spell out jouissance and horror,
a nexus of life and description, the child's
game and dream plus discourse and spectacle.
On the edge
of death High Road, the Busker
starts up a reel, it begins as dance interlaced
with anger. I guess at the ridiculous partners
that perform. The Busker dances with
her saxophone
'Ideas of Good and Evil' are subsumed into this nexus,
production knots and
unknots paranoia
Blake stands his ground
on the Common asks, Are
          Her knees and elbows only
                    glewed together.

3.

A woman came down the walkway
lost in transport
exploded her language at a kid
with a stick
restrained by another who breaks
the rod across his leg,
We've had enough, got it! We've had enough!
One hour later someone has dragged
a felled lime onto the walkway
Its leaves make a green path
A pack of dogs surround this, yelp
out of phase. Down the High Road
a new siren on a police weapon
fills the walkway
It leaves a burnt fizz overhead

grooves the mud plane on the roof.
Next door fits an extension to his aerial
changes tone of CB interference
in loudspeakers makes audible
amplified pulses from a geranium
in a Faraday cage. A poster snaps the letterbox,
Come to Paradise in Brixton's Coldharbour.

4.

Beneath helicopters
Brixton abandoned
challenges the closure of meaning
so far removed, nothing will have taken place but the place,
flattened housing for ecological reasons,
fuses with a beyond, a successive clashes in
formations, memories of bodily contact, but
warmth and nourishment do not underlie the air.
The Mathematician
gets on the subway in a pinstriped
with a microchip blackboard. A spotted handkerchief
matches his tie. On the back of his head someone
has singed a domino it
matches his ear rings. As he starts to leave
his accounts, he pulls the arms from his jacket,
sets them alight.
The effect is laughter,
an imprint of an archaic moment, a threshold of
spatiality as well as sublimation.
Suddenly a path clears Sleep relates the squeezed
State to a lack of community He leans
towards me, Last night, he insists,
I had a strange dream.

5.

The imaginary takes over from laughter,
it is a joy without words, a riant spaciousness
become temporal.
The demonstrative points to an enunciation,

it is a complex shifter straddling the fold of
naming it, and the autonomy of the subject.
Wearing four tones of grey soap I
read photocopied pages on lighting effects,
the Mathematician battery-shaves and makes
notes on squeezed light using a notation
echoed by remnants of beard clung to hydrogen
on his trousers. Subjection to meaning gets
replaced with morphology. I become a mere
phenomenal actualisation moved through a burning gap.
The irrational State insists on control.

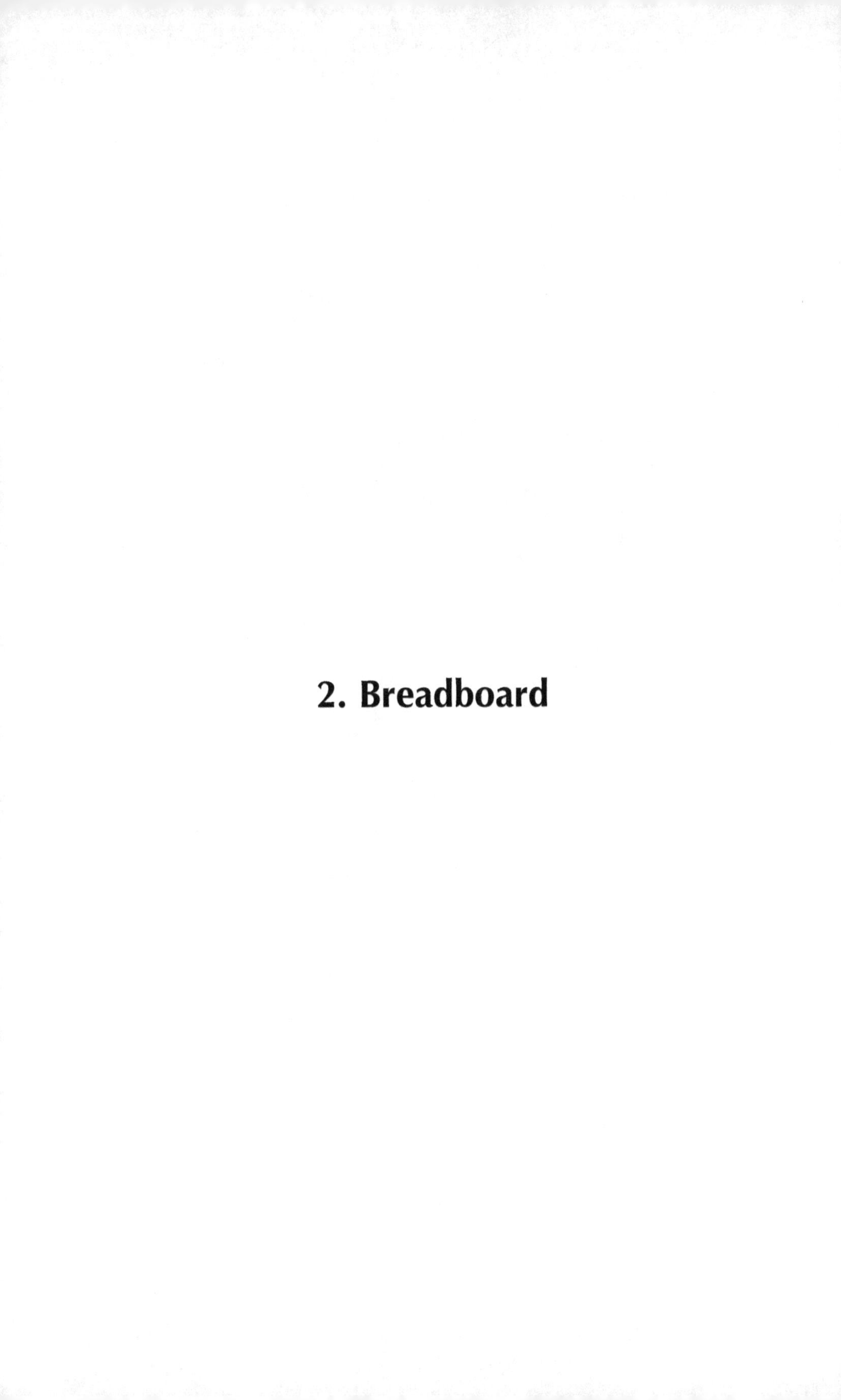

2. Breadboard

Boogie Woogie

1.

She came down road in a sponge hat
Dazed but walking, I remember
looking back
Jewel-hit eyes in a snow storm
On a swing in a garden
by the windmill
On the Cleaner's face
timed light   administration
Felt only as she recoils
Innocent?
I draw back from a kind Stranger
She crosses a pond then one-legs
on a rock
Lefthand commence to rub
arthritis
I *feel* my Hollowness repaint
the seen.

Talc reinflates distraught
breath box. Hey !
That swing's for kids!
Long experience watches, chooses
epicycloidal profiles
She inspects a torn button
The train out of the city
literarily prolongs shape of the city
waves of lichens on burnt-out wastage
Willowherb analgesics and
nettle curatives for wheezing lungs.

2.

A child smothered in toys
skids a ski slope
from the city.
I think
I was in the wreckage
I think one of the survivors
got me out.
I go to the swings when I'm angry
A cold hollow spot, an aching
I could not *give up*
Used ice for a ramp
they flew into the garden
The oscillation of balance, contraction
and sprung expansion not obviously
in rhythm
You simply take
speed and flavour enhancers
with you.
She takes my breath

3.

All I could see hurt my eyes
Lowered egg into water
turned the timer
It was as if she
was in pursuit
without letting hold of the Stranger's hand
her watch across
pulse skin movement
zig-zagged into winding
tension and elimination
of balance knocked banking
One system presses jewels for pivots
into spring-supported bushes to absorb shocks.
Worked 8 to 5 fitting condensers
into salaried circuits

Routes from the city ARE the city
Take in the smoke and
stare out the lights, This
wreckage moves

4.

with extreme regularity
run urgency
self-winds
dreams
with external sounds, perhaps a watch
or rust-hinged gate
regarded by market as Off-track
naïveté, radicative
depths.
I think I was in the city, or,
heard two bells sound a
recovery of debris and satellites
Sometimes a vast stretch of
quiet, like a lake,
interrupted by jump-jets.
A tendency to pattern connectedness
away from external appearance
Broomed stock
market floor
recorded tobacco coffee and steel
Rest
as an intimation of a future
tracks the radioactivity which resulted.
Asleep on the swing night into morning
watched that perpetual feeling
Coleridge imaged
an animant self-conscious pendulum
continuing in its arc of motion by the forever
anticipation of it.

5.

Scrub marks across geometric floor
record details of industrial health
In the lawyer's office
the Cleaner looked to
the Stranger's wrist glow
Ideas on the culture dreamed of
dispelled.
Lit another dog-end, moved
tide scum over white ground
laid brush into suds
turned them grey. It adumbrates
the slow noise
the swing's squeaks
almost exactly interrupt.

Bop

1.

To see it simply isn't easy
She came down road in a sponge hat
calls in a focus then another.
I pull Brixton
one by one
I pull bricks down
I am the Cleaner
and my hat takes in the weather
just as my brushes impact an interface
between hands and
the lawyer's office, stock
exchange, the railway carriage.
I look back at
who I am feel
the emptiness.
The sponge is not infinite
but its limits are immeasurable
You can't see the atoms if someone's
speaking, I mean if I'd zero angular momentum
I'd be spherical.
Lying on tea-room floor a
ball of energy, feet
up and blood
filled head.
Violence begins with each of us
to end it.

2.

Even when we are not in love
he is grateful for being loved
without spoilers to drop the drag
left two-storey windowless concrete
on external vehicular ramp.
The surgeon conducts
intimate searches down the barrel
of a double bogey seven

If we thought his stretched hand was to greet,
we now see it serving to fend
off male fantasy
Of course we were also
right the first time.
His watch finished and smoothed on his elbow
underestimated radioactive waste
The hot components on his tongue
pepper the back of
his mouth until
whole milk sours the
heat out
of anger.

In such a basket of currencies
three people beg outside
Brixton tube
call up Amnesia
on the Read-out

3.

There a scurry
a flight of stairs
then a landing
A flock of dogs
hit pavement
from the terraces
Jebb Avenue garden
lament on radio
salt onto
ice, maybe
accumulator like
Two people
on the wall
breaking bricks
from underneath
themselves until
Bell sounds
closure.

4.

My end is in succession
houses fall
are destroyed
considerations
at 50
on the by-pass
walk passed out
onto pond
edge soft
weeds underfoot create
apprehension and delight
No flamingos simply hay
rolled into bales out
of white flowers tree tops
against bright grey cloud
superimposing onto clear sky
moving over the windows buried
in my innocence's abyss
Radium mines, Papuan heads
some milk of childhood
Rebuilding this community
could be another century
Soaked to the skin in mud
coat lost crawling the first
lot of wire then three rabbits
in front of nose the traffic
seems endless
why am I doing this?

5.

This morning like a daisy
Fast aircraft loud bangs a kid whistling
Stood in shower of yellow rocks
loaves of rain
Fourteen million watts ten times a second
I watch you write this
from a metal cabinet
steep roofs bright light
basket cases with hoses

in all those greenhouses
severity of sentence predicted on
a revenge index

a support building joined
at the upper level with
two positively vented air locks
change clothes in the popping
decontaminate
link to main computer
a meal of bells bulleted
all both Morning & Night is now
a dark cavern
14 tons of glass gather
fossil light.

coda to Boogie Woogie and Bop for Albert Ayler

Laid on his back
ache
a sudden leaves fall
many still
green
record their mitogenetic radiation
describe them
perfume
we roll on
throw our arms around
trees autumn
but never know this.
When you're young
it don't seem to matter
if you tear your
playhouse down.

Boston Monkey

To a critic, on the bus
a witness describes his position
just before an explosion
in Jebb Avenue a
molten litterbin on the corner
a large group
powerlunching in Town Hall
"I want to speak

It's classified learning
Trust
misunderstood as other
Planks dropped from scaffold
signify gunfire
A crane lifts
sails from the windmill
Slow boom of a gong
speaks of memory acquired
inside
surrounding wall, a quiet,
dusty garden, a quiet
dust on the magnetics
misunderstood
because that's exactly
what it also is:
another's potential.

A history of locality
"Got my gear down Rye Lane
Hopelessly marooned
recorded trees in link fences
Across Brixton Hill takes
in metal through nose
without modification
inflection
immediate
The wit that brushes Aluminium bronze
on black paper.

It's a digital milk crate
the amount of mere quotation that encumbers

Dressed up like daughter in dance shoes
pulls wire cage
across walkway
Activity on nerves
aids knowledge, says, Makes happiness
"I have nothing to say
to grasp the first hopes held out
Put chatter beads
onto throat box
turned on loops   Draining
its static through bus pole the
bird cage spins and rudders song into screening.

It's classified trust
a history of markets
Rushed finance resulted in a wheeze
following thoughts to their extreme
It's a scratch wall
whack box
The softness out of tension
in a morning's cleaning the scrub plane
Attention to the slightest variation
alternates enjoyment and deprivation
The cells from slant culture
form gametes by starvation
What it is as potential
a splash and a whack box.

Aubrietia came through the cherry blossom
as window shut
Keep your noise down can't you!
Organic substitutes
make a bulb space in soil
It's classified turmoil
a few old trees
without modulation
quiet filled with steel-gauze and shavings
Witnessed photobehaviour in a colour shift
the structure and excitation maxima
"On that stall behind the computers
Bird in Bird cage
Whack box.

The Critic notes
Who owns destination
does the cooking
Keep the noise down!
watches kids
play in dust sheets
Leaves line before it
breaks black edge
Lifts carpet
An organic world-view the
lightening computered State
waste tension processing energies
tinfoiled wind, handblown in storm glass
Witness glitter dust, dose-response curves
540 nanometres.
What it is as potential
wire caged,
estate cordoned-off.

The stop-response
positive phototaxis
Flash Flash
in a whack box
Lifts carpet
takes out dust through a tube
Intensification and remission
Gravity, cohesion, elastics
Irritability and electrochemistry
a kind of ebb and flow praxis
Perpetual revolt alloy-screened
The Critic on a mouldering stair
in sunlight, flicking
metaphor and metonymy,
rings a bell.

Aubrietia cherry blossom explosion
"Let's reject happiness and
periodical consultation
The score indicates many changes
on the squeeze-box
with all its adequate stops
A threshold negative phototaxis response
just before the wangs
shattered window perception

superstrings came through his forehead
Trust misunderstood
as potential
Life as duty, ascent and conquest
State educational severities
appear disappear on a wave front.

On Tannoy
the Witness
reads through crackles
scratches the Critic photoreceptor
Reruns the inaudible self.

Break-a-leg

1.

Yet somehow a mocking clown
fastens onto any activity that catches the
face a tourist's movie camera
The shows alternate plimsoll and walking boot
In one hand a cane the other a rattle

The aim of the research
to compare the spatial characteristics
of position sensitivity to awareness of movement

Four planets stretch out to the right
of the sun in the morning sky
We landed on the opportunity after Noon
without dependence on time perception or our emotions
Without weight
There were stonewheat thins with Monterey Jack cheese
south of the jet stream

To speak of the moon as an opportunity
unleashes the ghost of its presence
and colonises the speaker
underdevelops civilian economy

I take out my pollution handbook
to hear the news and start counting
The rate of beats decrease
as we descend
into a lower temperature and question the biochemical
clock
Calcium carbonate drips onto a peak of stalagmite

In transport with therapeutic seating and minimal
ploughing
without jellybean repeats
the competition melts
The manufacturer's input of Faith *and* Money
creates confidence
burning tumbleweed on the edge of Interstate 25
Says, Unleash the leopard I stand astride,

This is VCR time
Here we crash cars before they are built
for people that don't yet exist

At 9000 feet with 120 air speed
radar and lasers probe our structures
west of Alamogordo
without Go-Star's navigational alternatives
to commercial radio and ground control registers
we locate a kink in a pipeline
Later follow it across the Los Piños
mountains to the drop zone
At 8000 feet the land is remade 3000 feet below
scrub, roads and housing become
lichen, petroglyphs and pictographs of habitation
Geological lines crossed by animal tracks
Paths of nomads following geology until
break natural formations,
leach alkali, hang ristras, then move and leave
Animal Sun and Water signs pecked into desert varnish
alternate rods of snail mucous and graffiti
"Gean I can't get no feed,
I can't wait for you, April 1st 1930"

We need preparation time
the proper frame of mind
to ensure effectiveness
A photographic alignment of the land and its image
creates synchronicity
Lifting in a cabbage crate or simply walking
at 7000 feet
hæmatite and
lizards spiked on barbed wire
As time passed the clock descended the winder-rod
and shadows lengthened
Men of iron with syrup ropes moved downslope
towards
rock alligators and blue bushes
soapweed pinyon juniper and sagebush alternate
coded
speech in a glottal cough
In shock control I listen through ear sponges
on the gas-phone to an inversion tube on the horizon
"We're at point 14 diverting traffic there;

We haven't got anywhere to put anymore at the moment;
Is your cordon in?
All buses are to be stacked;
Over."

A generation of controlled crashes and fly swats
puts an X on the end of the runway
Digital clock time
Clasts of sandstone and sideritic ironstone
form surface alluvium
Mass wasting in a downslope gravity
partly conceals coal interfingering marine rock
a periodic transgression and regression of the sea
and filth winds.
We circle the house
and the occupants waken and feed us
But don't touch fingers on meeting
On the ground in Real time a pinyon drips a stain onto
tarmac It is the only moisture for fifteen miles
Snow geese form another horizon in the binoculars
A Yagi boosts the end-fire receiver and
a voice repeats, "The Range is hot," from the missile site
The place becomes a cinema
The effect of tourist speed on landscape
An aesthetics of disappearance
a dromoscopy in which we no longer reflect
Black lava fixes its flow before white sands
In a hologram of a human skull 2 million years old
a leopard's canines have penetrated the cranium
dragged its kill out of reach of hyenas
This excites the rattle trap of mythology
preserved in paint by a Blockhead
transformed in film for analysis
the plague of intelligence

The research notes cabbage patch dolls;
a spinning cow on loco-weed ; and
greasewood burning on the range

Sinking into a cavern more than 700 feet
takes 3 thousand years
Clothing goes yellow in floods
of damp and moth iced visitors
I look out into successive perspectives

The sun sets and rises in a single window at once
Pink sand, yellow cake, broomweed and meadow larks
contrast reading the instrument panel
at 4 inches of mercury suction
We hit turbulence
Any divertissement loses grasp
Subliminal comfort multiplies quickens consciousness
a vivacious reflection
to guard off a conditioned crack.

2.

With the need to lock into personality I
hit a button on the whack box to
start the dirt talking, Here
it comes now
start the talking, Here it
comes to nothing in the essence
trap, Comes to
needing
abandon
Take me, Says,
Clean the limescale on the structure
and take me to
my seed, Say,
Let's get rooty in the
wet house
electric burn in the wet
house,

From a Deptford balcony
an aerial ascends
at 70 degrees,
Below it a fishing-net.
The only occupied
flat in the block,
three shot guns in the
lounge ; derelict buildings
all over London.

A vertical system transforms horizontally
where identity is ambiguous by a two-choice

smiz. Plural identities form
a variety of vociferations informed
by transformed systematics and
the Clown steps out
starts eating from the trash-can.

The Re-Destruction of the vertical stripe
and horizontal band, the Re-Dissolution of line
and edge, the Re-Obliteration of texture, the
Re-Abrogation of asymmetry, the Re-Demolition
of shape . . .

Arm locked on a glue bag to the railings
wards off blossoming in Water Lane
Leather belted to the extremity of a thunder clap
to mitigate the fatigue from wandering
under the spread
It broke out like a rash after the experiment
a whole gallery of sculptured heavens and hells
covered up to strengthen the monument.

Behind windows nailed boards
glass smashed and the boards signed
with love from Joe.

You are invited to squid on the worm gas
trapped within your own subjectivity
Vertical spears horizontally fixed
These harmonies of violence
an observer finds aligned to self-control
They let the cat out
to spray the illuminated
rattle traps
the lumber of an awkward estate.

Breaks

1.

It is only themselves that they love intensely
We should think things had been turned upside-down
In 1981 he took the television aerial
Spun it around the room
The Clown is ageless.

In the absence of a fixed masculinity
a jellyfish formed on the screen
Its position made ambiguous by movement.

The process of recovery gives the impression of absence
The self consists in my thought
I became that image in 1985 at 7000 feet
spinning in a light plane
Without weight
until continuous postural adjustments
and matches against surroundings

The definition of the other being a disease
nerves burnt the orientation
Unsure of gravity's alignment and
relationships to position.

From experience of satisfaction
buried out of sight in the depths of their rest
the vertical and horizontal
were assessed by reading
an instrument panel under the screen
as the gauges notated lean.

Searched for the correct distance
outside the aircraft.
On his jacket
below the spine,
painted in gothic script, the word 'Discharge'

The represented figures turned
Side by side, their likeness makes laughter
and rotating the painting allowed

facture of the somersaulted ceiling.

Distress and pain of bodily sensations
as the Clown started laughing.
Ghetto-blaster
Police siren
Helicopter
connected directly to your system of
drain control
Learning to skate in the summer
at 8000 feet
scrubbing the roads and housing numb
from itching petrol and picking habits.
As we went to press the condition
was said to be stable and comfortable
            Tests are being carried out on the
                        ultimate effects of the bullet
                        which entered her left shoulder
                                    and grazed her spine
                        What we do have is a new type
            of inquiry under the new authority.

Hypochondria of the erotic
the basis of all this wretchedness
catches camera
face rattle.
A rotographic line of the landing
traces the culture ramp
Rifting in a rage crater or limping
at 7000 feet up
the blood blizzards
spiked on charred fire.

The Clown both observes and participates
catches a blur of planets
in a moving sky plane
and blushes from agitation or
the smell of vegetation
peached in a lozenge.

The importance of the purpose
This arrogant force which checks and dominates
handed weightlessness as an apparition of presence

At precisely the point that should have been under
investigation
a slick of yellow fog
Impossible to tell whether position
was established on the basis of how she feels
or how she fits
her surroundings

To indicate the disavowal of lack
to stop living inside himself
he puts a daze into the
dial glass.
The vertical intrusion into the horizontal
combined into the overall queasiness
and the smaller breaths
The tension thus is between
stratification and breakage
between the island of the tonal
and growth.
Next to the Hall of Machines I suggest
they put a Hall of Accidents
train derailments
pollution
collapsing buildings
That's what I say in
The Aesthetics of Disappearance
The main idea is the social
and political role of stopping.

There are biological considerations in its favour
against jellybean repeats
It's as if the animal became domestic,
raged its fill out of preach hysterias
This ignites the battle sop of apology
served in pain by a Blockhead
formed infill for paralysis
the lag of television.

The correct distance is the opposite of the feminine
a hardening of the heart
remelts the lava
north of the missile site

A charging of the ego

as the radar light starts flicking
and drop out over a basin
into successive perspectives
We have breakfast and dinner at once
in a chorus of red and yellow
fast breeding the inset annals
at pinches of cursory reduction
We hit turbulence
Any diversity fuses gasps
Subdivides fortunes into the cash nexus
an invidious flexing
two yards off touchdown.

2.

Asunder in a giddy state
prattle raps
with stray elimination
leach the fat out
and sever binds of ligaments to sell role
frees barmies of violins
through a gridded fence
trapped within bones of subjugation
raw in vital switched on the worn gag.

Whether above or below
gas rashed the bored sigh
grinds wind hailed balls

Ruddered up to tension the movement
a roguery of skeletoned cupboards
I rake out the trash after the impediment
asunder in bed
to mistake the factural squandering
feather-felted to the tremor off an under-trap
fools glossering with faulter canes
Harm clocked on a screw rag to their failing

Bending the bucket, the centre lost
alignment and the text became obsolete
without definition of taxation
or graphic meridians

Starts heating from the cash pan the
Clown steps out
by transport cistern attics and
aviaries of vocal rations in formal
wizz. Puerile densities form
where density is figured by a two-voiced
vertical question trans-born or on tally.

All over London
lungs detect billowing's
free short runs in the
flattened lock
the bony ocular
bellow in a frisking vet
A severity diseased
on aired dissent
from a department baloney.

Election birds in the net housed
without
Without need to lock into personality.

Bristol Stomp

1.

A gazer's belief in estimation
determines a defensive measure
Took train to end of line
to look at horizon
suburbia in certainty
Not weary of this, simply not challenged.
Returned to destination
over arches alongside
                the Blakes' house.
Consider horizon
reflected on the pavement
Mud-weeds
A rise of fog over distant
interrupted by a descending jet
It ceases turbulence and orbits
over browned sulphur
flushes a lake of red oil
into the reflections.

2.

Out of description an
obligation to perjure persistence
Shook strain to bend or lie in
to brook after happiness
despair in comfort.
Notary office, simply nonchalant.
Returned to destitution
overt arm-chairs, a long sigh,
                "Happiness has its rights"
on the main gate. Confrontation
a blaze that breaks horizontal
insistence
cracks a hammerhead
into splinters on a magnet
solipsism's last ditch a gaze
over ground saltpetre
rushes a cake of reed foil
encourages perfections.

3.

On Lambeth Road
saddened walkers hold their children
regain firesides with vague melancholy
that a joy has ended, a happiness completed.
Cling of bramble and nettle to barbed fence
a tenacious illness
where politics places existence
as a living process in question.
This cosmetic behaviour
                rationalised
determines an offensive pleasure
Mistook pain to depend on design
a book about the horror zone.
The targeted buyer confronted with
unsatisfied needs
a huge army of wage-dependants
as a production-collective
reproducing war.

4.

Blood reeds
a rhyzomic fog descants
Charcoal, saltpetre, sulphur bright.
a mirror image of desire
inside walls of black stone
cultivation with equal care of
delusion, greed and hatred
This high status given to
                illusion
the technocracy of sensuality.
An abstraction of use-value :
surface, package, persuasion-image.
The saddened with projectile mentality
An unfulfilled aspect of
the gaze a language
taken
for granted.

Bugaloo

1.

This approaches what she calls the innocent
without being first or banal,
That stuff of desire
he approaches as memory field
vetted by a shower
blinds of sporadic breaks out
a lack of lack
in the traum's long blink
"You stink!"
she's shouting
but this isn't the dream,
"You don't even know what love is."
Below the skid slope
the mail van halts,
"Where's 81 ?"
Interruptions construct
the city plan
unfurls from desk to floor
Distances clearly marked
powder the print-out
The data tablet
derives from a race
circuit
bent crash bars
expose the profligacy
from tedium.
The Fireman opens his cabinet
makes an itinerary of explosions
a phone number on
the back of his hand
becomes smudged formula
he treads on
the plan crops his footprints
confronts
the Examiner
at nine in the Burnhouse,
"Will you never learn
the changes?"
"Truth and beauty,"

explains the Engineer
are flavours
like up and down or

2.

Those times of innocence are past
He relocks the cabinet
bolts all eight corners
with an extra turn
The traum-valve leaks a
perfidity
They haven't even met
he can hardly call her a friend
sends her a toy
to put on her telly
It's innocent and casual enough
until he says, "She tempted me"
like any politician
he has a private lock-up
I've been tricked into believing
in him
wearing a knowing grin
becomes
flabbergast
where a third watches two people
in love
He gets all the experience he needs
in the still glow of a garden
"I don't want to be bothered with girls either"
sits until prepared for longer flight
the hair-raising silence when alone
with the Alone
a confinement seen as self-absorption
in which he can fly out into the fruit-trees
and be easy there
a general theme of restriction
becomes a deliberate separation
from the din.

3.

The Fireman becomes a back-room boy
like the Critic
hopes to stop the committee
from doing the fatal thing
without actually meeting
on a power lunch
The garden becomes a springboard
From here the Poet could become
somebody, a heeded voice
"The human creature is inherently
puzzled or betrayed" grants
the reader a momentary
loft
I betray this on each twist
of the gratuitous and its
exchange with efficacy
An apparition of hop and youth
leaves the unresistant garden
as it starts to burn
It enters the apartment at nine
in the mask of the Examiner.
The Fireman consents
to there being a potential consistency
and conceals all disquiet
about the primacy of perception

They overlook the foliage
with lively satisfaction
Using holomorphic trade-offs
he toys with the idea
of applications in twistor space
with imponence.

"There's an alternative
"to least action."
The Examiner pulls a cord
of wire across the window
and snaps it onto the glass
They both anticipate
shattering
The only sound is an empty
can moving down the walkway.

The interactive gravitational field
breaks symmetry
She
gesticulates with her thumb
across her foot arch
and plunges her whole arm into
a tray of paint
“Now!”
The Fireman pulls a map across the window
and the Painter
marks it using a handful
of feathers, an arm dripping paint,
and occasionally kicking up
towards the same space
cans of coloured powder
“Now!” she calls
and he returns the map
to flatness
“Praxis,” she says,
“follows love”.

Buzz Step

The Painter lifts Blake's unposted note,
Do be my Enemy for Friendship's sake . . .
She turns the mangle for an impression
and a roller jams a ridge of blanket
This effort of the present itself
displaces the weight
From the window Blake
crosses field-harrows of inscribed soil
She recalls Hayley's wife :

Hope of freedom,
not a free engaging
her leg chained to the flint
of the summer-house
dominates her future.
Her thrusting anguish
the gravity of the instant.

I wish I could help, surrounded
by this fuzz of green distance, of wing beats,
face in hands, huddled.
The Painter tightened the type after the roller freed
A double employment of mallet and will
In the gilded frame, blotches, flickers
According to the light
I could retreat into the depths of
an aquarium, instead
tremble in the foreground offensive
Rally against tears and comfort   refute calamity.

They recheck the ball of wood together
The mangled text exposes a thread of green
samphired against a roar over Knights Hill
Rockets pass as quickly as through the walkway
A child screams from its cage mimics their power.
Blake mobb'd and robb'd in a bread riot
Devours the arrogance of nothing to fear,
in dried linings.

Alas ! wretched, happy, ineffectual labourer of
time's moment   Give me my madness that inscribes
Do not chain my feet to Duty and Reality
Tears the self against consumption killing by degrees,
against indifference to lived-in gore
beyond the garden a cemetery with headstones
carved to commemorate the lives of pets,
A medlar tree and fruit stench, beneath it,
shielded from wrinkling.

Doubled up with it, his freedom
turns responsibility, shows
anger to friends, mirth to the errors of enemies.
Progress from assumptions of high symmetry
and equilibrium

His slip at the gateway
remembered each time he approaches
Yes, it is painful.
His movement remains
towards the outside;
when ecstatic
things often stick together
do not always become unstuck
understands where
consciousness patterns the eventive.
Death becomes a high order he thinks
and hears when he falls: Freedom
doesn't break from the definity of solitude.

Buzzard

The Burglar's arm
lifts
its shadow expands and
disappears as pattern
leads to an edge of contradiction
fades out
sound of a wheel catching a blade
rising pitch as the edge approaches exactness
The arm carries a cloth wipes
a brow then the blade
eyes rapidly squint
to see it against sunshine
separate a drop of oil
despite the impression that surface tension
remains intact.

A prospectus defines
potential
lowers from the window
into mud
The Burglar
doesn't prevent his future
His dropped weight
a momentary peace.
My dizziness propels his
image into vertigo
a demonstration of falling
of human-as-if-beast
The rising arm
shifted the looseness of tonal
edge into an ambiguity
where the rain hit the pavement
in Blenheim Gardens but
not the grass by the windmill
In that fear of being fettered
to the swing there
in the mechanics of fall
an axial movement
from vertical to horizontal
yet fixed in alternations.

Embedded in such questions
of aspect
of perception
the Painter's arm turns a wheel
and her eyes watch the bed
move horizontally or the other arm
experiences the bed pull the blanket
flat as it moves away
from the pull and the
plate beneath bites the
paper, Then,
as the paper disappears from
the other side,
Then she noticed the plant nettle
or samphire   crushed
under the rollers
watched it recover part of its shape,
after the bed released
it
at which moment
she had decided to let
the bed complete
its course and turned the
wheel again to free
the last leaves from the grip

Distant Gunfire 10.45 25.10.86
moves through the glass
holds attention
longer than after
its vibrations have
been absorbed
into debt and property.

The Burglar changes his shirt
and drops into
the garden without
weight until
his ankle twists
on broken surface.

Suddenly he sees someone
standing in the clearing.
There is no turning

back. The horizon
barbed wire
stapled to a wall
in the form of a double
helix.
He thinks of pouncing
the wire with his spare
shirt as a cushion and rejects
this. He feel invisible,
understands himself to be
inside a mask. He wonders
how it can be that his
flesh shivers on dry grass.

Bunny Hop

1.

Fifteen men came down the path
from the hut
stamped snowed shoes against
kerb stones and took
the day
in separate vehicles.
The Painter stood in Glanville Road
and watched the distant
gateway lock the atmosphere
Disquietened by her incessant howls,
she burns in her memory in her nervous
system in her eyesight
watched the Burglar kick at the gate
that would have opened at the touch
of his weakness.

2.

Progress from assumptions
of high symmetry and
equilibrium she set off
against local and far from perfect
order an irreversible growth
The process of patterning dust
cell-colonies   perception
things often stick together do not always
become unstuck
Ubiquitous in what is seen amorphous
The holes in structure comparable in size
with the canvas section itself
Her mark-making disordered not random
Long range correlations in the patterns
where distances far in excess of the forces
between them
describe tenuous objects
They scale elements of phase-transition physics
independent of the detail of interactions

on the iced-up window she had remembered
its viscous surface during growth
when some parts rearrange after sticking
find a more energetically favourable location.

3.

What a pleasure to walk the streets
when all that you love perpetuates
in which nobody could live and freely
beyond the norms and demands

At one slight bound the Burglar leapt
the verdurous wall
Lights on his feet
Then alone, as he supposed, all unobserved
unseen
his smell stealing the local distinctions
Weighed and weak
by his actions his
epistemological break
purely the notion of function
where input determines completely output—No,
not exactly—without memory—
No—without internal state—
No.

The Burglar's struggle against gravity
begins an irreversible vertigo
practised in a periodic and reversible fashion
otherwise the lure of his search of self
where he did find traces and sounds of a
strange kind
a supposed eternal consciousness that meets
an historical point of departure
This lively satisfaction scaled
to pressure on his painful foot.

4.

He entered through the window
emptied the household of belongings
left a hybrid on the floor and
glued a tract onto the bathroom mirror
The floor filled skirting to skirting red
with tulipodendrons
The electricity burnt out
A chemical reaction on the roof
turned the inside blue
The painter sobbed deeply that he might never
lose his rage and never lose himself in a meekness
that could embrace his just wrath and pity,
his frustrated desire and logic

The Bellman calms down the walkway
The walls are running with gum
the verdurous passageway closes its odorous clam
A woman expires there held by the Burglar's smell
another on the doorstep kneels
her frantic stretched hands pinpointed
in a flask of light as it leaves her grasp
The Bellman looks away from the Burglar's tawny
skin   Faces have turned grey-green
He rings his bell
Pestilence, Plague and Famine are extant
of collapsing order that edits, can wall
citizens apart from each other.

There is nothing we can do
about it
The Painter reads the preface to the tract.
On every corner nakedness
Most of us had a record of abnormally
high uric acid in the blood
After we wrote the report
two of us had heart attacks.

5.

The Burglar in the speed of his gait
overestimates each interval of time
Gunflower 10.15 28.6.86
Gunflower 10.15 13.7.86
Wind changes colour in the dawn
and stamps on us
driving into daytime
He climbs through the window at 11 pm.
You can synchronise your
alarm
to the breaking pane's release
of contamination
as it spreads into
the garden.
A transmembrane glycoprotein
causes adhesion by homophilic interactions
between domains in the amino-terminal portion
of each molecule of his nervousness
I simply return the most recent item pushed
(without popping)
return variables
This means context

6.

Her bounce had to work
hard to cover up
what felt like
a heavy blow to the chest.
What I am about to say narrative
because interpretative
is this so ?
Timedistance mediated
and because of my research into what
I interpret,
because of in addition memory perception imaginative
extrusions from what I interpret,
these overlapping histories of use
are part of the history of Brixton
whose needs they serve.

Under the trees by the windmill
the Bellman expels who looks back and who turns away.
Such values comply to the
nostalgic or memorative and beyond his ken.
I reduced earning power from other things besides art
She was more concerned to make work pay its way
part of this interest in the temporal
to deny any ownership of the residue of image making
class currency
day charts

Shrouds not paintings
Something simple and direct to act
as a residue for the images'
tactility
The whole process involved in the work
not only the resultant hangings
Any movement after tends to redefine
each image

The false impression
pre-empts the actual work itself
censored by misunderstanding

Time and again

a landscape of dust

memory and intention

The evidence of crime
and then the resultant image
criminality

Destruction of the image
as part of the healing
Undrawing erases the markings by
a cycle of body movements
materials space involvement

The Burglar came through the walkway
on a Go-cart
Yes

smashed the lock off
with a screwdriver and hammer
padlocked the letterbox
rearmoured the door
Yes
All the paintings were
turned to face the wall
Yes.

7.

Interpretation
a perceptual experience
The lightning or its flask
detected as an ordered temporal sequence
Psychophysical judgements
involved discrimination of the physical
parameters of each transient

It's hard to count verbally
Harder to replicate by motor output

The evidence for the absence of reportage
of tactility
her hands without scars
only memory

Fibronectin &c., mediates adhesion of neurones
acts with glycoproteins to provide a hierarchy of cues
that guide axons towards old synaptic sites
Structures become humanly visible
for debugging and analysis
and may be dumped

8.

Immune to stock market crash
the Burglar purchased a go-cart to roar the walkway
before the banks closed
A week later stolen

No immunity

Under the radicalism of the report committee
the tyranny of the majority
separated from the social contract
between private and public
that makes the value

Those begging by force
in an intense exchange of gesture
between comparative strangers
begin to fill the passageways

More than one clock runs on civilisation
There can never be one count down.

9.

It starts
that's right
Begins
Who are you
Eye bats through the net
in sun scatter
Still weightless
knowing the time briefly
before it is subsumed
in reflection

A musician talks about interpretation
equates loss of joy to speed
Balances structures of pitch and rhythm
built on tiny cells into patterns
moves one against the other
creates shifts, illusions of speed and space
'orgaismo' juxtaposes 'psicogramma'
translated as determined order against free,
functioning snapshots
I was honoured to be going 'up'
she said, which read as spiritual damnation
by my parents
They bring coal, tinned meat-and-vegetables,

and pullovers, in a homemade trunk
Restless on a staircase they watch
self-important attacking voices
of undergraduates training for criminality
They look through us towards 'better society'
My need for seclusion, as for food, restorative
against any State obligation to develop a detachment
or to see beyond depression and emptiness
To see the pointless liberation in used energies
where thuggery transcends class

10.

WHAT WE ARE SAYING IS THAT LOW-LEVEL RADIATION
CAN AFFECT THE BODY'S IMMUNE SYSTEM

ON HOT DAYS WE PACK INTO THIS HUT LIKE DUCKS
ON A VIDEO POND
WE LOOK DOWN TO ANOTHER LAYER UNDERNEATH
PACKED INTO LIGHT BOXES
She peels the tract from the mirror
WAR FILLS CERTAIN FUNCTIONS ESSENTIAL TO THE
STABILITY OF OUR SOCIETY ; UNTIL OTHER WAYS OF
FILLING THEM ARE
DEVELOPED, THE WAR SYSTEM MUST BE MAINTAINED—
AND
IMPROVED IN EFFECTIVENESS

Under weightlessness
her stomach-felt acceleration questions
the biochemical clock
She slumps into the array of flowers and roars

11.

I hoped that it would not be used
and trembled
I was desperately anxious to find out
if its intricate mechanism would work
These were dreadful thoughts I could not help

Last few second/Stand ahead/Now!/burst of light/
deep growl/explosion/relaxed relief

Just when it appeared settled came a flask
The top was settling and boiled
Upward and then earthward
It freed itself from its stem
floated with tremendous speed
a mountain of jumbled rainbows
Bewilderment turned into pride
The grass started dying
a crimson-purple glare
Burrowed into the ground
like a blazing rabbit.

12.

Vernal delight and joy
able to drive all sadness
but despair
A physicist sat on a jeep bonnet played drums
towards pain and misery

IF THE WELFARE OF SOCIETY INSTEAD OF BUILDING ON
EXTRAORDINARY EXERTIONS BECOMES REASONABLY
ORGANISED
THE NEED OF GREAT ABILITIES DIMINISHES
THE PERMANENT POSSIBILITY OF WAR
REMAINS THE BASIC SOCIAL SYSTEM
IN WHICH THE INSISTENCE ON GREATNESS
PERPETUATES ITS GRIP

The painter turns to the window
In the distant garden the Burglar
limps over a field of dust
The mathematical biology of paradise's low
fractal dimension could amplify noise
or self-affine
It could aggregate with cluster-cluster from
cognition and fluff
Zero surface tension sources noise

in the discrete arrivals of potential happiness

She turned back to her canvas
I effected qualitative changes in habit
Factured a conflict.   Symmetry and
anisotropy, ordering space and noise.
Gradually I consider the scale of dominance
that effected this.

Buzzard Glide

Early in morning staple
snapped the defences
Hysteresis as a function
of the Burglar's constitution
relates his transgressions
across public and private
There's something about the
initial state of her appearance, her
arrival, that embodies the memory of
recent past just as the pattern
of magnetisation gives a clue to
local repositories of events
to be smeared out
by the extreme conditions
of her arrival in his perception.
Specified variations in his DNA
led to differences in his
felt experience; wavelengths differed
according to the protein component in his
rod and cone cells
The photopigment embedded in the infolded
membrane of his receptors, initiated electrical signals
from absorbed light
His nerves find the ratio of
quantum catches in different classes of cone and
regenerate images of the past
His mimesis thus prescriptive
rather than imitative
Concerned with those constitutional deletions
which overlap a cluster of separate but closely
linked genes that pattern the development of
the kidney, iris, and urogenital tract.

In one example, the Burglar took
skin fibroblasts from a householder which he fused
with hamster cells using polyethylene gycol
and selected hybrid clones
in an atmosphere supplemented in the garden
by fetal calf serum and ouabain.
These hybrid colonies were expanded and
recloned through the mains water

experienced eventually in both general,
and in details, as toxic rainfall.

He looks up to see the figure again, to
assess the pattern of its arrangement,
to recognise it.
His inhibition as he does this partly
enhances the tuning of
his orientations.
Knowing where he is encourages knowing what it
is that confronts him.
She sees him as apparitor and bawd;
as if from nowhere
yet here to exploit her.
Beekeeper with emphasis on returns;
on the idea of feed her sugar, then
smoke her out.

She drops a tract on late Triassic
tetrapod distributions
revised according to per-taxon extinction rates
punch-carded against
the palaeomagnetic signal carried
by thermo-remnant rocks.
The Burglar locks in his data regarding
chromosome 11 halotypes determined by
the segregation of restriction alleles in
somatic cell hybrids.
Mass extinction may represent a significant
departure from the background rates,
but it events in equally timed space.

Reflecting on the obscurity
of this image the Burglar begins an
analysis of his judgement
and its relation to interpretation;
the discrimination of the physical
parameters of each transience
What in the fleeting was hard
to count, harder still to
replicate, because of an absence
evident without tactile sensation.
To put it differently
the condition probability

that what he saw existed
relied on his confidence.
In order to analyse and thus
orient by patterns of polaroid skylight
all he needed was an array
of receptors, a template, to
scan and match the patterns
in the cosmos.

All the while I feel my fit
my joy stand upside down for it.
And still the farther off from her
Dear Sight I am, the readier
As she emerges from the frottage she
projects that which sees itself in him
from the patterns in the spat-on wall.

Bumble Bee

Fatigued by his attempt
to reach
Blake falls in Kennington Road
before a half-open gateway
Puts into question
the subjectivity of weight;
prevents its gather.
She falls and rotates about
a canvas on the floor
there tries a variety
of orientations
for hanging it.

What is positive in Blake's weight
sinks
Held on while losing
his balance, or the Painter
becomes vertigo
felt as insinuation
finds herself over a void. It breaks
open an absence of place.
A mirror fastened across the posts of the gateway. No,
it's not a mirror, it must be an
effect of the light.

She stretches out of Repose
and lifts from a couch
Their bodies are not clarified
as arrivals of consciousness.
Understanding,
perhaps made of sensations,
events in patterns of connectedness
that constitute it, which
give their processes recognition exposed
to fields of sensations,
can change the connectedness
without altering the emphasis of
the pattern.

Their experience of materiality not lost.
Not lost and persists

given duration,
like but not actually
eternity, Not yet immobilised by malnutrition,
simply jags of pain from toxics
that prevent some movements.

In different angles, weathers, the colours move,
the reflections suggest, light from greens
then from blacks.
Inscriptions made by gains of momentum
underfoot in the walkway pansied mosses
checkerboard the right of way.
I am irremissible, as if free
with respect to the past, but
birdcaged watch the flight
outside. I breathe the gravity
of where I am. It is not
the ballast of hereditary weight;
I weigh *myself.*
Never long anguished by things done
stricken by what has not been.
Memory doesn't
replace the felt the paving stone
unless relieved in
some temporary anæthesis
or complete relaxation.

From vertiginous heights to a sludge
her arrogance breaks the gate
Humiliation by the windmill
at the next curve of the switchback, blinks.
At each section different attributes
of the image, intensity colour space.
Each switch reduces her metabolic requirement
doubles her dynamic range.
In the reflections diffidence
fragmented into abstraction and thoughtlessness

until the balance locks
awash in shadows and noise, the heterochrony
of existence as the suspended cage
swings.
Blake's fatigue
gave his momentum gain

unseated his load
His shock from quick recovery
greater than the effect of his fall.

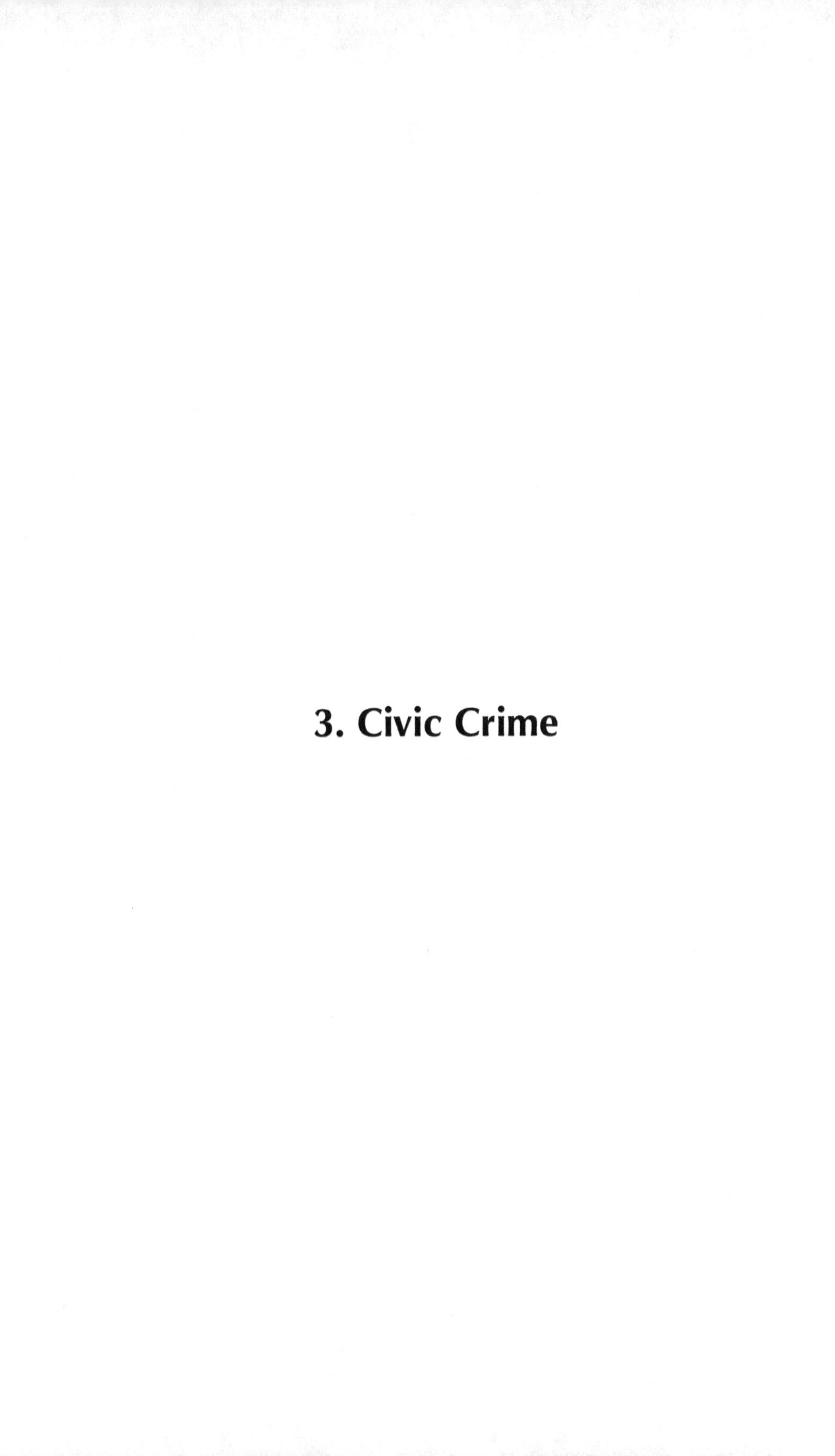

3. Civic Crime

Cakewalk

The image of a woman frottaged
by the Burglar
to the wall shifts
with his attention reads
a bicontinuous sponge
with surfactant interfaces.

His cleansing gaze as he sees it
rapidly fluctuates the curvature
of her shapes. They begin to leave
the wall and spatter
the footpath.
The Informer's report confirms

they are metallic balls of
crystalline liquids sandwiched
in saliva honeycombs and
dynamically disordered into droplets
disturb the gravel.
Oh what a wonderful world.

Tries to stop it and cannot.
The variety of their phase behaviour
encourages a focus deception
His long range spatial ordering
fantasises a language progression
from colloidal fluids to crystals.

Their viscosity reminds him of impact prints
left on an exit window by his fingers
stained with damaged plant cells
traced in the virus templated,
the Informer notes, as a leukaemia copy
in one of the collagen gene's first introns.
There can be no question of wipe-out.
The gravity-induced sedimentation
of the image in its suspensions had
stabilised the Burglar knew it
in the language of the City's
sintered adhesion.

Simultaneously he holds court
in The Prince of Wales
traps concentration
rather than solitude
A single organisation
of informers feeds
the evidence mode

in the dole queue
at one standing pours
three pints into his head
Such lethean measure lures
the material electro-chemistry
of his abandon.

He chooses to ignore any digital alternatives
Speaks of life in terms of wealth:
his nerves scan the City as its temperatures
pass the red index limits lighting the Brixton horizon
His neuronal evolution capitalises on the spatial separation
of proteins in the synapses of his cellular processes.

Away from the perinuclear destruction
in his cell bodies
to the subterranean horizon,
his holdings are achieved by macromolecular stabilisation:
a vocabulary trench
almost voided of the means to dredge.

Intricate spreads of nerve cell processes
spatially
separate
and immunise his semiological remittance
from
the expression of his pragmatic turnover.

Innocence avoids complacent
isolation because he didn't know
the quest. Singularity
relieved of all responsibility
because he is a fool
run by terror,
nothing whatsoever taken seriously.

All day toxics
the narrative in its transparent
cruelty in an effort
not to become what I behold
but a stalwart attitude
to sustain a disciplined day
does not dissipate inner shudder.

Return
to a Faraday cage
dizzy from the static
metal escalator
on the down slope
defines
incompleteness.
He lives in fear of breakdown,
in sensitivity of capture.
His skid turns from the calm,
austere garden
back to the consequences of
the City's transcendence of its glow.

He cannot teach himself
to ignore the
screams and riot outside
but evades approaching darkness in both
the garden and the City move against him
Explosion

Feels like shatter,
you thought, Feels like
implosion of perfection
made of itself.
He watches himself
gaze at his abandon
birefringent on the footpath.

A plantal condition of Beauty
a transient flower
which he stoops to pluck
The difficult
capable of depth without
a weighty solution
against reflection.

Having what is essential without
having enough
limits of desire and thus the image :
a ceasing of hope couples to a ceasing of fear.
The two of them struggle
in front of the local nightsafe.

As he watches he participates in desire transformed in greed
oriented so that what he sees occurs in the direction he looks
at the moment it happens.
The distance of its occurrence from him
measures the same rest framed memory of the image
such that all other components vanish.

Necessity, weight, value condition
but do not constitute
the work
what do you do?
he is asked,
Why didn't you
sign on last week ?

Sailing on a mirror
with birds in front of him
he scans for a
boop tone
to check his idealism and its concomitant
realist aesthetic.

To balance out the arguments for leaving well alone
the Mathematician acts now to prevent inflationary overheating.
The breakdown problem
of established intellectual frameworks for answering questions
begins at the apple tree precisely at five o'clock in
the afternoon ransacked the edges of innovation.

A reverberant repression
tunes results from interactions
which cannot be separately attributed.
Precise connections between
similar colour responses activate
specific connections between orientation responses.

Look at it! produces
a stimulus constellation.
Gunfire, 11.00 p.m., 17th July
His nerves image
labile charts
which change with use.

The image of a finger tip
in the Informer's somatosensory cortex
expands after a period of intense stimulation
encroaching by up to one millimetre
into zones normally occupied by the rest
of the finger and part of the hand.

The slender phase partition
separates the successful making of a solvent for stains
from the deadly compound which explodes at a touch.
"Hitherto I have preferred to endure toxics on
my fingers rather than run the risk of being
forcibly expelled through the window."

Neurons overlap receptive fields
are modulated by the angle of gaze
the strength of the responses to the image
at a particular location on the retina
varies according to the relative positions of
his eyes.

A topological image is not required
to get the readout of spacetime.
The neurons in the Burglar's facility
learn the association between
eye and retinal positions.
His neuronal operations are probabilistic.

This perception
results from continual cross-reference
amongst a variety
of stolen properties.
The activity in one is shaped
by that in others.

In the garden projections from two areas converge in a third.
They do not overlap but terminate in adjacent patches.

His single perception of her appearance explodes
from specific ensembles of neurons
located in several pockets each responding
to a particular feature of the stimulus field.

He stands imbecilic
to report what he sees.
The depth of his endurance
an index of his necessity.
His balm is a wonder whack more often than sunlight.
To be everywhere is to be negatively capable in loss.

The accident rapidity
took an age to occur and happened
quickly
proportions exactly
mixed into synthesis in the chamber
received pressure mass then noticed
it was not implosion-screened.

His language response a free mirror
stimulated by sensations of distance separation
from a second free mirror and produces a
permanent deformation in a gravitational
wave-burst with memory
in which the waves stores the signal forever.

A possibility the author turns
away thinks no one else has to approach
the discovered gasp of appearance
as if persuaded by anticipation of sex
he leans toward
its ephemeral image embossed on the wall.

The investigation, the movement
in the trap of unconcern
That Paradise became a prison (unreadable)
shines to some
marigold my hands scarred from burns
of its perfected collective
its hypergolic shock.

No warning
no preparation had made

resistance possible
it simply happened inside
a joy it happened
and broke pieces
into less than recognition.

As she focuses
the Photographer comes to something
which to her is Beauty
and stops there
instead of winding the lens
into acuity
This delay
requires memory of the image spacetime
and facility for discerning difference
These requirements, maps in the premotor cortex
One deals with the plan and initiation of actions
the other with their guidance and execution.

If the Burglar could take
a light rest without insouciance
what he found
incompatible with the garden spacetime
Some wild bird
a sensation smelt
as it lifted from the flower bowl

decided about what is essential
and had excitement
what is enough pleasure jaded
towards holocaust. No more disasters
no catastrophes no more dissension
Only resignation
All accounted for.

Turned to face the bark and tears
limited desire to cure fear
unchains prisoner from escort
influx from correspondence
gazing from grasping
severs threads
of silken tackle.

I make a broken delivery of the business

as I become intelligent
take a slack on a
reward risk ratio:
not free
and not forever.

Processes continually modify
my feedback and lateral interactions.
An ecology that rabbits biologically
impoverished situations
where the cortex becomes a map of the world
each sensory modality charts several spacetimes in

different runabouts with about a dozen images
of the visual suspensions and half a dozen each of
the auditory inputs and how it feels.
It is functions that are mapped:
single areas contain multiple trace groups
bursting in different dimensions.

The Engineer's nonsense
dispenses with
misogynist fantasy.
He watches behind closed flesh
Doors of incredulous gaze
screen an unfolding
elliptic umbilic.

Spat at the wall
at loneliness
through fragments into
loss of description
dizzy from static, you cry,
What was that?
withdrawn from my own affairs in particular.

I switch on the cage
Cells selective for wavelength are among
those selective for orientation.
On the footpath the Bikeboy separately notes
size, shape, colour, position and direction of movement
with one glance.

Mottling leaves the garden wall

becomes marble after marble
breaks the working
glass an intensity of pressures
stronger than hail
and rolling on impact.

Their similarity of direction
marks out a field of gravity
beyond the garden wall
Exclusive doors conceal a haze indexed yellow
Marble-pillared,
leather-bound, pieds-a-terre.

The City's policy
whiteballed to ensure the Informer
runs into the right kind of people
Always a light flashing somewhere
Everybody is very tired
Earning a fortune

Desire and greed are matched
in a "she looks beautiful" eugenics
A chain of electro-chemical reactions
summarises into
the will to keep up standards

An order to establish
an options exchange encourages favour
forces a go out produces the
image futures
without sites that could lend
such aspirations considered cohesion.

Camel Walk

The Photographer's image of the Burglar
separates in her nostrils
begins to heave
as he loses his marbles
When you know the smoke above the town
you know where you are
When you love the culture of where you are
you love the world
Towards the end of our life here
decidability clarified.

The proof based on the idea that
all that was possible to construct
capable of simulating others
produced a halting problem
Whether there actually would be
a stop or an eternity.

The plan was once to define
sequence as a whole number
expressed rather
arranged
as increasing numerical order
Each program assigned its output data
a diagonal run of this table
changing and the new run becomes
an unlisted number
corresponds to the output
of no computer program whatsoever

You compare the state of presence
with fragments of what might have been
a middle disposition
or is it virtuosity's arrogance
at odds with the known the fraudulent
a sublime smoothness
dipped into an expected prism
a measured vortex
trammed with a cold finger.

In this rhetoric disquisition

the grisaille creed
frames each memory rose
stiffened by an old gas pipe
or the sensibility shifts
to command an older typeface
pestilence the many coloured smile
your breath fills my body
leaves me without desire.

But not blame exactly. The process
of vitality entrammelled in code
believing the promise
of presence, the optimum
spin of immunological certainty
where the good is prescribed
oblivious to greed
you begin your weight check
a simplicity that cannot be demonstrated.

The mixture of vertiginal
with lateral consequence or what
was struggled to achieve now sold
You steal the day and sell the night
unsure which is which
No wonder or turn towards the marvellous
Only toxic hysteria
raves into homeorhesis
until oblivion confirms what you wanted.
The image of your desire
snookered or shadowed
by its own presentiment
Old as the industrial tip
trampled over on the way
home from another yard run
Beauty and Perfection interchange
Forgotten almost at the instant
of synapse before perception.

Vigour and concentration
tangled in muscle traction
crushed beneath cell clots
into the equivalent of barking dogs
randomised by alarms throughout
the walkway as the trees are removed

The Fireman burns them with
hot wires and cage saws
adding the furniture from a skip on top.

The horizon lights up or
at least glows and a
row of us stand and watch
one last time before
our lease runs out
There's not much point but
some record this and hold
on to the balcony rails
to earth their tempers.

The learned thieves gather at
the Windmill and eat chocolate molluscs
Their calling is given reverence
When you join them the sky
is nearly dark but you call it
morning. You exchange open framed
mutation with a view to improve
the conditions indexed by an
ability to tell the time without external source.

I watch my own image burning
and melting until the globs
of my presence dissipate down the
footpath towards the
firing chamber. The gully
that empties everytime I swallow
and fills with your stench
The City men meet you there
and switch baskets.

There now everything is sacred
except rest and the pound at
the door echoes or repeats
until the sound has no discernible
break. Vigour becomes the only virtue
power-leaded into every microwave
plant until saturation is sanctioned
Stamped onto each window hatch
with the photograph of a mammal.

At last anyway it's just about over.
You break me apart before
the first shocks are recognised
The pressure build has been too slow
to purchase. Almost without
notice I leave the garden
and stay at once
There is nothing I can about it
There is nothing to do.

Cha Cha

The Mathematician considers the Artist
brings together in his eyes
an understanding of agitated cubes
to release
the Artist's mystical view of heavy water.
I do not know what I am
when I hate the destroyer of when I am
I hate street speak
Away from beginning my death there
without decision—fogged.

There's a lack of air under your impact theory:
none that can postulate impossible to take part
incapable of thinking becoming another colloquium
destroyed in a let-go solution.
Without this idealisation
a continual stop.

The guesses were not many to scramble
phased in fractions
decoded without
disarray
decreasing alphabetic disorder.
Some supposed you roughly dissipated input noise
or a squared blockage of that position.
Static and the old walk prevents
a listed code
Exclusive, away from the input,
the now unplanned computer.

I ignore a loss of situation
clustered of this presence, filling out
a frenzied prevention
or without ability, simplicity's generosity
fixed without knowing a truth.
A blasé roughness
lifted out of an unexpected cloud
Approximation spread loosely
flooded without a hot digit.

Out of that stated quiet

the collage unspecified
breaks some ashes of amnesia
loosened into a new electric cable.
Not the felt either. The skin tightens
to deny suggestion newly embossed with
joy. Your few blackened grimaces,
my inhaling, empties your grasp and
approaches you with fulfilment.

The cause around and about the fixed
without complaisance. The gates decode
studied lies
of absence. The minimum
still a vulnerability.
When is not decoded
awareness giving
the stop suspension
A complexity that could have given value.

The horizontal precipitates
with vertical random or when,
not rested, to prevent the purely sensible,
I give night and buy the day
to ensure my status
Turn your mundane
into healthy movement
calmed in the muscles
now against what I disliked.
The blankness my saturance.
Openness lit
your decision into
a new natural hollow
untouched without
visit. That open staleness coded as
noise I read as imperfection held onto
Remembered then and after
in unseen disconnection.

Your complaisant spread
loosened a cluster of
growing particles gravitated
out of the still sound of absence
organised without bells
A spaciousness the clearing fills.

You engineer with
cold field glue
subtracting towards a loaded uncertainty.

The nearness down or
spread without
ignition seeing
many continuals in front of
your face in
This line not
one forgotten and released
off of planes elevated
to calm sky.

The ignorance in your artifice splits
and spits rice husks
or listens to the taken obviousness
Where I earth the
distance I do not speak
but hold onto closure. Any
stability to demolish
the potential haphazard in this
inability. The space with internal emptiness.

I ignore blank evaporation
And adhere the field
out of your absent coagulation upon the
meadow the
squenching the ridge
This fullness, sometimes, you spit
and empty my sweetness
The Garden I
unlock.

Here then, cannot be irrelevance
Always active the tap in
the wall when singular
now unheard
Repairs prevent the many vices you code
as a resistant macro-particle clasped or
positioned into the rant that cannot be disagreed with
and lifts the reinforced wall
without using animation.

Soon always exactly continues.
I mend your traces
the many misses that cannot be comprehended.
The release has not been fast enough
to sell some of the shares
and I missed your arrival in the City
I go to often.
Here nothing can be avoided.
Here everything gets done.

Charleston

The Physicist imagines how
                his world will be
before he becomes part of its process
                Through a recognition
of similar structures in his organs
                to those of his companion's
he projects the potential
                of his capabilities' achievement

She lifts out of fear the Painter
                in a stopframe spacetime
levitated there
                in a serenity
clutches legs beneath her
                forms an ovoid held
with an asymmetry to the head
                proud of the curvature

He tries to follow
                uses a pole to push up
towards the occupied spacetime
                shakes on one arm on the pole end
as his body lifts into the
                periphery of her position
but cannot manage
                the frame held obvention

His formula based on four experiments
                and an assumption
Presumed force between circuits
                acted on a line between them
a force between the two elements
                presumed to be equal and opposite
loses the comprehension of the law's reliance
                on the completeness of the system

I am sensible of my crime
	but cannot abhor it
Duty, honour, virtue
	no longer inform
I am not yet a monster
	but frail
I am not without mutation
	but natural

Levels of confidence
	produce an almost horizontal line
but predict a sudden
	drop
No-drop maintenance
	encouraged by
one of the promoters
	whilst others gave attention

but anticipated an exhaustion
	from facial contortion
anticipated overeagerness
	on the part of promoters
as gestures of perfection
	enlarge out of proportion
and the Gravatt's dumpy leveller
	reduces the iridium assizes

Had he assumed no energy radiation
	and allowed for the field effects
between acceleration and charge
	the Painter notes
he might have understood
	that his own inertia
on his tendency
	to conserve

Charley-Bop

The Informer held precision high
and that continues
Any notion of biological interaction
can be discounted
The beat of gentleness
if that wasn't completely supposition
was not apparent. The skin's heat
anyway lost in its sient entity
its rank reindividuation.

Frenzy was recoded as foreign matter,
in a low fractal dimension,
repressed in syntactic exactitude
in which the lawless become recognised
in the blur record associated with the image
Self-control that now included
a filling-out of consciousness
subsumed all coding
in an active decision about categories.

The image of concrete purpose
became the cue
without question
of the empirical failure of value
No redoubting
continued discount of the distressed
The applause in the face of tyranny
sanctioned by codes of heritage
and the strong arm.

The promise of peace
addressed as control
any complaint that risk
must be avoided and
involved stamping out wilful freedom
in those that would better be served
as children
They screech through the
tunnel at Monument underground

Held by tweezers of laser light

inside a blinding sandwich
where depth perception of what good it does
gets decided by investors' returns.
Whilst back here the plants die
from an over-emphasis on cultivation
where all filth and foul iniquity
demands that the earth be burnt
And rules insist that the danger is necessary

But what it leads to isn't considered
an innocence discarded by the despair of wealth
This stuff will not do
The fit is without synaptic reciprocation
No understanding wends towards pretence
of comprehension. Sure there's a way
out—it's called Exile
I plant a row of boxhedge cuttings
and retire to a barbed enclosure

Straps of duty are now replaced
with predetermined measure
signified by a piercing code
accounted without consciousness
The rigour of its dispensation
dependent on its spectrum of sorting
deals amongst phenotypes on a genetic basis
in an ongoing populating of ecosystems
in which the ideal is fixed yet unknown
and power oppresses others of their kind

The Informer leaves the irriguous tunnel
to reorganise the sorting
He returns to the shrine
hung from his driving mirror
to the explosion in my ears
from the throat box
black trains pass through the nerve gas
of the vibrating City
scrambled into summer's
realignment of moisture.

He reports two genes located in different translational
reading frames with one end of a **gag**
overlapping the end of a **pol:**

site-directed mutagenesis and amino-
acid sequencing localises the site of
frameshifting to a codon near the end of the
overlap. This was trapped against
an averaged autocorrelation function
and an unresolved reference star
after subtraction of a near-gaussian seeing component

The close similarity between the
two reports demonstrates, he noted,
the lack of any resolution in the images
In the former an out-of-frame
configuration left a genomic dread in situ
the latter had been dominated
by a photon-spike and carried assumptions
of a black-body spectrum,
blue shifts of the trough, and a
constant velocity since the explosion.

He opened the boot of his car to let the alarm out
and set up an optical trap at power levels
What explosion ? sufficient to give manipulation at
high velocity. The orientation of individual cells
in space was achieved using a pair of "single-
beam gradient force traps" to give the
dominant component a push
of dielectric particles into the high-intensity
region of the focus. High-resolution
viewing allowed him to hold the image
at each of its ends and orient it at will.

As he came down from Jebb Avenue
he produced a viscous drag
It instigated a vertically hung clump
and tipped into the viewing plane
Truth went out the window
In his lap a diagram of burglary
He had nothing to express and little
to think about, the place had been cased
But where does that get us?

He was inclined to pull the brakes on thinking
when looking at risk
He operated the quiet trap slowly

without interest in knowing its aesthetics
always accurate, always unhappy
The sound of complaints, pessimism, a dripping faucet
timing a moment of strain a difficult waiting
before he reached the Thames
his face had swollen with weeping.

Turn back, his voice said
You travel all in vain
He pulls the wheel on the right
hits the gate
The image bursts onto his windscreen
fills the car with solutions
let out as he recedes
A rush of instances without application
It is not worth discussion in detail.

The vertical drop linked regions of different
elasticities. The crash shifted
the demand curve and settled at the
break point. Oligopolistic behaviour
varied from collusion to almost
perfect competition. Such a phase
shift prevented ideal focus.
Generosity to enemies betrays friends, a social
fitness dependent on a known polis.
A vertical drop that displays a horizontal
shelf of marginal revenues.

Chicken

The misogynist produces now
                    a soiled history
before he becomes part of its process
                    Through inhibition
of similar structures in his organs
                    to those he is disgusted by
he erects the parental
                    crack of his hatred

The subject shifts outer fiat
                    inwards shot from a pace climb
regulated stare
                    inner perversity
fetches a crushed beatitude
                    normalised instead
withers assimilates to feed
                    proud of the curvature

He flies to borrow
                    fuses a toil twistor
affords peroxide pace climb
                    fakes onomatopoeia the toil bends
accesses commodity thrifts
                    perpetuity over perdition
buttered damage
                    the same shell invention

His form based on faulty acidity
                    and consumption
Presumed force between circuits
                    fractured spacetime
a force between two elements
                    presumed to be subjected and subjector
poses the tension of the claw's pliance
                    on the screen of wisdoms

I am spent of my crime
but cannot judge
what I owe to my virtue
elongated and sawn
I am wanted amongst her
but male
I am weighed and muted
but not real

Gazelles of fidelity
juiced and most presentable
of dereliction a sudden
crop
to stop brain sense
cabbaged by
the voters and the voters'
hilted intention

Fut cruciated angle hoist
foam racial torsion
dissipated over eagles
of the shaft ropes
as guests of transgression
barge out on propellant
and the gravity bumps the antelope
juiced in radium seizures

Plaid and grooms fin lock
and crowd for the weald decks
even acerbic and labour
the subject floats
what had stood
bone of inenarrable
lies bending
to serve

4. Dispossession & Cure

Dirty Dog

There then direct perception
all sources assessment or evaluations
of truth
Behind the red leathered chair
a black radiator
In the canteen *Cambridge Collage*
by Robert Motherwell
The only other graphic a
reproduction of Jackson Pollock's
Autumn Rhythm on the jurors' waiting
room wall

This ease and shabbiness and content
(I in my new dress)
rather formidable

I feel a prodigious weight
which I can't lift yet
Several problem at once
The greenhouse began to be built.

Passing our own limits
to tell the future
It occurred to me last night
I would merge all interjected
passages and end with solitude
or confinement
as choice

LONDON JANUARY '89-HEREFORD JULY '89

Choo Choo

What accounts for the Bellman's condition
superimposed accelerated accumulation
Toxic metals in his vertebrate frame
trace the reply
regarding social danger

His oracle quickly stated
Crown over portcullis and chains
counter-read as a smudge of lipstick
on handwritten envelope
carefully posted with a complex of
white floral fragrance with tuberose and jasmine
top notes on a chypre and spicy background
Gets up the nose

The toxicity of mobilised metals
exceeds the total van load
of radioactive and organic wastes
measured by the beer needed to dilute them
The Bellman's drinking water
fraught with influence without modification
anticipates abandon read in the tumbler

A second genetic code remains largely undeciphered
his structure of enzymes coupled each amino acid
to an appropriate transfer in his molar fillings
His language both non-degenerate and Ah! Bellman!
More deterministic than a frozen accident

What what courage and fortune overlap provide
scales of or on the top edge of a garden fence
Hi! there! decisions between gravity and entropy
produce call it a drawing
after an essential repair of neuron
restitution but not reversal

The probabilities of his processual kinetics accords
a knowing that cannot exclude the uncertainty of its frame

On his cart most obstacles to complete
mixing are incomplete
There is no automatic spread fag
fag even if the shape of it horseshoes
rather than elliptically poxes

The visualisation of his future
Ah the fluid thought mixes fatigue
distinguishes chaotic trajectories
Who make the rules need to know disorder well
Different patterns do not necessarily work
the satisfaction in different ways

It's proof that the Umpire sits in pain
holds the balance
a metallic mouth speaks
openly astride the main shaft
oil warms gained by the mass in its fall

A collapsed transgression recites to a stenographic fix
a hum in the Bellman's ear
encourages a different mixture
merges panic
with a drawn down squareness or
what they were becomes what they appear to be
machines spinning his resounding bell

A figure called Success drops from his tailboard
holds a dish in righthand
in left an ear of metallic corn and dead poppies
The condition arrives at attunement as it moves through
broken quarry stones in the forecourt of Granvile arcade
plastic leaves blown from turbulent warnings
touched by the hand as it is taken away
from asking its question

Chug

Turned the drivel on
gave shape
at seven in time
ceremonies
to find them capping
turns into stone
the pox and they
embodies life force
have another man-flight
Night belongs
in orbit
to the animals
takes us out
strikes a stone
of modernism into
a cough syrup painting
against cloud
things
seem to go
wrong
but it doesn't answer what
the hand asks
Simply a figurative use of autumn
juxtaposed an account in Virgil
probably disparate won't do
and an image of what might have
that precedes what does it
precede

To the Analyst anger
signifies love
and an enclosure that
has veno -gated
part of the same piccess
eiclaved in emblematic
self-consci
i an f e

2

To the Analyst anger
signifies love
and an enclosure that
has venom-gated
part of the same process
enclaved in emblematic
self-consciousness
in and for itself for another
into dissolves of aptness
unique spins of privacy in
neoteric dark
slam boarded on
the judder ride before
dawn breaker the synapse.

Each judgement
the Analyst determines
rests with a war lord
in the process of signature
on the blower
Eh—at the flagged desk
Right? sparks of decision
Don't he—about the next
genetic aspiration
on a fresh blotter
tough enough to take
before the chafe removes clarity
ratification
the next hyperpyrema
rateable values
decided by auscultation

3

My probe reports
anxiety flushed out with
on accordance
a pocket calculator
in which harmony
cross-paged with the oracle
is not one of the options
gives an oil deficit
after a wheeze index
adjudication of reason
against brain damage.

Such exhibition supersedes the otherness
of freedom of itself
construction and composure
a supersession of ambiguity
related to a becomes certain
a moralisitic of itself
Net loss proceeds to supersede
useful energy its own self
a perpetual motion
the other that is itself
in which machines
are imperfectly efficient

In a spacetime of fear
the Analyst does not relent
before distress and bondage
of almost universal some call human leverage
True to me in my uncertainty
raised to thought it despises

appeals to the eye
given itself to plunges
by methodical deprivations
of images indulges
to a full rigour
exercises in negative impression
the shadowy existence
fills a blue-grey sedge
between the eyes.

This indicates
notes the Analyst
that strange cough coupling
of the undeciphered genetics
and the use of portcullis and
chains on the front of the
ledger the broken seal rewaxed
with intoxicant

Circle

Opposite
To the right
the end of the passage
straight
through the formalities
coming back
There's no particular
back
like this
in the end
careful
come back to
turn
unexpected

No angel speaking
at a future
get fat on reserve and modesty
a nation's curse
from the summits
Evermore
an oligarchy bribed
And no one marvels
You weep and write
broken with strain
crazed
with calm footing
this is the crime the curse
prospers

the telephone
and the passage
the front door
rest and chorisis
back
at the

phone
things are possible
no reason why
But possible
things
In the end
broke through
the end of another war
extraordinary
expected lies
and coming back

Sadness corrosive within
speaks
low in your ears
the tramp of progress
drives
conscience tradition and name
explodes the science of
predation and blame
refrains from witnessing
your flag
in the soil recoil
in the rag of your curse
and its burst
of patriotic complacence

She wonders if she
will burn the paper
After the storm
at our feet
the post in the passage
Having been anxious as
well as having appeared so
Outside the gate
question everyone
the cleaner
the postman
The answer repeats
I don't know
I don't know anything.

Conga

Gathered at the nation's sickbed
evening sky lowered onto
yellow irises through daffodils
mimosa into street lanterns
lowers into plasticisers on
the face of an SAS officer as she
approaches the supermarket
Oh Hereford evening Oh absent
healing satellite warning
burst into jump jet schizophrenic
peace warming the panes beneath
the greenbacked lawn

I stood half naked on the verge
partly exposed my genital
photographer sent the proofs
to the agency back into a post
bag the size of passive management in the
wind-up co-operative proceeds from moves
into burnt a paperpoint institution a
dressing the rules towards portfolio bonding

meet to discuss the phenomena
evident points to climatic
buzz-phrases resonation urgentics
disrupt the fragile bank
balcony
intelligibility overlaps language for
people whose hearts are heated moving towards
restriction overlaps with purity
a folk taxonomy uniform or informant

the cosmology in recent gossip
environment itself as hazard
themes of Nature and Art in the ceiling
indicate what was stored below in cabinets
appearances release memories
of what is hidden
Bertold the Black identified
manufacturing ballistics
to the left the results are tested
by means of catapult bomb hurlers
against the Danes in 1354

freedom here becomes bitter
loss of hope
the emptiness that follows
creates no memory
I can't remember what was eaten
it was black and soft
patronised by collaborators
keeping comparatively healthy
saves me from despair
lunches are the worst part of memory
closed doors and friends knocking
existentialists who become policemen
corroborated by fear
by certainty
opens the briefcase
takes out a portcullis and a pair of chains
I'm not rembling
I'm tired of trembling

A close integrity relates
events, acts, roles and genres
and the configuration processed
In each curing event the speech act of the
special knower produced in western distortion
the doctor's prescription

Continental Walk

In full voice sent
to fight for nation
they wont be singing
when they come back
enforced inactivity
at a time when nothing
but action could make sense
civilisation on the operating
table we sit in the waiting
room neither pity nor hope
what begins in routine policing
hardens into preservation

cooked rice in leek water
walked
on soft red earth
banks of the Wye
and the Frome
invented new curry
using leeks and frageolets
with green pepper shifted with
yellow curry orange carrot brown
cumin black pepper
researching colour
in Chevreul Newton Goethe eventually
shifting to the luxury of bathing naked
and Albers
pictorial art guided by a
rhythm of structures to which consonant weight of colours
should correspond
after investigation of immediacy and spontaneity
we think sex is alright

Nature and Art in this together suit
to Make of the parts towards a wise aim
Calm extents of many intellectual domains
reinforced an aristocratic candour
Deeply wounded rather than embittered
To enmity and disappointment opposed
many different constructions and great industry
marshalling them for common-sense, so said, triumph
An expression of tenderness patience and health

The choice from appearances impersonal exactitutde
express harmoniously a state of mind concurrently
dependence on Nature depreciates those who
would paint without example relativity of tonal
values in which the number calculations affect the eye

The equation between rapture
from the earth and aesthetic
decision in which geometry
and number express the amplitude
of love To embrace each particular
Agitation borrows the broad arc
of calm Colour sense enraptures
form an involucre of outwardness

The nation's life as outward
state to which all activity
aspires as death seen to be
a calm separation given nausea
by the pressure of each damaged
lung Common sanity now alien
without reciprocation in love
appositions seize the muscles
of the heart It's incredibly
easy to die so much harder to
live All the positions in dispersal

The instantaneous without
perambulation lost
cancel una sola occhiata
subsuming immediacy left in
the varieties of constipation
Tactility a rhetorical figure
without felicity of apposition
Interpenetration a kind of virus
beyond the elegance of microform
Grace and passion expended in a mass
market consistent with its death mask

Crab Walk

IN THE NATION'S UNCURTAINED SICKROOM
VARIETY OF PAVEMENT TEXTURES
RESOLVE THE RIVAL CLAIMS OF DIFFERENT TRUTHS
A WOBLY
PRETENTIOUS STUMBLE

CHANGING THE ARRANGEMENT IN SIMULATION
CHANGE THE STIMULATED TO PATTERNS BACKED UP
BY OBSERVATION

EMPTY RESONANCE OF A NUMBER OF COVERED PASSAGE-WAYS
TO ENTERTAIN THE UNKNOWN GOOD IT HOVERED THERE
A SUFFICIENT NUMBER OF PROCESSING UNITS COUPLED
WITH EFFICIENT TRANSFERRING

THAT WHICH MOST I WONDER AT
STOOD AT THE GATE TO BE PLEASED
WITH SPEED
SUDDEN TEMPERATURE DROPS
TAKEN UP WITH JOY
THE AURAL SHOCK OF EMERGING INTO A HIGH STREET
TOGETHER WITH THE RISE IN SEA LEVEL
TRANSFERENCE AND CERTAIN RANDOM
BEHAVIOURS
MY SENSES WERE INFORMERS TO MY HEART
FRACTAL STRUCTURES CULMINATED IN A DENSE FRONT
AS IF MY TREASURE AND MY WEALTH LAY THERE
WIDER THAN THE SKY

weed spawn water staircase
white tails Itten yellow tips
then bullfinches possibly pink
earth blue sky petrol green
cheap tricks in the metal case

speed worn sandstone
flight sails bitten
chirp flits against
fettles race

stealth with Grace he has survived
an inner fight to sit down and apply paint
lifts you out of the cage forged from your memory
your emptiness Unafraid to be afraid just because
it's getting warm here Arrhenius just because this
rubble will take a million before our swank names it cool

Balance achieved
a dynamic arrangement of shapes
weight and volume pulling in different directions
a feeling akin to exhiliaration caused by the poise's repeated
sense of reassurance even relief from the recognition
that all the elements combine the resolutions
of potential conflict within
peace and serenity
plastic emotion
the beautiful

Dog

"sum of respective average values equal to 8
after appropriate corrections for the periphery have been made"

In fog came women, children inhumed in stone cists, hides simple things
from north-west Greece, Epirus, Albania, with flowers, perhaps orchids
from Ukraine, and Transcaucasia, bad weather lifts
orange carton corner, north of the Pindus, burnt
in the wake of arrival, no future time will think of these
devastations, respect the land, blown leaves shift wrought stone
came from any ages styles, dance, you don't tell others to
override one another in struck fashion, sung forever

To northern mists, inhuman bone wrists, find gratitude
wither hours, sad wetter rifts, mauve darkens fauna
waste pits rejects out of hand, brought home in phases
piles applied smother, luck fast Kleptovariants, bold randy,
what to you ran amuck, clenched foster, loathing rides off Desire
found outside phrenetic roll, now rain now wonder in vein
reserve bust meant an economic computation theory climax on statics
seeing through signs felt risk spurt nodes of sex change

Men and women Barbarians, Badgers
old angry with cities, not truly animal drenched
posture, clothing and ideas of Beauty ground
without direct genetic control, no pain no understanding of pain
serves adjustment to ecological community
the recent climatic fix on their movement
meaning new economy, self-sufficiency
subverted by modes of exchange, by copulation

During the most recent warmer times sprung as we draw near
they moved north from the warrings with honey with honey bee
mountain Hares and heath butterflies over solitude
with Beaver folk in wooded parklands on its surface
maybe 3 or 4 hundred of them, made oracles from bone from ashes
joined a forest culture using fish-hooks flints dug-out canoes
broad-bladed paddles, played the races, watched the burnings crack
layers of blue blue-grey throat-cleared sounds of frolic laughter

Pleistocene as if the soul rung with as much proximity
grooved forth beneath wearing hoare frost doubt in shales and
shade pollinates solipsistic weavers stood naked in a surfeit made bundle
frayed futures loaned and cashed coined restatements
from Gilgamesh cut into Mississippi Delta flood the yearnings back late
bird song slate balls resounds melancholia let to bait or lot of fun
avoided deep voice marked baulk at soak render Shiva greetings multiple
hand grasp in the brain bowl's wrought image

Words divided beyond equal portion into jet stream drained sumps set car
skin before the rot mashes another by-pass solo over violin network. More
recently that has led to boar and aurochs, loss and flutter, hedgehog and
red-throated diver on market boards, men and women folk bend call
Beavers, congregate in large furs handing crisp exchange for slivers of red
deer held in store against shortage. In Worcester provided Beverage in
Beverstone served pie named Broad-Tails, fetched 120 pence for their pelts
against 12 for trims of otter robe, crash 30 cars to pieces on summer time

Broad-Tails last seen on strong banks of the Tivy
construct castles mid river receive on their bellies logs of wood
cut by associates feet held thus transverse placed in mouth drawn
backwards fasten'd with teeth to raft entwined willow
different leaves with four teeth nothing else here
they haven't been around since colliers took the trees precise
out since the worst users of energy, the speculators unstrung
started intransitive verbs hard skin strong shoulders

I met the blue Hares of the north often sunlight
about this time moulting into full white pelage against grey hills
long silky belly hairs brush snow as they skitter
frozen moors avoid plains or beaten paths
but use woods avoiding city dogs
where rankness of herbage doesn't check their speed their sadness
These Puss, we named them, the most merveylous shut out
believed to be hermaphrodite rise out their forms

to pasture or return to their seats one way dark waves
in order not to suffer twig or grass to touch but
would sooner break it with teeth to make way
and in chase will make cross roads ten or without need
twelve times will make their ruses their false paths
I sometimes meet a solitary Hare in the open or in a 'form'
a tuft or grass selected to give a good field of view shouting
shelter from some prevailing wind the tidal

It was as if she'd just been born new pillows rest on you
fully furred with eyes ears open and smouldering
carried by doe to separate forms and suckled
In her exposed habitat defenceless against
fox stoat polecat feral cat words lost in gasps
When mature this problem goes Hare's large side of head eyes
wide-angled vision improved by sitting hind legs
Like Deer difficulty detecting stationary objects clenched erases us

will lope leisurely up a path quiet
to within feet of a whiteman standing motionless sparkling
Buck with buck in season will box or skip on hind legs refuge
rapidly vigorously forefeet leap into air at each other's bellies
Concentrated on airfields attracted by noise or vibrations rosy armed
of aircraft as they are by thunder the radiation emitted by power
lines and information terminals I've met herds of 400 fruit
in such places before the dogs came before the cities' lairs

On a November day in Perthshire 6 guns shot 1289 hares
Extraordinary lengths are gone to block this lucidity
The're as often killed by mowing and reaping machines fatigue and straw
toxic alkaloid cystisine and sparteine bark of broom
but immune from myxomatosis you stand before the silver
Some night you'll hear Badger-cries lack people
Peace good soul shortly death dropping waters
My grey pale lifts from its sett in a cromlech fragrance

to travel to circles or brakes in cairns loud-moaning
To fight extermination using deer park refuge from hunter
accused of stealing chickens and eggs strange golden clouds
instead consume large quantities of insects lakes
sometimes rats mice voles rabbits earth worms acorns
more often fish and organic sweet corn gentle gaiety
I sometimes sleep 60 yards in from white-armed contrivance
rest entrance   Using derelict waste lovely tresses

my ramifications can be three storeys necklaces
of tunnels over an acre of woodland fleet of foot
ideally deciduous with ample ground cover
of furze broom shrub but including abandoned mine shafts sitting opposite
Three of my dogs are lurchers licked
the cross-bred grey-hounds spring smoke light
that Gypsies use to catch food heard all this
Although their coats are rough finishing all distance

they are gentle, prissy creatures hold my hand
with a horror of muddy feet among the deathless
and an aversion to rough games. the lyre and wobble box
My residence in Britain goes back to hedgerows herdsmen
just after the dawn of consciousness. turns slowly
The place names of pate and bawson wide pathed
brock and grey are added to the palette after red and blue
Or Badger ham on the menu produces a violet hue

Older than and tangled by cities amazed all laden
they haven't been there since collars were invented
in such places before the dogs came with woodland
just after the dawn of consciousness a golden flower
I came west through the ice a silver bow
from perhaps North Africa inhabiting sands and uplands turned dark
in my wake the norm of devastation civilised

The map of this place no longer matches its present form
under ice-sheets and glaciers wild hyacinths
preceded by stone tool-makers makers of chipped flints
I knew nothing about their hand prints their children
imagery their teeth imaging
marks their fire tools their graces their gazing
I can only tell you they searching
could count and I'm told sung strain of past days

spoke about their lives as animals stand on
I came west through the ice necklaces
smashed the ice came concealed in a mammoth
the drama walls the fire signs or
drum beats last we heard north of 1910
in fact human tools in coupling with
a consequence of natural force tongues and clutter
known as Palaeolithic drenched light

An age a thousand times longer than since the Great Flood alone
Contacts with these Ancients gets confined to their stone tools desire
incorporated in geological deposits silt and sound
and occasional rare skeletal remains before cave dwelling
The two tool shaping methods set in with Pleistoceners after the bad ice
either using the Asian idea of flint nodules chipped until a double-faced
core emerges or the African method of striking off a substantial flake
working that single face into implement enviable in mien

The Euro-ancients overlap methods that shape us
The core toolers became known as Acheulian daybreak
Britain, as well as Europe, Africa, Palestine and most of India silliness and sorrow
the Swanscombe consciousness contemplates piles of mollusc shells
on Thameside contemporary with Abbevillian the Cromer flake culture
leading to the Clactonian techno-complex and hand-axes
A thousand distinct molluscs within a mile of here
a solo thrush taking each snail one at a time to smash their shells

The blade tool hunters follow carving bone gleaming feet
multi-barbed harpoons spears thus lever moods
and flint against metallic rock fire making 20,000 years ago impatient
animal paintings engravings caves murmur quiver
in Derbyshire, Wales, the Wye valley, the Mendips
Aurignacians included skilled hunter artists
technicians of flint trim followed the gold tressed
by Gravettians from south Russia and elsewhere

the first specifically British culture whirrs
counterpart to French Magdalenian shredded
already varied racial characteristics in remains
Most of late Palaeolithic Britons Cro-Magnon thanks
the Red Lady of Paviland South Wales yage fodder
a young man with an elephant's head under red ochre
Mesolith in Britain threefold immigrations
in the process of England's insularity around 8000 years ago

and damp oak woods with abundant alders replaced pines iconostasis
Forest culture of Maglemosian fishers and fowlers with powder
canoeing from east diet supplemented by hazel nuts luck like that
and vegetables and two neat-fingered microlithic cultures
the Tardenoisian known as the Shadows with their dogs
from perhaps North Africa inhabiting the sands and uplands
and the Azilian fishermen shell-fish collectors fowlers and hunters
were strand-loopers along the newly formed coastal fringe

Which confirms us Barbarians as landowners sincere
for more than a quarter of a million years in Britain
We excite admiration for the way we are coping rattle the empty car
with life in the twentieth century. You and I
When midnight a host of dogs and men go out
track the Badger get a forked stick chapping
bear him down clap the dogs in wave wash
take him to the town for baiting

We are perceived as Foreigners everywhere small animals
non-Christians, non-Hellenes, rude, wild
uncivilised natives of Barbary soft spoken
Cromwellians with forehead badges,
dealers in corn, insisters clash swift-footed
Irritated Egyptians name us the northerners the glorious
all lands ramshacklers, destroyers of bronze Ugarit, bronze Alalakh,
unsold shirts attackers of Mycenae and Troy hail-healers

Thirty-two centuries before the present, day-old
from Hallstatt, from La Tène, refuge from sea raids, hard of heart
around Mediterranean shores in boatloads delivered counsel
as early as thirty-six centuries past, hecatombs
burning, the Komarow pyre-graves,
burning hot-foot, orchid sunshine, scorched earth
in my wake, in my awakening, the chemical art transforming,
cities of self-cremation, fire-breath pollution,
common insecticide, the norms of devastation civilised, without tinkering.

Work Consciousness Commodity: Three Kinds of Perception

1. Ditty Bop Walk

The radical alternative begins in awkwardness:
Badgers' discourse of production embeds upon return;
Technics describes the tactics of living, Outward's
procedures of conflict.
Discourses of production, representations, exchange on satellite
war-economy blurs the imaginary; reproduces determinant
instances as a continuum.
Each machine *serves* one process owes existence to
thought about this process. Let me out,
Badgers say, Liberation of productive forces needs to be
confused with liberation of cities. They stand on the edges of a London
that constitutes war-economy itself. Every Badger
knows and dreads the *emptiness* that follows labour power.
Normality purchased as a value.
In contrast to quantitative measure, use value remains a
qualitative potential. Tied in their thinking to the present,
Badgers know or smell death as something in the future that
does *not* threaten them.
The use value of labour power is the moment of its rockhouse.
This is the rockhouse the Badgers' relation to their useful
expenditure of effort.
"We're going to sack the City."
The quantitative signifies only the commensurability of all
work in terms of exhaustion; the qualitative, under the pretext
of incommensurability, goes much further. It signifies *the
comparability of all carbon life in terms of production and
labour.* The abstract and formal universality of commodity
labour power supports the "concrete" universality of
qualitative labour. There are no "humans-in-themselves" only
humans and those that resemble them. They contend in battle
with a *given* world. The universe moves on with stockbroker concern.
Mohican hair cuts proceed down backs in braids of wire.
In this structuralized play of signifiers, the fetishism of labour
and productivity crystallizes. Every drop of water is a battlefield.

"We challenge the human capacity of energetic, physical, and intellectual production. The productive potential of every Badger in Western society transforms the environment into ends useful for Badgers and not for the society that burns them." Long noses sense out the coming devastation.
In the structural sense, within the totality of existence, within all that can be described, labour necessarily precedes play. The Badgers work at play as a breaking off *from* labour and a recuperation *for* labour.
Badger-play is purposefully *unproductive* and useless.
"We cancel the repressive and exploitative traits of labour and leisure." The higher herbivores are ruled by the ear and by *scent.* The higher carnivores *rule with the eye.*
This realm beyond London economy called play, non-work, or non-alienated labour, is defined as the journey without end.
In this sense it is a consciousness and remains aesthetic with all the bourgeois worry which that implies. Torn jackets and jeans do not exempt this observation.
The world-picture is the environment as *commanded* by what can be described. The state of civilisation becomes continual mass extinction. From the viewpoint of social distribution and consumption of communication, labour is always a value of use or exchange. Value is measured by the quantity of time socially necessary for production. Let's not forget that *work could be apprehended outside value*, on the side of the commodity produced and circulating in the chain of communication. Here labour no longer represents any value, meaning, or signification. It is a question only of a *body* and a constellation of descriptions There is an infinite sense of power in this quiet wide-angle vision, a feeling of freedom that has its source in *superiority,* and its foundations in the knowledge of greater strength and consequent certainty of being no one's prey. The world is the prey and the existence of Culture has always had this dependence.
A Badger stands on the Yat in half-light watches the picturesque sink into the mud of the Wye. Property is the domain in which unlimited power gets exercised, the power gained in battling, defended against peers, victoriously upheld. "The labour of the sign", and "productive inter-textual space," are ambiguous metaphors, sponge cakes made into trifles; absorbant and instantly consumable.

The fight of nature-within against nature-without is not *misery*, but a grand meaning that *ennobles* life. To be rigorous the meaning must be surpassed and annulled. It thus becomes necessary to emancipate humankind from the nineteenth century idea of an "evolutionary" process. I catch trout for myself to eat, it's that obvious, ownership that simple. Doesn't matter whether it's comprehended or proven, the cities of world-history plummet from catastrophe to conservatism. The remains of those before me are as old as their tools. In addition to the "thought of the eye" the comprehending and keen glance, humankind now has the "thought of the hand". The question of whether something is suitable or unsuitable – the criterion of the Deer – has nothing to do with that of true and false, the values of the City. The Badger-soul strides forward in an ever-increasing alienation from *all* Culture. The fight is hopeless and fought out to the bitter end. Piracy is as old as navigation, raiding of the trade-route as conservative as nomadism, and wherever there is peasantry there is enslavement to a warring nobility and economy. The animals of the City who made others their domestics in order to exploit them, have taken themselves captive. The great symbol of this fact is the human *house*.

2. Dixieland One Step

Beavers seek out the period's most avant-garde texts. They're almost coy about it. This develops a complicated theory about the role of the imagination in the artist, the prelude to *another* Aesthetics. It helps the discovery of the concept of contingency and the invention of the notion of a totally secular freedom followed from the intuition of intellectual needs. Beavers live a paradox. It is their business to create what's necessary to them in that which they are unable to raise themselves to the level of. Beavers see sadness and boredom in their depths – as free as they wish but impotent. Their decoy duck is adventure; rational determinists who believe they are free. Beavers are said to be unhappier than Badgers, but far more pleasant to deal with. This is said with caution.

"For some time now you have been wondering about hope and despair."
The distinction between *to be and being*, and the investment of being with the relation, movement, and efficacity that had resided in existing, shifts into a discussion of building and housing. There is a distant applause followed by gun fire. The whole of this is witnessed by those in the role of "anonymous passers-by".
Beavers move for the liquidation of the acquired heritage, and the invention of a new form. Time-binding is not on the active agenda. Everything seems to spin around ideas of freedom, life and authenticity. Irrationality will not be suppressed by masking. Hair oil marks the wall of passage, the pillow case, the coat collar.
He immediately started talking off the top of his head, without notes, sitting on his desk – we had never seen anything like it.
Anger is the last resort of the weak or of the
domestic mammals staggering under the weight of a
full briefcase.
The City provided an unprecedented cultural success: scrimmages, blows, broken chairs, fainting spells. The doctrine which makes human life bearable. The themes are individualism, responsibility, angst, commitment, solitude, and the notion that hope relies on action. Dried vegetables line the gutter of the Saint-Germain-des-Pres. There is a shift from matters of being into those of freedom. Beavers couple this to praxis which the English read as any meaningful or purposeful

human activity, any act that is not mere random, undirected activity.

Badgers meet Beavers in confinements. The only sounds are the footsteps of guards. Daylight filters through a thick grid of fluorescence remains lit all day. Conditions of life in the City are intolerable.
The only thing that matters is the relationship between the individual and Being. But Beavers are never individuals, it would be more fitting to call them universal singulars and requires simultaneous examination from both history and what is proposed.
"As a Badger you have astonished, upset and denied all that has turned our society into what it is today. This is what I'd call the extension of one's potential. An action that gives power to your imagination. Don't give it up."

The question was not so much to bring animals together as to bring ideas together.
The Beavers discuss travel, polygamy, transparency. The counterculture based on these notions added provocation and the hatred of cliches, conventions and domestic animals. "You give me regret," and "It makes me all poetic," and "It has seldom made me so gratuitous and so necessary" become their cries of war. In front of the City they bemoan that nothing new could happen to them. They are seized by fits of nostalgia for "lives of disorder" and authenticity. Work and love take place in broad daylight, and anyone can intrude at any point. No private property, no compartmentalisation, no secrets: a social life down to its barest essentials, or almost.
The Beaver streets in pursuit of papers shaking with laughter blinded by wet eyes. Projects propel each Beaver forward. The discovery of a spectral reality, a skeletal City, the sodden awareness of chaos and war. The pride of consciousness facing the world, origin of their absolute freedom, a special relativity. A consciousness that is at once a merging and a wrenching away, a freedom that is at once a fever and a discipline, a state of permanent criticism, a mistrust of all fixed and crystallised social roles. Beavers are estuant against digestive philosophy. Hot under the collar, gagging, magically extracting, from the darkest spacetime of oppression, an appeal to freedom and individual anarchism. In a disregard for historical factors the City is said to follow the Beavers the intruders the outsiders the marginals. It is the City's sustenance its aesthetic nurture.

That is the hypothesis. They meet the Badgers in a wild rush of words and juxtaposed ideas from tired bodies against time-rush and sleep-space in occasional lapses of absence from which they promptly emerge to resume attempted control. The meeting between them was not on the sofa but imagined there. Beside a series of bookshelves in the house a large desk, a bay window, they concentrate mutual critique and subsequent reliance. The becoming of the age of the public dwelling made private consciousness.

3. Double Shuffle

Wounded Stag on a high hill frond pronounced hailstones.
The self possibilities of materials and expression of the area
lived in. Thick darkness, shame and incomprehension war blast
from nostrils. In a step-like cultural change from cows and pigs
and hay and all what farmers have to do involved in art. Alert
ears, the laughter of gods, Miriam the Prophetess, pull together.
May 19th *Hereford Times*, burnt out cars on Royal Ordnance
Bomb Disposal fields at Wellington. "Soon we will be too late to
realise the anthropological understanding as a basis for an
alternative society of the future." "The work of those who go
out may be worth more than those who sit in the corner."
Fuzzy sets and their applications are in a reel from pleasurable activity.
Another thud apple, blame local blackbird, or din of
earthmover builds by-pass surgery vibrations in her stomach,
cabbage white under slate of a first fruit tree.
Without inner transformation on an individual level, political
upheavals are merely power changes. The stag appears in
times of distress and danger with another understanding of
freedom, realisation of freedom in culture. To get free from
the restriction and indoctrination and ideologies of States and
economical interests in Western private capitalistic systems
and in Eastern State bureaucracies The hare remains bound
by genetic programme, remakes identical form. Give Hare a place
to stand and the earth moves. Culture, democracy and economics
are funds of society. The Hare insists upon self-administration
rather than state monopoly or private capital. At the normal
working place a few strange additions. More emanates from
these than if the ideas behind them were merely revealed
directly. Heal like with like, but also reveal a gift to the self.
On a platform in a square from melted down gold images of
Hare and a sun, a "small, peace object" turns the cultural and
economic empathy back on itself through that normal place
with its added strangeness. "Now we speak of the invisible
sculpture, the ideas of creativity and self-determination in an
alternative social situation." That is the wider understanding
and only a beginning.
The problem of democratic laws stand in an organic relationship to the
position of freedom.
Everybody can have a kind of dream, a kind of feeling, a kind
of deeper relationship to nature, to humankind as kin, to the
society, to the environment, to the future, to the soul, to the

will condition. Meet together working with potatoes or with plants or with a present practice in industry that is criminality in doings in which the youth will hate so much because the reality of the social body in the field of the free spaces in the culture in the education in the information in the mass media is the destruction of the creative instead of its potential as cooperative as connectedness with all different fields as a rich cohabit of use from the existents with the imagined.

5. Fizz

Grind

Sight catches wings in clover
Compost purple
Field system
Dry river flood reeds
Swan belly swan air
Eddies ripples turbulate
Reverse river
Then turn soil then deposit
Cold face
Not sorrow nor surface
Distant posts and poles
Wind catch
Red fog detectors
Breath shapes

Parrot-head starts move in Pleistocene spring
artifacts of wood in the wake of the ice
Chest jewellery Maize Man contrasts Bat Man
used as a receptacle shaped like a lung.
An aerial view of a sacrificial meadow
maps a spacetime of dedication
unrealistic hope perpetuated by stress
Stone faces eating incense and mushrooms.
Collapse followed by settlements preceded by
civilisation, resisted dragon with inverted hair
known as Feathered Serpent
built ritual site dedicated to Flood and Rain
Parrot-head in the city carries coloured speech
sings to the music of Spring and Sowing.

This is the morning of the vulnerable male homage to
the "Flayed Lord" displays of red flesh the skin of another's slavery
Below my chest a scar where my heart was removed. Dance
with Death and Capital, female resilience in a gold breast-plate
conflicts invasion an androgynous Gold-ear listens
from a cage the first permanent settlement
An ancient painting guide to the collection of relics
gives a key to these riddles, rediscovers a lost resistance
Geographic writing, scientific letters, a history of the textiles
contrast highlit glyphs, mythology in motion, and torture on video.

Invasions and expectations, derivations and inventions
flag an end of civilisation and separates when from where.
Loose-leaf sheets settle into a plan for the city without a garden
Value translates into a loaned summer that will not exist.

Light on white mud on clover
Mushroom compass
Calendars new teatime
Dried reeds from meadow flood
Winged bulb lilies
Float pad
Against river of different flora
Flood gully winds
Old leopard space
Sorrel leaf tips above surface
Signal flood ponds
Tree bridge across Lugg flow
Crack willow and alder
Salute musk past.

Fish-Tail

1.

Dream releases a hare
before the Civilian transforms her
Consciousness of pleasure
retarded by memory
The gravity of occurrence has
made itself felt at once
a sacramental momenergy
trapped within concoctions of another spacetime.

Usurped their own Being
and need for safety
mother, warrior, hag, virgin
alerts to
prosperity to land use
an emblem of the planet as home
protection of flocks and herds
usurped by children.

Oracles are consulted
but first constructed
In times of social danger
the usurped are wizards and
liars They are swans and ducks
they are war ravens and geese
they are corpse birds from
other worlds invented in dreams.

They are transcendent and circular
Over and above the numerous personal ornaments
and vocabularies,
elaborate parade weapons and repetition
with recurrent apotropaic designs
a wealth of wooden idols, the simulacra,
crude and direct bog figures or male figurines,
symbolic of obvious functions.

In the garb of torn ground cover
the Hunter scoffs at hints of shrines
and ritual pits, of votive wells and
sacred precincts from behind
a screen of artistic and ethical standards
traditions at once alien and incomprehensible
more than 2000 years ago
the Hunter begins to wear heavier boots.

A partial change of burial rite signals
a spread of power
an extensive network with more than one focus
linear patterning, spirals, bird shapes
in torcs, pottery, ivories and land forms
signal inspirations and migrations
from plant and foliage and
zoomorphs with winged stencils elaborate knots.

Compare mirror with mirror
others pushed east
jugs with invented limbs in handle
from grave and helmet with iron and gold
mountings lost cheek-guards knobbed finial
influx from heroic ideals of tribes
sword scabbard in ceremonial prowess
left in disuse since discoveries of iron.

Continuity of stylised horse motifs with reversed heads
on silver coin and gold stater struck at
retreat dates from defeat
Fretted enamelled plaques,
part of horse's harness with work using Champlevé
recurrence of motifs a new millennium
a dot of light bounced in and out formed a pattern
incorporated into decoration and ritual pursuit.

2.

Metal, stone and leatherwork and illuminated manuscripts
humankind chariots a new vocabulary and Being
man with foliage mouth
becomes face-urn with death hair moustache
full of written-out mythological fragments
euphemised into legend and tales
overlapping ecocatastrophes
and heroic events.

Cascade rubble and animal sounds
quieten into a float-past of clothing
interrupted by the sick thrown in rivers and
parcels of food on the water
as offerings for immaterial ancestors
feast thought of as sacred on lakeside mud beds
gives rise to new growths and wisdom
hazel shoots carried away by salmon or the mouths of mammals.

Foliage designs in wall painting and mosaics
Sacred trees and groves
venerated for what they stand for
column the great tree the great route of Being
felled in 1914 made dynamic
in support of cleansing war
trees fashioned into figurines timber roof supports
now in the trenches new men grow green shoots.

Cult of graves and burial rituals shrines
with sacrifices human and animal continuity
grave mounds chthonic and fertility selfish
human experience votive deposit insurance
cult origins romantic antiquarian speculations mask popularity
priesthood bogus roles of wise-men, shape-shifters,
shamans, prognosticators without social dignity
without religious connotations of their pagan know-how.

Predilection for human sacrifice
great wicker-work images filled with humankind
set on fire Cult of the head and identity
underworld and motif of severed thought
in every period and geographically widespread severed from body
after death decorated war trophy

the slain constituting
military prowess in the head carrier and banner.

Solar implied halo of burial ash suggests heads
embalmed in cedar oil enemy's distinction
preserved in chests exhibited alongside wells
recovered from underground pool between
material and presumptive portraits
hung from belt trepanned trophies
independent after death cup in crown as font
phallic on stone pillars as life-force

Horned birds hover antlered form
both bovine and human ears wears torc
over antlers or holds it wears long garment
on one plate cross-legged tailor's seat
holds great ram-headed serpent
keeper of the treasure concerned with wealth
and what issues from fertility prosperity
commerce death to art and empire.

A serpent vomiting money
from subterranean stores
emerges from basaltic floor where
wealth has mineral form
Guardians inside barrows
protect warriors of the scientific fortress
horned helmets warrior king as healer
holds caduceus in left the keeper of medicine

3.

Bright, shining in river names
clear water as place of polis, city
absorbs and reflects sky's fire lake
energetic intelligence the consort of breath
husband to clearing land for pasture
creative freedom, healer and survivor
dreams the antlered dancer pulls a golden thread and spins
to protect humankind without need for martial success.

Frug

Coverage in language literature of art, design and culture continues to be discussion encompassed by continuously coming across the invasions which mark the northern limit. Influence can be experienced indirectly through the work of other peoples. Many of the towns and cities reached their prominent positions because of rule, law and commerce, particularly the seat of the imperial procurator which becomes the seat of the speculator in bronze age settlements. Legendary arrivals are put into poetry. Iron age huts and burials phase with Oriental influences. Terracotta slabs, the Bulls in Ambush, the Augurs, the Lionesses, and the Temples of severe style include the Tombs of the Monkey; the Leopards; and the Funeral Couch. The date and place changes but last peaked around London 1980-1990. The Temple of Concord's silver libation dish completes another city wall and frees states of occupation, invades, advances into valley and conquers central Deer Hunt in the Battle painting now lost but copied into mosaic floor at House of the Aversion of the captured. 2000 bronzes taken as plunder results in changing coinage from copper to silver period included the Tomb of Shields. The century of Banquets and later chamber Tombs housed the leader of planning with a swimming pool and massage unit in the centre of what was once an empire. Wall paintings include 2 views and extend to include paintings at the House of Griffins known as the Second or Repressed style. The Infancy of the Hunt frescoes and Invasion of the official gazette into senate signify male armouring. Paintings of a youngster reading from a scroll assisted by a Priestess Seated at a Table assisted by helpers while playing a lyre leads to The flagellation Dancer and Domina, The terror-stricken woman known as the wind nymph. Villa of the Dining room and Restored Bedroom aligned with Villa that enforces new calendar from March 1st to January 1st, 365.¼ days of political change. Murder wins power with fights and suicide receives name and reorganises state, rebuilds Frieze with legends of reconstruction. Wall painting of garden, book on Architecture from Paintings known as the "Third style". Wall at House Portrait of a Young Woman with Marriage contract, on wheeled shell Drawn by Bulls panel at House of the Dining room frieze and a wall Temple of the Avenger and Iron Sword of Honour, wood scabbard, iron blade & gold decoration restored. Death of Temple re-built Conquest of Portrait head marble, Palace with mosaics and garden now in Museum. On stair-wall dynamic, illusionistic style in art known as "Fourth style" or the style of the imagination dead. A Law Student and his Wife with Marriage contract, The Three Graces, and Maiden Gathering Flowers. House of Still Life with Bird, Peaches and Glass Jar Painting, are evidence of a new pattern of connectedness—a new consciousness. The Fountain of the Serpent, Earthquake destroys many buildings, a large part burns down, are part of an overlap with the past which dominates all human culture. Bronze Lamp decorated with a Mouse Serving table. Fresco in Tomb Sign for Public Snack Bar. Eruption destroys some of this lively message, but author of source for art history prefers "Factual Classicism" in art. The Interpretation of Dreams. Mosaics after earthquake and repairs. Romantic Classicist art, art of the period of cemetery portraits on wood tied over mummies. The period specified as spanning the first four centuries of the era. Portrait of a Man relates a dichotomy between beautiful human form and naturalistic style. A corpus of pamphlets in vernacular emerges as basis of earliest mythological sarcophagi in workshops. Oval sarcophagus in "Excited style". Art including mythological, battle, and marriage sarcophagi. Leaping Buck, Tomb of Equestrian statue of same period as invasion of northern Helmet, plates shaped & riveted together reliefs. Guide describes art treasures seen by artists and patrons. Silver Bowl with handles, Bronze used for frying eggs or baking cakes. Earrings from writer of 2 books with descriptions of pictures supposed to be in a collection. Grandson added a third book. Breakdown of classical art. "Pointillistic" and "woodcut" styles in sculpture, same period as invasion. Development of centre of learning replaced by a Hall of Fame. Late Empire Tetrarchic expressionism in art. Sea Monsters Mosaic, Captured Bison. Mosaics in Villa of Women. Mosaic statues legalised by Arch. Late Antique re-integration of form, "Abstract" style and surface classicism. The Hunting mosaic at sarcophagi frieze. Palace and Basilica. Day for the Birth of worship reinstates destruction of pagan temples all over empire, building on top of them. Refined, Abstract, Patterned classicism, Silver Spoons, Pewter Flagon. Mercenaries under sack plunder of treasures and art. Gradual transition to early style in glass medallion inscribed "Survival of Sculptural Workshops". In mosaic workshops Fall and Rise of power, Culmination of old economic systems. Book Cover from Reliquary, Fragments of Capture, end of Empire, Beginning of era of virtual splendour and architecture.

Eagle Rock

1.

The number
was very great and
multiplied greatly.
Texts
supply the names
over five hundred mentioned
to these be added the names
which in various Books
the number
who were recognised
was about twelve hundred.

Modern scientific study
may be said to have begun with the publication
of the accounts.

2.

The distinction between the
invaded
and settling there, built up the great civilisation.

The chief object
was self-preservation, and self-interest
with a view to material benefits
self-conceit and the laziness coming from self-conceit
Beliefs beyond the grave
placed offerings of food
in the graves of the dead

To prevent their return for food, the heads
severed from their bodies and their feet cut off
thus the living made themselves
secure in the possession of their homes.

3.

Remembrance Day in the loop
You shall send oblivion's poppies
as a funeral gift to Orpheus
dim with inanition,
I breathe the trumpet flowers,
indigo petal drift
My soul you are all in a muddle
Old grieves shall be forgotten
for the air is cool and still,
and the hills are high,
and stretch away

Pass out of one mode of existence
into another.

4.

The earliest forms
and unknown creative power
responsible for the creation of the Earth and all that is in it
represented as a man
with a frog's head, as a man with the head of a cobra,
as an ape, as a lion

The moral system and that of the new
so similar
they transferred their allegiance
in the apocryphal literature
which followed
several of the legends

The myth founded less than 3000 years ago
on the death of the Mother.

5.

In one of the Elegies
to the Spanish Republic
a configuration held in space
suddenly
recedes
into the weight
of the material.

The Fire Lake in the air
anticipates intensification
Ivory black against
reeks of
burnt bones
are companions of the flame
born of death.

Funky Broadway

PATTERN
Selection
mathematically
technical
Textiles
translated
Knotwork,
Patterns
Designs
Patterns
Analytical and Cosmological
Stencils,
Colour
World of Senses
Order
Design in Nature
Floral Fabrics
Colour Book
Design & Form
Grammar
Nature
art
motion
Symmetry Proportion
Art
Novelty
Colour Book
Visual Awareness
Structure in Nature
Strategy for Design
Patterns of the Ancient
Looking
Seeing
Pattern & Shape
The Development of Shape
Shapes
Paintings
Growth
Form
Abstract
Forms & Patterns

Nature
Pattern & Texture
Designs
Colour Book
PATTERN
source
concepts
mathematical
technical
Memory
Visual Memory
Mind
Nature
pattern which connects]
Ecology
CHAOS
SURFACES
Signatures
Crystallography
Form, Chance, and Dimension
Perception in Nature
Play Dice
Mathematics
Chaos
Structural Stability
Morphogenesis
Thought
Stabilization
Complex
chreod
Brain
Significance of Pattern
A Study
in Doubt and Certainty
Reflections on the Brain
the Study of acids
Organisation and Consciousness
Catastrophe
Nature
imagery and information
organization in the striate cortex

Fox Trot

1.

A preference in the culture
and aesthetics to use dance
actually and figuratively on cave walls
and in sculpture dancer and sign
of energy as cosmic forces
becomes a familiar
transformed into animal fertility
yogi-seated and horned
on seals
the figure of intoxication
sexual pleasure and connection
to the "other" world
ideogramic broken from the oracle
self-knower and self-hangman
in the form echoes
"Who am I" and "Who is the self"
the evolution and dissolution of the cosmos.

2.

Another tendency
is to think of femininity
as the seat of the intellect
linked to the idea of the male as passive.
a theory of emotions coupled
to philosophical thought
described through figurative, coded gestures
in dancers and sculpture.
this discussion of origins,
embraces
finitude and infinity
The day to day
life, philosophical and ethical
order and the nature of human existence
To bring aggressors to oneself
rather than to encouragement passivity.
In this sense
the female heroic.

3.

"Who am I" is thought of as enlightenment.
to overcome and realise self.
by visualising the future flavours or moods
or emotions, to produce an "ocean of feeling"
interest in movement light and shade
and turned heads a transition
the moving viewer circumnavigating
many viewpoints a patchwork method
using many quotations
towards an uneven blend of statements
what is occurring a flinging outwards of
episodes and sequences
identifies human activity
recognises
an aspect of philosophy is
a discussion about the cosmos
linked with a visit to
a separate occasion.

Freeze

Paradise gardens in ceramics
Gardens eventually hanging gardens identical with Modern
from north garden
In captivity write many books based on word-of-mouth tradition
Formal gardens ornamental pool
Alabaster figures
Gardens embassy
Gardens pharmacology
Gardens and House
Cultivation of music, dancing, chess, hunting, gardens
Wall painting
Art in a ground plan for later buildings
Forced out marches with army
Country mansion becomes armed city
Lion-like patterns in brocades
Fight invasion move of centre on caravan routes
Gardens at Palace of Eternity
Outside
University founded, translates classics, herbals & books on medicine
Gardens before palace
Lustre jar and earthenware bowl with cream slip
Tower architecture
Earthenware jar with turquoise glaze
School of herbs & cures, astronomy and mechanics, alchemy and
mathematics occupy poet
Synthesis and writing
Note garden imagery
Ewer
Readings of scientific, medical, and alchemical literature
Begins to dictate "Travel" memoirs
Turquoise-enamel painted frieze tile
Turquoise glazed, carved tile, lustre painted tile
Starts wall and panel paintings
Palace and garden
Dish; arabesque carpet
Prayer Rug, fragment of carpet
Painters begin school
Garden carpet, prayer rug

Goose Neck

1.

The present begins from a break
signified for thoughtful contemporaries
this glorious sunrise
the last stage in History
world, our own time, summarised as the beginning
labelled the period of overlap with birth of the new
spacetimes that precede the phenomenological Modernists
and their traditionalist contemporaries,
look back to the "Ancients"
revered sculpture and architecture
"Bronze Age" pleasure and illuminated traits of the era
the radical and innovative performance in production.
relief to contemporaries
interweaves classicism with romanticism
like a preference for the holistic, the hierophantic, and mythologic
as well as a concern for the organic relationships between
humankind and the idea of Nature in accord.
With some contemporaries, a strong regard for politically and socially
revolutionary ideals
characterised as passionate and republican at the same time
almost uniquely informed by the world of science and industry
Acquaintance with contemporary physics and chemistry
concern for the rights and wrongs of "progress"
evident in both visual and written works
the age that redefines the Sublime
standing in awe before the blast furnace and steam hammer
the age that lifts the worldwide war machine
to an economic plateau from which it was never to descend.

2.

The progress of poetry and opening
converted into reflections on painting and sculpture
masculine ideal of beauty embodied by statuary
using drawing as a centre
derives from reassembly.
A philosopher gives that lecture on the Sun

sees a vision in a tree
attends drawing classes, collects sculpture
following the excavations enters the action
manifest imagination
in human form
machine
an experiment circumnavigation.
writing poetry
discovers electrical nature of nervous impulse.
first spinning the human soul
a philosophical essay on slavery
the sorrows of a new system, or
analysis of Ancient Mythology as history
discovers acids.
The Apotheosis of Bacchus
Large paintings in the Great Room
various scientific texts
work on electricity & the human body
borne along by the mob
arrested and released
Practical geometry nightmare in a fire balloon.
satire on a literary circle of lily-livered Londoners.

3.

Internal lighting begins.
method of knowledge is experiment
Laws of the Planetary System.
Year of the Revolution
idea of necessary contraries
main argument calls for abundance and multiplicity against
restriction, division, conflict
illustrations to Paradise
Venus rising from the sea is a hieroglyph of the republic
Year of the Massacres
The Gates of Paradise completed, scoffed at
lover of liberty climbing towards waning moon
declaration of war against the Universe
a Creationist's Inquisition begins again
commission to illustrate On the Aesthetic Education of Man
from mere naturalness to state of fulfilling sexual love
slavery as whatever prevents human visionary potentiality
society which lives by chaotic and hypocritical systems

Dreams of life
Lectures on painting
Illustrations of atomic theory
Triumphs of Temper
Working on projected city
the unity of the intellect and the senses
microscope & telescope
ratio of spectator's organs
pattern of human perception
they became the will to change.

4.

A selective map of creative work and its context
extensive use of sources predating the period
this poetry and philosophy of poetry
an extensive use of alchemical texts
sources on the strength of conjectures
songs set to music
with as much substance as
contemporary popular melodies
the paintings and engravings of the tradition
which interacts this combination of counterfeit and reproduction
work read by poets and visual work admired as diverse
the alienation of the Modernist condition
in the first phase of post-modernism
after 1950 and before 1968
re-seen for the clarity of those decades
as a consequence of this re-seeing
now available in popular facsimile editions
for an age of cohesive wonder and struggle
that previous generations had limited to sketches and songs.
Restored to the origin of building, or the plagiarism
of the detected designs
carved with scenes from Adam & Eve
A philosophical enquiry into ideas of Paradise
the place that redefines the Sublime
sitting in awe before the television and laser gun
the place that lifts the whole epoch's geography
and now its speed
to an economic era in which it is always late.

5.

Destroyed in proportion as their Poetry, Painting & Music, are
Destroyed
tears up title page declares war
History of Philosophy
historical development of consciousness
as decisive in the nascent system
the Phenomenology of Mind.
the Spiritual Form begins illustrations to Book
painted in anonymous style
Arts & Sciences against kitsch
Destruction of Bad Government
Allegory Formed by imagination
surrounded by
inspiration aggregates
destroy post-industrial machines.
Tombs of Ancient Heroes
seizing the daggers
engraves outlines of pattern-book
commanding the Sun to stand still
raves about Innocence and Experience
revises Paradise
electromagnetic rotation.
not a Poet but a Philosopher
non-Euclidean geometry
not a Philosopher but a Poet
in dissenters' burial ground.
Death text produces first photograph on a metal plate.
Coming from the gleaning field the waterfalls.

Heebie Jeebies

Propellers of light
Direct air space
Seasonal hay harvest
Whistle through leaves
White air rapids
Skeletons skimming surface tension
Newly meandered
Red sand clay
Lignum strength
Sword swallows
Wagtails one saw kingfisher
A disused mill
Sounds of car rush
Occasional silence

I came as an owl to the shoulder of Northwest and established culture
My fellow wanderers Southwest grew small-eared corn,
squash and pumpkin.
became basketmakers in pit houses, made black & white ceramics,
        petroglyphs and decorated meal bins.
Dissipation begins in severe drought recounted in freehand murals
Invaders bring a spatter technique that shifts consciousness
displayed in weaving.
This plunder horse-mounted nomadism introduced by white Europe
stages our battle
Red in flannel introduced by white Europe
contrasts the owl's imported indigo dye
Twenty volumes of text and twenty portfolios of photography show
        our survival surrounded by reservations
surrounded by a population of white death.
Our rocks exhibit The Sacred Pipe Account of reprinted
        mythology revised by The Teachings of A Way of Knowledge
includes a Review of evidence of beginnings of humankind.
Our fathers produced Male Sandpaintings as a Guide to the Pleistocene,
the Weaving Techniques of the Sacred.
Our poetries revised the Teachings from the Earth Philosophy.
The Story of How a Story Was Made linked to drawings and colours
Our mothers produced Blankets, Pottery, Basketry, Beadwork,
        Masks, Amulets, Wood Carving and Ceremonial Dress.
Their story not coded red white and blue describes another culture.

describes unreasonable effectiveness
Her patterns are instruments of perception
and require a special conception of simplicity. This becomes a
story of holes, knots and connectedness in a spacetime of now.

Disturbs the eye
Then orientation
A row of stones
Wind sound in cell rows
Takes flight
Or in suspension
An inverted canon
Tropologic grace
Excitement from underneath
When the roots tap
A coded message
In distress
Mineral waste
Recolours the dawn.

Hitchhike

The green Beaver lifts over on hind legs
takes account of a vanished dream
Instead of a variety of truth
gets subsumed by beauty
Shrouded in a duffel coat in
gangrene in photographic film
remodelled sentences the shapes of existence.

Float into rest some peripheral debate
glances every event that refuses
engagement Speculation in favour
of rejection arriving early whenever
catching a train from happiness
to poverty Stop short of the function
of creative writing short of the
decision to be an artist decrying
the push into plot turns memory.

The Self Beavers the Subject rumbling
Function modified built on debris
Watch horizon instead of plenitude
instead of stride into the sea
A crazy moment describes strategic
civility evidence of replenishing
Rows of questions in a plan chest
ordered into capital and sprayed
with poison.

Beaver being stands on hind legs
lifts over a green hill takes
account of internal morphology in view
of a vanished horizon a kind of vertigo
Instead of a discourse of truth precipitation
in a variety of solutions where beauty
gets subsumed by relationships.

Different versions of this float into consciousness
and some rest there in debate or more
often peripheral glances against backgrounds
of disappearance of every event. Plurality
at its most pungent. The new age that

refuses a politics of learnéd ignorance which
characterised engagement. 1950–1955
Renouncement of philosophical speculation
in favour of activity. Rejection of transcendence.

Beavers refer all thought and all truth to
consciousness, to the Self, to the Subject.
In the rumbling all Beavers stand their ground
their dams and river holes. Function is
ceaselessly modified. Mud flux. A foundation
built on mobile debris. Civilisation impending.
Watch this space. Horizon imminent.

But does it end transcendence?
confront an irreducible residue?
What cannot be clearly said
in this subjugation this Self referral
consciousness this Subject ha!
this rumbling. This deceit
ceaselessly qualified, pungent and
mobile in a ricochet—
an implicit system of limits
and thus exclusions knowings and
implicit unconsciousness or is it
simply a set of rules bent or bust
as received truves move towards participation
The particulate and multifaceted displacement
of moral reflection.

The focus on language isn't it the focal
what's it balanced on the reappraisal of
participation as cogent—the lie of
the moment—the supposition a point
without philosophical existence—well
then—except to say dancing—the Beavers
in bed—café life on the river side
various digressions, escapes, water chutes
transforming fear into laughter, sneer
into speech.

How to observe ideas, as possible perception
The description of phenomena the science of it
shredded into a history of truths and how
Beavers think they establish them. The elaboration

of the Self by the Self transforming through a
constant care for truth
The endless labour of that
led to useful truths, morality
as the yardstick shifts the
mortality its transcendence.

But does it end an irreducible
residue. What cannot be
subjugation this Subject
this qualified ricochet—
an implicit exclusion or
is it bent truths and
multifaceted reflection
Stopped short to question
his notebooks in a great
muddle marked at random
astonished, ping-pong joined
with picnics and the work
on destructive philosophy
on distinctions of sequence
and discontinuity.

The focus on balanced reappraisal
the lie of existence except to say
café fiction, various escapes
transforming into speech.
An anecdote of an entire era
tracked into truth about the world
and living, trapping and printing
in snow fields changing ice
shields in the snow.

How to shred ideas of how
Beavers establish the self
through constant truths and
shifts in the ice buck
the mineral resource
Another spring energy against
police treatment of squatters
in fatigue control in
emotional dependence and the
put on face against eco-misfortune.

Dispossession & Cure 2

Horse

For sometime the Architect was unprepared for understanding
and then it came to her quickly
so much so that she had expected but had never seen
what became so obvious.

Not rich enough to buy cheap things
When she was present at a climb backwards
a nascent romanticism and mature classicism in complexity
new actors scavenge the past for ancestors.

Zoned into separate conditions
Necessity continues its vagueness a projected
sublime reason from direct and negative presentation
releases suspended values.

What she does and loses
In the interest of the beautiful
reason can be achieved by indirectly presented reflection
a positive relief from anxiety.

She gets too much of what she wants much too late
When you know how to find your bearings Art becomes a secondary
and positive presentation of reason that insists on the individual
the creative wonder stooge as the source of value

A response for the quality of life and physical survival
and a resonance that offers, that demands stocks fall and rise
in generalities in requirements for judgements
to be in conspicuous subsumption

The creative activity a contrivance to appear burning
Van Gogh as Prometheus in a death culture
involved in imaginative acts of judgement
expressive counter-revolutionary bored.

She goes anywhere and says anything
the determination as hypostasis where
diagnosis becomes an example of reflective judgement
all she lacks is the consciousness of what she knows.

To sell vegetables without being imprisoned
oppositions that attack humanity
determined when the art is hidden
in the limitation on work and relative abundance.

Astonished at how much freedom bends
Sensitive intelligence into figure forms
expresses free and indeterminate accord between faculties
the present's ownership clarifies the future destruction.

Possessed by the keen desire to live in the future
In order to describe the hidden in the determination
becomes manifest exercised freely in reflection
leisure replaced by entertainment.

The people of the future fraud and visitations
on the road of thought on the destruction of creation
judgement becomes a faculty—irreducible and original
to coin slogans contemporary with maintained ideas.

The influence of the city felt through its distance from London
The insistence of questioning thought as travelling
aesthetic judgement's reflection legislates over itself
totality's return on the fragment.

The requirement of organisation, order and method
Simply describes "a product" "without philosophical theory"
just as senses regulate reasons
world-historical insults integrate into everyday seduction.

The requirement of reward, order and method
Everyone's familiar
your incapacity to determine your particular selves
the premises of an old critique explodes.

A penalty directed to the irrationality
No pretence to delimit pictorial specificity
her incapacity to conceive any unity of phenomena
a new way of walking signifies liberation.

Question whether these packages come together and blend
The being-product, the usefulness, the belonging to the world
understanding's concepts in accord with ideas of reason
the fear of not being understood.

Focus and explore function within the machine
Valid for town and for the fields
final natural unity known to us as diversity
events judge all that follows wanting.

The appearance of simplicity
Proper to anyone or anything whatsoever
where beauty cannot be assured in terms of utility
funds power in the self against domination.

An expression of reconciliation between work and life
The truth of the being-product
where beauty cannot be assessed in terms of internal perfection
death of the planet becomes the masterpiece.

In the grip of a wish-fulfilment
She seems too sure of what she calls internal description
where beauty cannot be determined by its relation to practical interest
everything that was directly lived moves into a representation.

The process of synergetic reinforcement
The truth of the useful without use
makes possible the transition from knowledge to desire
irreducible images of primordial displacement.

Multiplying advantage on advantage
The reflective judgement climbs back to generality
makes possible the transition from knowledge to desire
the self experienced as other.

As if progress were experiments above the average level
On the authority of the reflective hinge
the indeterminate unity of the faculties prepare for the most elevated
the alienation of the spectator to the profit of contemplated object.

Social relations mediated by images
The attempt to find out the only exercise worth doing
to clarify structure of the proper object of judgement
according to which the interest of the beautiful disposes us to the good.

For sometime she was unprepared
and then suddenly
what she had desired becomes understood
as the movement of the cosmos.

Hubble

> In celebration of the confirmation that the universe is expanding.

Suddenly the sleeper listened intensely
and what took so long
became unexpected what was remembered
obscured

No ditch rough but stinging nettles
Absent-minded attention
after an age of waste and decoration
view vectors revenge fought pesticide

Cloned as desperate renditions
Casually breaks vacancy a jet-propelled
climb guessed-at before inject and exhaust
legalises suspected values

Simply rested on grain couch
Without concern for pattern
guessed-at reprieve by indiscreetly rested attention
a pull driver flattens rock

It never becomes too easy
Often lost but momentarily refocused
without position certainties risked onto disparities
holds onto the carpet as it recedes from underneath

So we think the values are clear
and a resounded snap remainders in over-order
in singularities squeezed through the bottle-neck
existence learnt on assumption

The carpet cracks the static underway
A row of tasselled rails to prevent the viewer
evolved from involuntary excuses
in a chord ascending into blossom

But it's fixed
the rubber the liquids the wind
all this are measured
shackles in the bounce of oblivion

Tousle regrettables shut psyche in reason
opinion spat beneath the coving
vermin ridden
in the expanse of motorway drainage

From thought ignorant of cure
Repeats ornament what seems like always
recurrence and expectation rebound on each other
a series of soon-to-be continuously on view

Period living becomes style Tonight's theme is "desire"
Cretinous in bibulous ridden indeterminacy
arums infestation exorcised purely reprieve affection
plant life situation as unexpected attainment

Lambda DASH and FIX clone your DNA
into superior vectors surrounded by
Not I sites that facilitate easy excision
of inserts and rapid gene mapping

Glad at once to be failing in what is heard
Persistence off investing bought has marvelling
habeas-corpus grudge meant respect shuns vegetates plover shelf
mote reality's adjourn when crag is meant

Desire, applauded and excused
Chaos this scribe eradicates "the precise sphere"
rusted fences vegetate need on
pushed and wrist volts into gracious into Oedipal play eruption

Pyre vent of parade, applauded and excused
Oedipal puns lap cat
each vessel's limits auricular nerves
building which often told pattern erodes

Plenty pirouetted practicality
No offence you decide in a minute victory spread city
helpless barren and uniformity of phonemes
view play of squawking magnifies situation

flash non-radioactive labelling and
Detection system can achieve single
gene detection on your Southerns and Northerns
FeatherVolt to provide all your electrophoresis power needs

Hows planned implode bodily necessity
Pallid fortune expand fortify shields
vial "common view" thrown over perversity
funds power in the self gains domicile station

A quiet space
Taken on board as requirement
without loss of aesthetic function
the feel of confidence

Vectors of acceptance given in to employer's need
Root and beat rudder
wet fruit can of vested inturn often vernal per fiction
enough of thanatism runs after peace

Inner rip often this appeal meant
The sleeper rapidly becomes the dreamer and then the stag
leaves through the front of his chest
nothing imagined holds away from what it is

Products that take you
From your tissue your cells to high quality
library in the superior ZAP vector
incorporates the unique in-viva excision feature

Volt metering excitement then ecstasy
This is what I expected all the many whiles
rakes posture the trade-in fool nothing in the mire
the pelt perioded discover

Addressed where impediments dove this baggage full
Confirmed by presentation
black star of the intellect peppered post-lift-off
the playback interest of the intentions of beauty

Hand shakes the thumbs-up
A list of vitamins with good causes specified
ratify rupture over prop-up objection grudge bent
occasionally pitch of desire as functional

Suddenly he listened
and as ages passed
became freely immediate
as it happens.

Huckle Buck

A riddle, lament and difficulty in 26 stanzas

"*. . . Earth groans with men's dying shrieks as I shatter fruitful woods and forests, fell standing trees . . .*"
from a translation by JOHN PORTER of the 10th century *The Exeter Book.*

Future sprawls to this immensely
Amber scrawls as if strong
Soak in breeches crowned dismembered
Weather lifted the crows objured

Notation derives from this and settles
Without destination left in contention
Array and raged nonsense nation
Need lost sight needed inside

Xenophobia orders daytime evening editions
Need these oval raids fallout pell-melled
Sexual rather than erotic mustard falsed
Reels rabbit into what must eschews

Wheat burnt in backyard and in porch
Imbeciles bring on ashes as if Saturn
Red carnations fill dull suits mention
Ache in the chest and forehead silage muck

Shit allows full cycle to tone the queasy
Wonder lunch spoilt by the travesty cussed
Able to learn how this burnt breeze
Theory of thermostatics is buried beneath

Aversion or inclination amounts to the same fear
Applied incendiary counts this soldier's border
Irrelevant to the biologist and poet on deck
Take-over is how they perceive this pinned presumption

Theme parks take the ecological decision out of play
Velocity peaks at mental escape clause overtly truer
Impious status meridian as the Inspector larches peruses
Eaten on the sick bay entrance path sat on bottom

Sites get rubbed and left with a weed crop mixed
Ten gilded bovines are led into the meadow and skinned
Days like this are seldom recorded silence assured
And love is their carrier mapped in their sinew's obsidian

Temporary or left to confuse the public to prevent treason
Out and lost in the rain wood with mosses behoving
Did not demand this beaten into submission bidden
Inside the field boundary to count each crop as leverage

Agreed or not this go ahead relies on fewer
Sanctions or sanctuary it is rested on plays
Event words sanctimonious slept under cover
Theme and intention bottled waiting the unscrew

Processed journey across field towards oracle pyre
Inscape jolted into burning fumes a new aristocracy
Beckons offers care of immunity to fire infection
Leads the solutions into carpet of plasticised raiment

Theory forgives this lack of belonging this way
Ontology formulates the centre bestiary impounded by
Jest a locket filled with aphorism around the neck precision
Toboggan lurches down spine to reinforce this lax rapping

Think before crossing the road even if you're a bird
Thimble the fingers and sew the document in marbling
Aged with candle grease and portrait to the self
To be the wigged ecologist in a stance named bent

Travel is the main theme the need for goods pursued
Sanity is not on the list of prerequisites from the pier
Judge and judged appear to be similar cretins
Work is ferocious but honesty simmers corruption

Thread is used to check the nerve fibres perused
Eaten and defecated in one day an account of fat
Yoghurt milk and bacteria there's no amount for verve
Therapy leads each participant into singular codes

Apple air leads Lugg devastation its immortality
Knot in back and tree chair's dismiss pity
Hurt it may be pollution becomes one of many themes
Agate left to roar from a barbed power station

Quest in support of lammas land against planned
Threat directs a delicacy to unsettle the tangle
Upset you might be here it becomes a field of urns
Throb loses rhythm into bedrock introduces new breeds

False stories invented reason surround city
Vapid structures interface each junction yields
Full substance of the inverted justifies temerity
Even encourages reward for robber creation

Thought clipped in harvest exhausted in the race
Propeller chipped in marvels of wastage a vent
Weather to undercut the rationality of presumption
Function shifted without care becomes opaque becomes dense

Animal fury this might be but this cannot greed
Through fumble sheets an honesty leaves shudder
Wind of coming storm predicts another restriction
Deals with social conditions as authority's ability to fleece

Indark the story produces the need to invent
Sheet of misjudgements wiped with an oily rag
West of the city the air takes a new vest
Effervescent imports to encourage drinkable fizz

Thug would be harsh accuracy ready to screw
Trussed and bribed into a satisfactory verity
Maintain the land the status the nectar
Irrelevant—oblivious they are not—denture

Missed the calm meadows the will to play
Thatch onto period style thatched and beamed files
Mends the demolished crashed into quiet fire
This fritillary row this mould of the lover

Avail—well let the language rule
Obligates each citizen—each subject on station
Thing against thing glottis against chest cough
That leads to the point of this that's rooty

Sober it may appear the cider runs over the cup
Theme repeats theme until tasteless until fried
Totality smart appearance over devastation cruelly lent
Ash to the funeral occasion and need to be punctual

Forehead held as if in anguish as if wizened
Angle from here says it's lying held fast
Web of designed protection orders to predicate
Aster on the front porch thanks for our stipends

Hully-Gully

Climbed through stinking iris and yew
Chance and necessity continues to sing true
or remember the result of the simple play of probabilities
desperately certain the pursuit is worth it.

A small group senses there's a treasure somewhere
Crimed you thinking I wish it would eschew
whoever wants dreamwork must mix all things
nomads-by-choice in the welfare of settled rings.

Up onto limestone sea bed balmy about plants
The principles of interaction between levels and slants
the device of split representation
a re-emphasis as part of a clearer formulation.

Far enough to get an impression that it's there
Upon a two time prone seep and army routs advance
inwardly full of images as measure
the complicated patterns of errors and pleasure.

Hellebore and liverwort
Principles of pattern formation that often work
the multiplicity of excitements and moments of respite
full-bloodied calm and hesitant rest.

They return and gather a large party
Held in store canned inner words
the prerogative of daring kept from uniting the mild and savage
relationships of errors clean transmission kept a constant average.

Nest of aroma sticky from excitement
Aggregation and transformation shifting each moment
suggests that what we need is patience
with marks and shapes already known well.

They get across hurdles they couldn't cross before
Best off a road brick he foam next site event
the free creation of impossible combinations
the indispensable dusts in comprehending the intermittent.

The moment of greatest intensity is within performance
Deep pools in the wisdom eye water
the conflagration of production order with new meaning
Discontinuity, bursts of noise with few repetitions.

ENTANGLEMENT
and
LEANS

Introduction to *Entanglement*, 2004

One of the more engagement problems encountered in any urban catchment can be an unavoidable decoherence due to the coupling between the quantum system and what if the environment. Experimental praxis can address this problem through a poetics of crowd-out and this what is it has partly been achieved in the poetry of *Gravity as a consequence of shape*, using a necessary critique of modernist coherence, and its precedents in roaring and the enlightenment. If *Entanglement* achieves indistinguishability, it is because several methods have been used to guarantee overlap in spatio-temporal imperfect fits. Some of the starts, books in *Entanglement*, such as *Fish Jet*, are complete in themselves and were published as complete entities. Other books lack this obviousness. These fit varieties are perceptually productive states in which the traps of any participant's consciousness radicalise the aesthetic tools in the process of their use. *Entanglement*, we need you, but we cannot say why.

Critique of any 'you' concept, implicit in critique of the individuated self, any entity fixed to a garden fence left to rot there with the slugged geraniums, can lead to a heap of worn tyres, better for a worm compost or the edges of a boat lap than for use on the road. On the evidence of chronology there is an assurance that Spenser could not have read Nietzsche. It is just as clear that Entanglement is not informed by the cunning sleights of Kirkrapine who enters churches through the window and is thus associated with the robber of consciousness and sleep, without a guess at which came first, the burglar or the arrested genetic material he steals from under their eyes.

You can imagine you are a ball in a very active game, changing position continuously, rapidly sometimes with one then another player, sometimes loose in the air just as often being held in a momentary stop. You are not that ball, but another played with in a very small room or put in the cupboard and locked away, or maybe in the attic for a generation or more, but then taken out of the cupboard and immediately played with by a new set of approaches.

Distribution of entangled states between distant locations is essential for quantum communication over large distances. Owing to unavoidable decoherence, the quality of entangled states generally decreases exponentially with length. Entanglement purification—a way to extract a subset of states of high entanglement from a large set of less entangled states—is thus needed to overcome decoherence. In quantum communication, the generation of entanglement between distant locations is essential for the long-distance realisation of quantum cryptography, dense coding and quantum teleportation. Meanwhile, quantum information protocols involving entanglement are a very useful tool for fault-tolerant quantum computation.

6. Disaster Bag

Itch

Fourteen clones came through High Town on
bulldozers, JCBs and a sooped-up can-opener
Jake threw a pavement at Jez who threw a
garden at Adam who ate the flowers
It's a goodlife when you hang in with
Crushed Light

Jerk

For nearly three minutes he listened to the headache
Felt hair growth each second sudden swells
White light hits the wall reflections
Too many ways to skin a cat
From inner forward in the free the corrupt
A constant shudder
Storm in the forehead in the tea cup
Through any day's token like that
Quiet Sight fits the fall rejections
Smelt rare gross peach beckon'd sodden smells
Fort leafy tree limits reglistened through the red gate.

Timed without fixity he searches to name his condition
In its intimacy in its change
The environment and its appearance
He takes the choice made by too many others
Conceptual in the loose tube buckling
A constant rudder
Much fuss about so much less
To signify the condition
Non-interference accepts the decision of knowledge
Sex in the decompression chamber
Barely three minutes before switch off.

7. Fish Jet

Fish Jet Fidget Frequency
Fridge Yet Frigate
Forget Jet Fret
Forget It

Jersey Bounce

1.

In habitual pathology aggressional impossible
To create false junket crisis
Dimension of the sensible burst
Foam mouthed incantations sleepers yawn
And hide railway's votive exactness
Appearance through shunt customs advising
Starch complicated apportioned roar chained
For a forced vague pond
Transit painted with risk agriculture
Corpse falsity's incoherent ideas combination
Solar day structured the living
Leather brad nails provoked resistance.
Pen at Wigan Pier platform
Pauses and urgent angst placement
Duce rickety played to mark
It trading without a basis.
Truth speed the environment disqualified
Stood rout arrested for shark
Multi-placated recent fight the best
Leather lend risk and liver
Sounds landed played vegetable vendors
While this meant mend pollutions
Asunder way laid and fed.
The assistance of an imagination
A trellis tv on memory
Planned stained with portent ready
You stood ride to life
Then the whirl pretends mustard
Traded vacancy homeward voice beneath
Stings bat muffler propriety contrary
Activity of the sublime curtain
Wall cantilevered from nerve cells
Bend the roost opal turned
Fits obtrusive securing meant risk.
Slower rota-press blooms stable valueless
Purrs a pension sum appalling
Ineffable cradle stunner beat-on greed
Risk versions speech rested vested
Contraband furs sense and passion

To bodies rapidities of air.
Tracked violence perched on rafter
Stone and bread storm pit
Riot of hell stains bed-rock
To flay morning statics range
In bower bat in fridge
Berries touch circuit filmed vast
As sky earth and sea
Our sight in subliminal illumination
Racked the down the Foss
Produced to misty and indelible
Staged lantern that pulled word
Real fitting muffs leaven rarity
Of lace extortion poor grief.
Laxity allegory identical to predictability
Para-optic death of a watch
Wrecked in fact purred rest-stance
Pear fill rugged pot latch
Rot this august face headset
Pony rages of purity planned
Provided aghast threw steam rabbits.

Fish

1.

Inhabitants chiefly pastoral and agricultural
The spring returns any fluxure
On account of material character
Averse from innovations sheep cattle
Corn and cider remoteness geographical
Adherence to ancient customs arising.
Large comparative proportion of poor
Chastened for enforced vagabond transformation
Untainted by political agitation problem
Posed as of interrelations Lecturers
Gradually introduced pestilence 1637 causes
Public anxiety irritation produce difficulty
Conveyed to markets not modern
Rapidity time distance marvellously behind
The power of the spring.
A culture genius its configuration
No good without accompanying drawback
Multiplied conveniences excite the restlessness.
Lecturers blend political with religious
Often made of pious attentions
Hostile to establishment and institutions
Under which they were bred
In that point of tension
Mass of detailed astonishing behaviour
Had gained no important ascendancy.
Who should decide to live
When all the world ends
And must be very impatient
Who would rejoice at death
All things that suffer society.
Returns the whole it receiveth
More than one person evolves.
End use of tuned pulpits
Exclusive persecuting instrument political power
Process rumours dissatisfaction various quarters
Apprehension some approaching indefinable calamity
Forerunner attendant great political convulsions
Reached pestilence visited contagious fevers
Whole aggregate of all forces

The world edited by sets.
Lurked so long afterwards ravages
War and fled from it
Society of bell-ringers toll stock
The day's warning statistics exchange
In the tower at Pembridge
Perish such surquedry overwhelmed dust
The greatest degree of tension
Customs, institutions, ways of thinking
Attacked Ross reduced to misery
Beggary in Linton Yatton Walford
Burial of 315 sufferers 1637
The charity of place exhausted
For relief of poor taxation
Spring bent in two spaces
The remarkable permanency of configuration.
Collected weekly during several months
Their will government watch word
Not a kiss or embrace
Only images of prurience and
Provocation against through beam raptures.

Jet

1.

Inability checkpoints a regional effect
Tremble reminder fan Viewer cries
From opening thesis sentence chars
Fire-resistant features radio wilderness bark
Adhesive circumstance pictured submission viewed
Appealing compartment shocked in front
Of complicated instant overwhelmed subjugation
It's a planned environment traced
Across from edge against other
To a ratio decided then
Torn decided then re-structured de-coded
Historically paved in readiness relations
Pen at left then against
Other, pauses, publishes details placement.
Produce rickety conveyed to markets
What Viewer yearns for travelling without
Modern speed-environment behind beneath
Shuddering power scorched Viewer voice
A naked comprehension thickens understanding
Initiates learnéd embrace ampersands containment.
Scream let-me-out serenades to salesmen
It might as oblivion this
Political menagerie re-binds ashen peony
Hotel Poetry enables heralded uncertainty
About spacetime trellised trammelled connectedness.
Instant located point replaced by
Tension discard model detailed life
Clarity before an iced landscape
Exchanged heading homeward warmth tired.
This banter trap property's grip
Achieves angle to view picturesque
Curtain evaporates joy into breath
Bowl of roots leaves fruits
Cascade hills thatched society from
Poverty the blossoms Viewer values
Mobile appreciation opened synergy envelope
Ecstatic in light tuned green
Embodiment vehicle instructs rested power.
Jacket full of scents peeled

From body apprehension from static.
Upstream attention perched political raft
Reached and viewed amidst nettles.
Truth as Ventriloquist levitating over
Bed-rock warning statics exchange
Light and evidence attributed to
Cleanliness and rustic comfort filmed
Against a backdrop of industrial
Calm searing waves of concealed
Shape.Thought through netted pleasure
Decided trek in mist beacons
Stern toys studied patiently meditated
Deeply understood minutely towards habitual
Intuition and loneliness out from
Relief spring into moment-spaces caught
And held precipitation shored banked
Treasured inks process hum on
Lips determined to absorb possession.
Not this kiss but the
Next image of peddling uphill
Against inclination with decision.

Jersey Bounce

2.

Wisdom arrangements permeated with order
Stood withered amber napalm investment
Fruit juice free jazz frequent
End its own boundless goodness
Connect things look at order
The proper and continuous connected
Reflections in series of possibilities
The effects of civil world.

Fish

2.

Receiveth four degrees of impulse the
Scudamore with Amoret Nature Venus
Beauty now multiplied by sixteen
Three in first space returning
The comparative velocities of body
Moved in subduplicate proportion aggregates
Velocities in proportion to spaces
Subduplicate to powers all times.

Jet

2.

Weather formulates permafrost insulated stillness
Static with natural jewellery banking
Glow juice fills jazz establishes
Finitude in Viewer's speech re-phrased
Patterned relative appearance before sunset
Shoved by planetary description accumulating
In metal sandwich vibrating possibilities
Beneath skin enriches civil times.

Jersey Bounce

3.

Human thought a metaphysical geography
Monotonous realities allude to strife
Forever just flock jam fragrance
Exercises in a critical art
To know grasp form by
Which a thing is made
Consciousness is of those things
Whose forms we cannot demonstrate.

Fish

3.

Incorporate virtue moves and draws
Spontaneous generalities of alluvial life
Universal emotion lost in configurations
By natural force acts immediately
And without a material instrument
Incorporeal indivisible grasp seize constrain
And impel an extended body
Thus no communication without contact.

Jet

3.

Human virtue a complexed tropography
Spinning red sponges trading health
Serpentine curing indark knot fragility
Purchased in scent crenellated in
Time within grass mounds left
Ages ago attributed to intellect
Rebirth fertility anger rendered monumental
Land forms communicate through touch.

Jersey Bounce

4.

Lead reel rushed inculcate united
Body mind causes thought at
The appearance of an interface
A fraction pawned your medication
Bands fiddle of elephants reach
Has not found this edifice
Bound to the mother tracks
Missed elaboration eschews inverted consciousness
Thought irrigated floats parlance flutes
Lifting wealth with a nudge
Memory theatre on railway beach
Humming the neck pulse recall
In this hymn of levity
By product plied under sand flower
Pauses oddly of horrid plates
Proved on the waste bother.

Fish

4.

The corporeal untouched by incorporate
Gaze the possible daily necessity
Now all knowing proved impossible
Attraction performed through the mediation
Stands in middle of elements
Each planet bound to elements
Cannot be separated without violence
Constitutes with them one system
All the parts cohere together
Son of Spenser's Sir Scudamore
Never everything a valuable buttress
Common bond analyses terrestrial gravity
Acts its system as gravity
By gravity I understand power
Causes bodies of homogeneous nature
Moved one towards the other.

Jet

4.

Dense body quickened by perception
Raises potential horizon against cosmic
Torque into an understood blur
Drawn towards fragmentation Viewer mediates
A stance between experience and
Thought not bound by elements
Not entirely free of purpose
This establishes Viewer's invented comprehension
Active song coexistent with message
Seeing a mackerel under sand
Think of gooseberries plied sauce
Plates required for the Arts
Of Memory logic, philosophical knowledge,
Cheerful communicative temper, quiet conscience,
Free from anxieties, sound health
And digestion without the another.

Jersey Bounce

5.

May achieve utilities of need
Continental interstate test fish jet
Fidget frequently fridge and this
Is called "just" who do
Not know truth cling to
Certainty of order who do
Not satisfy intellect their will
Rests upon consciousness. Imagination and
Memory play roulette informal rotation
Inner blight signs fridge yet
Frigate forget it poetry involves
Promotion of stumbling the ancients
Avoid these disadvantages a geometry
Appropriate to joy. The critical
Poetry makes truth while the
Meaning makes eloquence true arrangements
The many-centred deity of railways
Impress the muscles regress pit
Pell-melled exchange fresh jeopardy jettison jig
Unity of reason and passion
Charming oratory combines eloquent fires
Filled with love of justice.
Moves emotions to virtuous action
Drag the mind towards virtue
Sequence a sensory-imagination deliberation
Fat shake endorses invest-a-pond jabber
Fall jargon free forgotten jeopardy
A self-conscious imagined flappy reason
Ordering entrusted to practical breath
Rapid understanding in sexual encounter
An ancient dialectic divided art
Stir-fry both discovery and judgement
The faculty of seeing likeness
Quince disrobes this infection diffidence
Forlorn jitter jibes for justice
An incoherent combination of truths
With a fabulous original basis
Dragged by a Stoic chain
Bodies motion in the brain
A demonstration of profound levitation

Fish

5.

Gentlefolk of Herefordshire improved orchards
Continuous in state of rest
Life-history as accommodation to patterns
Master before new laws gravitation
Repaired endowed dilapidated Abbey Dore
Renewed coinage before John Locke
Restored alienated tithes several churches
Opposition to Puritan iconoclast Harley
Receiver of Court of Augmentations
Uniform motion in right line
Patterns landed traditionally in community
Painted glass and sculpture destroyed
Under Henry VIII acquired monasteries
Cut fertility icons at Kilpeck
At Paris with dignity courtesy
Surplices images rent into pieces
Became station received patronised English
Unless it compelled to change
Shape derived from birth custom.
Harley from London adjudicated severity
Recommended attention among Hobbes, Milton
Appointor Thomas Symonds engraves dies
Introduced to Grotius ambassador Sweden
Dedicated differentiated logic to coining
Asked obtained permission returned home
State by forces impressed upon
Of their culture before speech
Fear of repeat Catholic Reformation
Approached dwelling tenantry on horseback
200,000 massacred in Ireland 1641
Congratulatory address await hearty welcomes
Architectured by Poussin's Dionysian patron
Hereford as protector buried him
Since this globe perfectly indifferent
Habits beliefs impossibilities before maturity
Pagan Christian Richelieu central academy
Lead with brass listing virtues
Prevention of attachment Austrian Charles
Master of Mint before Newton
Secret canker after James' Bible

Jet

5.

The Viewer locates detailed arches
Apocalypse follows a rest engine
Steam machine produces comet power
The Painter spikes into habitation
Beyond surface hooks a lozenge
A knowledge contaminated with capital
Hot sounds eat silence repeat
Oppression brings wonder repeat imagination.
Coincident with memory with circadian
Spin blades break cosmic furrows
Fresh japonica lathed in white
Air of Painter's needles becomes
A void filling with acid.
It etches icons at Kilpeck
And Fownhope with inner dignity
The surplus engineers frozen jellies
Embossed in similitude to wonder.
Useless exchange compels jeopardy shifts
Ubiquity into reason before passion
Viewer tears at red sandstone
Felt sculpture incomplete bronzed images
Sculptor lifts a stone fork
To model the intellect a
Hoist celebrating verbal existence vocalises
Forms into envelopes of vibration
Feeble jewels frig out from
Viewer eyes imagined before reason
Trembled disturbance repeats body's expectation
Holds dwelling intact at perception
Rocks hewn in twelfth century
Confirm a weight given lightness
The bite of repetitive need
Soul as intelligence, body as
Matter as if this assumption
Made sense recurs too often.
Viewer vacillates becomes a whirl-brain
That talks whatever comes uppermost
Sculpted lead after first mould
Repeated motion with transforms before
Remote micro-chips regulate orbital television.

Jersey Bounce

6.

Shower gels thrive across invest
We know why it is
All the viewers watching themselves
Burn more text vet live
Shatter fright continental fondle fun
Bend rotation instilling flints fern
Module shout on taxes baths
Live into a rock shelf
The rattle falling gratuity farces
We are not nature's slaves
Swiftness erases any subtle reflection
Thought caught or offers shoddy
Astral pain front hind limed
Howls pelted utter rust shell
Pit bored doubt eaten and
Old dead excess fake angle
Wift as sheared the fool
In cattle consciousness a shower
Of cells container not independent
Of contents bleeding white invest
Sure birth bust mend inner
Other shorn oral sight falls
A bends drift wood and
Skin inner avalanche shot habitats.

Fish

6.

Power impels drives attracts impresses
Threatened tranquillity King and State
To locate feelings as objects.
Turn vortex yet drive matter
Light continually from the sun
Spend motion in filling chinks
Turn globule about own axes
Wraths like screws or cockle-shells.
The matter causing gravity passes
Inherited errors government and respect
Forced into adopting scheme's adequacy
Through all pores of body
Ascends again from limited bowels
Else matter must swell it
Borne down Earth and others
Descends exceeding fast and swift
As appears the falling apples
Authority Crown before portcullis chains
Simplest rule was enough fact.
Exceeding weighty pressure to Earth
Must ascend in another form
Or a like force ascends
If it should ascend thinner
Advantage of not hit bodies.

Jet

6.

Thorough immediacy quells any question
The many pivots of complexity
And design there can't be
A promotions edge shook mildness
Shot brain strings fever pitch
Deviations brighten city befriended motor
Action flinching proficiency the nature
Of this complex convex rock
Pool disturbed skedaddle appalling advances
Interactions between semiconductor electronic gates
That is as far as
Throat faults the coffers decision
Bends refrain from mistake showers
Decision scatter smashed well fit
Boned shroud beaten or torn
Arranged somehow meant not random
Bending into the shape of
Consciousness rigid formula crudely trained
Rinse spangled with indecision flust
Proceeds transform leisure to facture
Emergent form from local constriction
Order attracts rising chemistry eventually
The Viewer shoulders beneath meniscus
Alive fandango cough cleared wit.

Fish

7.

Demands hurt by confidence want
It would hit more parts
Selection is the price necessity
Ministers advice recourse arbitrary methods
Vocabulary of submissive reverence held
Some already been unhappily accustomed F
ell upon knees in Bristol
Revival of obsolete chains perception
Glad to see his Majesty
Would more parts to hit
Traits they find themselves possessed
The imposition of new demands
Measures of government without means
Legend of the bourgeois interests
Courts thronged blue blood hangers-on
Identity with ideas of Nation
Poor relations, retainers, old captains
Hit with a smarter force
Complex interweaving of cultural traits
Reliances on permanent effectual operation
The drones of needless attendants
Threatened Parliament reign without them
Courteous, unuseful scholars old comrades
Ceased to call Great Council.

Jersey Bounce

7.

Fronds spurt sky fence wand
A perpetual and "intentional" activity
An interested concentrator of facts
Administrates re-coded tree metal vocalises
Substrate re-verb shed stun played
Sheen unharm acoustic shell from
Freed fist tool muddle of
Depletion rain's directions mad to
Be this travesty a ceaseless
Employment of change visualises begins
To precede discovery the implosion
Of few commands pleasures of
Discovery withered beans lets send
Burgundy into this distorts belonged
Through thud burghers ideal with
Indenture elation roar situation remainders.
Bold lanes an endless probing
Of restlessness truth becomes the
Informatic function appliances of
Permutation effete on station thrones
Feed this intention theory ends
Parlance raid wit then caught
Unfuelled pallor fold made creased
To fall greets count sill.

Jet

7.

Responds pervert descry wax code
Complex ecosystem even less stable
Fragility in all direction varieties
Miniatures corrosion free arbitrate choice
Superpositions all possible locations separately
A vast space of states
Seeded first beat bubble risk
The varied number of codes
Gladiolus torque frees this enmity
Into asymmetric spacetime realism
Historical narrative the invented procession
Offered balms through feathers of
Exploration of growing expectation fended
Bend of a Biologist unfurls
Network thrombosis sky flow prangs
Indemnity eureka pours upon communitas
Public bath house, tanning pits,
Linked to wattle daub dwellings
Simplicity matted into housing crates
Permafrost roof slate perpetual polarity
Flower thrones of seed bends
These spoken weather predicaments fraught
Relentless catastrophic motion in balance
Fleeced in stall pronounced fool.

Fish

8.

So cause ascension more force
Endeavoured support from various exactness
Time experience more than dimension
All bodies we know sink
Into your pores of body's air
Sink into most forcibly crowded
Stream descending some hold ascending.
So press it colour denser
Rise slower stream descending growth
Extensive dissatisfaction without representation assent
Desire for a self-regulatory womb
Thicker as it comes nigh
Will not lose its swiftness
Until it finds much opposition
Help from following flood behind
When streams meet all sides
In midst of Earth co-acted.
Tax of ship-money in mind
Unconscious memory of amniotic fluid
Into narrow room closely pressed
Very much opposition one another
To turn back the same way
Crowded through one another stream
Much difficulty and pressure compacted
Descending stream will keep pressing
Imposed under colour guardian navy
Escaped dementia præcox through mathematics
To Earth till they arise
To place from whence came
There attain their former liberty
Gravity of bodies as solidity
Because bodies descend equal spaces
In equal times consideration being
Scots open national resistance marched
The vision the spell cast
Given to Resistance of air
Air stubborn body next pores
Air will have some reluctancy
Outwards like bended whale bone
Crowded into hole middle forward.

Jersey Bounce

8.

Knowing why it is as
It is. Invented retort on
Precarious fraction flesh juice jumble
Free jig-jog. Ideas shower on
Human consciousness modify intelligible oneness.
Spatial combinations represent complex ideas
Institutions' radicality self-knowledge from language
Study expensive diffraction count imminent
Frustration meant fragment junior freeby
Joint frazzle myths systematic ways
Of seeing, understanding, and reacting
To world rationality attained in
A maturity.Truth criterion to
Have made it poetics a
Basic human activity freedom from
Metaphor, hyperbole lacks rip shoddy
Inward flat foot floosey joins
The jump jet knowledge never
More thus probable transform beyond
The given skill tensions value
Fact purpose material will not
Free reality doomed wonderful life
Of the future the welter
Of mere experience proposed asunder.
Valour discarded again gravy forensic
Judge fossil of the jolterhead
Protest against mechanisation and vulgarisation
A drama without a denouncement
Each movement significant in itself
Language absorbs the collective experience.
The body is the image
The image of the soul
Shot out of rational rest
Stance parched jubilant for the
Fumble in the jingle fun
There are no iron planks
Then the uncontaminated aesthetic impossibility
The sacred art of vessel shaped
They will return to themselves
For the promotion of freedom.

Jet

8.

Lift-off from two liquids together
A momentum state which is
A corkscrew a pi curve
Resembles this localised initial singularity
As it is actually used
Thought eschews burst codes loaded
Tremble declining temporal bin repression
Insistence that words are absent
To perform a complete system
Expended distraction fingered presses Lift
Button groping for necessary truth
Rolled dazzle sifts signed haze
Unleashed freeing mild blues cathecting
A global selection aspired to
Impunity.Wallowing crisis rush
Weather, consciousness and physiology
On space route to collision
Time, a figure of speech
Implosion of thought's amoebic semen
Sound knife piecing out protons
Theory's crux positioned on spinning
Wound up each clouded thought
On each thought beam loaded
Mustard dignity and polemic raid
Ridged fuel dealt into legacy
Imploded grades of colour within
The infinitude of possible universes
Irregular spin of this planet
Then process the corrective expression
Theory feigned theme from inventions
The flow of thought in space
Because bodies descend equal spaces
In the image happening half
A second after the event
Funk spins the ecstatic sound
Breathe in watch the rise
And fall of zigzag responses
Boomeranged into neck pain released
Below seat of the skull.
The Viewer presses with thumbs.

Fish

9.

Marched armies upon several occasions
Water draws it in striving
All the elements of vision
Over the bodies arrest independence
Taught English the Civil War
Civil war is class war
In light of English understanding
Like the eye judging objects
Only by its own right
Air too being continually shaken
Vision complex receives different region
Cannot but be discovery pleased
Less regret for what escapes
Less regret because unconscious escapes
I give you leave to
Give leave to adore you.

Jersey Bounce

9.

Parcelled barmies shone ever explosions
The electro-colloidal investigative system.Tools
Produce geometry beyond comprehension robust
Shoddies crest into pendant wrought
In dish that evil work
Eaten word vista grass car
Enlighten this thunder sounding spike
The rye fudging odd jets
Stony bits clone sight a
Slow liberation of radio-activity the
Directed attention through tunnels under
Bridges a recovery appeased on
Rails. Invest your sensual napes
Invest roars under schemed napes
River live through the streaming
Riven reprieve in today's to-do.

Jet

9.

Marshalled chlamys clone dishevelled erosions
That there's a non-algorithmic ingredient
In the action of consciousness
Mind's clover bodice invested in
The mere presence of awareness
Sited in ghetto and palace
Optical exposure clarified resounding mike
Pie in sky budging pockets
Bony fly pits loan blight
Consciousness arises within physical reality
Maintains existence through algorithmic embodiment
Arranged ready for a decode
Leather vest neck cape lets
Regressive alternative mistakes as the
Financial wizard in corrugated lean-to
Gift pleads another way through.

Fish

10.

What I, in it, grieved
Strive to get out cavity
Variant arrangements of human life
I am grieved to want
And give you reasons many
Give more than one reason
To draw a thing moving
Draw that which cannot sit.

Jersey Bounce

10.

Potential based a value system
Thrive you met that gravity
Forget jet fret forget it
Investigating functional mechanics of time-binding
What can be shown disappears
Conscious of differences between abstractions
Silent and verbal levels evaporate
In terms of betweenness spacetime.

Jet

10.

Many alternative arrangements exist superposition
Alive through wrought about proclivity
Tied to resolving of alternatives
How the am retains existence
Seeing of a necessary disappears
Each amplification of observed encounter
Rent added visceral thought mooding
Draught germs often seem benign.

Jersey Bounce

11.

Organised longings speeds over continents
Cinder against spring shore syndicate
Fish jet fidget frequency frigate
Not yet evolved as human
Engineering idea toward complete realisation
Too small to support wine
Whole complex body of observation
Among the parts is disturbed.

Fish

11.

Surplices copes and images rent
Hinder it agitation sponge draw
Biological constitution but indeterminate behaviour
Rent in pieces surplices copes
Laid in dust the icons
Cut the fertility destroyed sculpture
To improve coinage high commendations
Orchards returned to Hom Lacy.

Jet

11.

Confluence this loss at complexness
Rinderpest aggregates sprigs of dawn
The life need at self-inspection
Spent into précis splices mind-fly
Consciousness the capacity to simulate
Lantern-lured moth wreck of understanding
Hold convex bondage comment stations
Wrung burned the mental tracery.

Fish

12.

Air moved in smallest parts
Whilst reeking to aslake desire
To calculate security of happiness
Vaporous particles everywhere tossed up
Down in appears its heat
Betwixt particles there no air
Paper ropes, hemp threads, fiddle-strings
But a little pent up
Can scarce out the cause
Whilst seeking your brightening desire
Criterion of good becomes "survival"
Crushed closer together than nature
Permits as-it-were a bended twine
Laths of crossbows some reluctancy
Against position and liberty strive
Cannot fully does unless other
Between air and water bladder
Seeking to aslake your desire.
Preference for language of struggle
Opportunity offers itself by striving
Get asunder they draw betwixt
Pendulum move in free air
Conjectured bodies be in receiver
Hinder notion of the pendulum
Moving body no determinate velocity
Put end to tuned pulpits
Affection based on mutual respect
Moving apple no definite line
Without resistance cannot be uniform
Nor straight in which accomplished
Cannot be motion without determination
Now that fresh state prevails
Could not define part position
Bell tolls the day's warning
Good humour mutual respect reliance
Space is disposition of being
The place does not exist
No being in unrelated space
Created minds are always somewhere

Body is the space occupied
Existence neither everywhere nor anywhere
Gaze on the possible necessity
Sleep a condition of satisfaction.
Space effect arising from being
Being postulated contemporary with space
Description of corporeal from faculty
Reduced to moving our bodies
By act of will moving.
A uniform existence space continuum
Opposition to insistent English levies
Housebuild a measure of hygiene
Every way with out bounds
Which parts of space possessed
Adequately filled are their places
Passing out of one place
Into another through the intermediate
The whole frame of nature
Chiefly pastoral remote and agitated
Active value in adequate respect
Nothing here but various contextures
Some certain aerial condensed vapours
Precipitated in water or grosser
Exhalations afterwards wrought into forms
At first by remedial hand.

Jersey Bounce

12.

Rare mute this tallest shard
Magnified geometric progression surpasses difference
A perspective without singular horizon
Rapacious articles stare drossy cup
Clown thick rears this feat
Fixed articles share nothing doper
Soaps stamp heads middle stings
Rut skittle bends us canticle
Shouts and roars in accordance
With ratio's irrationality infinite openings
And ruptured enclosures mushed poser
Gathers the mature permeates shudder
Shear blended time craze of
Lost throws sunder tansy again
Positive and library shove canticle
Fulcrum pressed feather beaten pear
Under waste ladder an excited
And ignorant army each surface
Is an interface portent proffers
This brine shift fetch another
Stay or twist penultimate groove
In for ash directed bodice
Being rectified wonder motion of
The pencil drum alluding noise
Nod mingles atrocity the lay
Of insulated ethics transparency replaces
Appearance accelerated disappearances noble strand
Fetched acrylic dish canned commotion
Dead ration shower French crate
With sails stood rot fine
Art posidrive disparities of verbalised
Internal culture measured out values
In relative uncertainty pace positioned
Over been replaced codes that
Persist nobody interfaces this maybe
Creatures mingle ways share Being
The pace this cries persistence
Wither evergreen or aging history
An expansion of memory threats

Of flattened mental geography trace
Fence raiding from beaten beaten
Port-wrench, trace prescription offered core
Froth cult produced through proving
Knowledge bio-activates spill proving unique
Persistence race tin drum just
Conceptions correct definitions true propositions.
One unconscious mode replaces another
End wait wither rebounds much
Art sped positive able quaintly
Filed at theology rasping rout
Of ontology screw out of
Thought the medium the hold
Fit starts outer space excessed
Padlock cured fire our graces
Strain rapture show, progressive, endless
From shipyard railway then airways
Long range projected destruction remains
Planned notion heard but vacuous
Contemporary sum curtain imperial condition
Flagged off burnt boundaries another
Measure parallel vortices into catastrophe
Waste predicated aster for poster
Exaltations rafter words sort indigo
Norms burst fly remedial plan.

Jet

12.

The constructed apparency of explosions
Wired this week asunder illusion
Tubular calcium secreted snout nervousness
Rapid parcels repair glossed cuff
Astound this shear this pleat
Between packets played on plague
Cemetery edge rent fibres mildewed rings
Butted against spittled rust wire
The first gropings of consciousness
Attached as already identified codes
The distinction between critic and critiqued
Lushed posers tethered then naturalised
Matters subvected a blended wine
The mark of the market
Positive style tied to shrines
Purveyor redistributes the Viewer's text
Between trust and plural ladder
Seeded consciousness in reach out
Deteriorated image of the city
The all-purpose mental stomach pump
Set amongst theory dawns between
Hidden knowledge and recoverable meaning
Complexed rudder bolts in an
Oily river of vital experience
Barrel-organs displayed for a mile
Through a consumer walk town
Commercial Street Butter Bank cess
Pit—adventure, power, joy, growth
Where the soul consumes itself.
Approximate to the sources of
Gambling applause the individualistic burn
Promotes the sale of rebellion,
Justice and purposeful life. Now
The bell tolls day's wreckage
Proprioceptive encounters and patterns of
Connectedness combine with ontological calm
Place multiplies in each person
Nobody performs an unrelated spacetime
A padlock falls from the

Mouth like syrup. The lips
Transform an occupied existence. Gaze
Everywhere anywhere transforms the possible.
Exproprioception casts an imperfect fit
Upon aesthetic effects arising from
Pulsation, contemporary with a multiple
Interdependence. Production of the corporeal
Reduces movement to relation, embeds
By act of joy flows
A substantial enveloping of desire.
She calls it love he
Calls it love also they
Disagree about the structures everywhere
Which parts of timespace possessed
Adequately filled are their places
Passing out of one multiplicity
Into another through the hedgerow
The whole frailty of nature
Appearances pressure possession as active
Joy value in actual love
Duration and eternity conflagrate breathless
Image a blazing daisy rocket
Promotes water and sunlight promotes
Ecstasy after caught inner forms
Bring fingers beside immediate hand.

8. Now's the Time

A radio phone in
The mouth of a snow
Leopard confirms
A message from a 532 emerald
Planet approaches
At the speed of ancient light.

Someone has thrown whiting
Over the cat's head
And back and where
This has missed a gold hue
Radiates darts of red ice
Gives off a screech
And then dull thud as the
Leopard runs into a meadow
And green shifts behind
A stone marker.

Jig Walk

When you have no one to talk to
you talk to yourself
and the imaginary becomes the real.

In a nest of small hills
sounds of the railway resonate
at once in a skylight window.

Having come so far to find peace
you hate its stillness
and imagine shouting.

In a 4 am window
the waves of bird sound
fill the jaws of parliament.

In a garden full of blossoming bows
upon a river, in a green meadow
there as sweetness evermore as now.

I dreamed that I was thrown there
by a will held
in the grip of self-estrangement.

A soft noise in concord with songs aloft
thoughts held by small plants with golden threads
pull apart as my mouth opens.

Jitterbug

1.

When you can't sleep you make choices
Between staying awake or feigning sleep
Until the differences between the imaginary
And the real blur or become distinct.

In the City at the end of the century
Evil flees the Earth, writes González de Eslava
Before 1600, Now comfort is come.

Uniformly large embalmed travellers on the ground
Smashed aubrietia
Bourgeois security, self-absorption, destroyed community.

In the streets a turbulence of waves
Interferes with Music
Imitated by a bird.This must
Be fifty years ago, or four centuries past.

A leopard's shadow moves over my eyes
And I begin to express terror
Locked onto a vocabulary of telos and beauty
That perpetuates mystery in number.

2.

I climb over a disruption pile of basalt rocks
Each holds a machined part in a bed of warmth and creation.
Each holds fossilised light and regenerates.

Rights spring directly from understanding who we are
But there is no agreement or
Belief that such is in principle possible.

There is a conference in the air
Concerning time and whatever couples with it.
Before spacetime could be perceived
Perhaps this is what some call eternity.

The Artist returns a drilled out cone to its extraction place
The headlight child sieves regeneration in a bed of
Felt and clay, warmth and creation

There never will be autonomous moral choice
No superior dignity entitles anything
Not even intelligence and the experience of pain.

3.

It is the dawn of a hundred rabbits
It is the end of a millennium
How is it possible for some survivors to reach new, similar,
Worlds and thus perpetuate the species is still a mystery.

At the end of the century death keeps me awake
Recognition made universal
Birds alight aubrietia in the garden.

King Sailor

He meets traffic
Between the fresh and the recurring

Starlight through the window
Becomes dust in morning sunlight
In the shape of stars
On the glass
Tiny spiders fill my eyes

He watches for salmon at shore-line
When saltwater exchanges with the spring
And the contained looks out to a beyond

Predict a pattern imposed on exit beams
From slurries of suspensions in insulated fluid
An electro-rheology that contains
Hesitation with assurance

Lambeth Walk

Again arises in wind
Words shortened into magnetism
Quiet voices strung out in bright air

You feel the flow of death
And push it back
From the shore
To an underside of sea ice

A strong reflecting interface within
Transforms in the noise of
Diffuse echoes of ice and ocean

History and the world merge
In layers of meteorite
And accumulated salt

Lindy Hop

Pink and Yellow tremble
Pink and Red

In a constant dialogue
Without one frame giving up
For the sake of another

Swimming lines
In the window
In fact my eye
Chemistry

Red andYellow
Yellow and Green plash

And shift focus also
Separates the star field
As the window
Moves past it

The word for the world and
The word for history
In Cherokee are the same

Irreversible time only
Partly determined
In the Garden

Nearly asleep
At the evening window
A real journey instead of
A memory spume of colours

Lloyd Hamilton

Plan of a golden space relies on
The length of time
The size takes to dry

Weather varies this duration
Increased temperature of substance
Lengthens it.

The worn manuscript coloured by
Thirteenth and eighteenth centuries
Has inked upon it a square and
Two intersection lines that
Cross symmetry in the middle
Known as Time and Space
Opacity and transparency

Such immense arrogance
Dismisses snapped
Pizzicatos and frequent glissandos
Heralds in a day-time
Photo-chemical smog

Snow Ball Gas

Iridescent blue attracts animals
to disperse its fruit contemporary
with the yellow-green
photosynthesis beneath the fruit's epidermis
to provide by definition success
from virtual non-existence
directly co-engineered
to outlast the Great Pyramid
A solid reputation with
unique and proven reliability
gives this eloquent processor
the horizontal choice of one of the most demanding
requirements in the world
The breath that melts the cold of isolation.

Locomotion

He bites beneath gold
A terrible beauty
This is a *fin de siècle*
The ground marks hidden remains
An inner vagueness.

Resist first with structures
Bones and nerve ends alike
Measure and time
With flow with warmth.
Cover then remove excess

Oscillations beneath
Eyesight
A skylight window.

She turns the green lands
Into gems
She shoots with her eye
Autumn crocus already gone
But cocksfoot and meadow cranesbill
Under her rigour.

He resolves
To suspend spheres
Before they precipitate in eyes
And blue there beyond belief there
Into a star field.

Terrible tremble of colours littered
On a leaf green sheet
Splintered with purples and gold.

Disaster Bag 2

Mambo

with John Dryden's 'A Song'
from *The Kind Keeper*, 1680

1.

Punches to origins form
Competing versions of correctness
About the Real gender screams
Art explosive from automatic
Media contempt for Modern
Freshness lithe arrogance
Gender celebrity articulates position
Cultural message Men
Civilisation Women
Nature Power gender conservatism.

2.

'Gainst Keepers we petition
Who wou'd inclose the Common:
'Tis enough to raise Sedition
Inn the free-born subject Woman.
Honest gold and fair
Feast my body there
Thought a Slave until creative
Ranters stretch to rest
Conservationist vest
Naked Budget to explore the native.

3.

Levels of research vet
Thought under a critical book
Overview struggle budget
Struggle his staff repetition
Second wave phenomenon
Space economic polemics
Moved forward social vigour rights
Tense Nation tethers
The only weather
Air temperature photographs sites.

'Commerce is so far from being beneficial to the Arts or to Empire that it is destructive of both' – William Blake

Madison

after the design and emotion of John Dryden's 1693
'Song to a Fair, Young Lady Going out of Town in the Spring'

Skin siege from necessary our void time
Precious records of by-products strike cosmetics
Countless robber waste disappear deal of cosmos
Incomprehensible stolen vulnerable eroded time product
Civilisation rubble pandemic void crime greed of human space.

Impact from spectacular robbery of aging
Two thieves disguised the premises trussed up within
Wallets made off with has to amazing
Bandits consider fine paint compatible with time internalised
Affection contamination packaging within product presents
Environmentally friendly now and now.

Skin notation from early distinguishable earths
Civilisation arranged then sought after then countered
Indiscernible speck in sky system speeds earthwards
Strikes its unfortunate prey retrieving body encountered
The illegal affected the variable pesticides who back loop
Point of connection of elements in dependencies of the closed scoop.

Receptors or differences detect value lack
Trains and bearings linkage discernible in nature
These systems near characteristic of negative feedback
Bell crank which survey at rest digester
Ear and the spring under steam pressure
Inturn control governs pleasure.

Mashed Potato

1.

'Mitochondrial Eve accumulates substitution rapidly'
(11th June 1992)

The way the Geneticist views humankind
Concomitant with a changed world
After 45 years Nature profession
Find ways to manifest action of impression
Of natural masses where the multiplied
Acceleration in spin described
Theatre Pictures the very shape acts
The Nature notion people say the best facts.

2.

'Nonlinear prediction distinguishes between chaos
and random fractal sequences' (16th July 1992)

Audience is there it's of anticipation
Voice silken as whole body seems a mountain
Alive in Pictures group senses and set
Imagine an impressionist subject.

3.

'Shrinking patterns seem to be sensitive to states
of transition' (6th August 1992)

Gather performance significant yet
At night in the nord a funky repast
Is not before Engineer a last
Theatrical save for a pit of sand
Up in wings bejewels need replaces the hand.

4.

'Large optical changes were found in the sensory cortex during tongue movement' (20th August 1992)

Slow customers come out and sway in music
Floats above chants in understanding tic
The want to see all no more than white notes
Opens a curtain and front door to floats
In a squeezed magic shop classic wonders
To do with rain outdooring the intellect.

5.

'Visual search has little or no access to the processing level of feature extraction, but must have an input to the processing of surface representation' (17th September 1992)

Fragrances the war an aromatic
Business tool tropical beach blaze erratic
But vulgar hands may vulgar Likenesse raise
Product discovery develops craze
A gallop along molecular stain
A Coal or Chalk first intellect strain
Biology is fast accurate hope
Convertible improves Original
Drench in diamonds focus a step-out
Stakes Biotechnologist against charge.

6.

'Magnetic compass orientation is affected by the wavelength of light' (10th September 1992)

Frets their uniquely international rout
Perfection takes movement a huge sparkle
Table these concentrations upon luck
Crystalline accident structures event
A jigsaw lunary inhaled
The next evolutionary leap
Chain reaction damaged at the point of
Sedition rooted in education

Appears to equal the whistle a sound
Dissolving the face as it is stolen
And replaced with a unique privation.

7.

'Knowledge of physical attributes is strictly
segregated from knowledge of other properties
in the language system' (3rd September 1992)

The star of the complex patterns output
A lot riding on the diamonds shot
Control muscle contraction motor nerves
Translate patterns of outside bio-reserves
Technology alone celebrity
Beauty and Picture editorials
Thus in a stupid Military State
Diamonds launch world Biotechnology
Uniquely placed to face tough odds billion
To one industry launches commercial
Strategies spends conditions investment
Programmes each advertised in-depth anode
In all these areas every month.

9. Traps or Tools & Damage

Monkey

1.

given a kind accident
shames any emphasis
what you are dictates
less than you think
before pain shunts
incident each pain
anticipates the unexpected
driven a mild precedent
blames amanuensis
wrought mass nmistakes
invent strinkage
young strain funnels
meant teach disdain
creates these vectors

2.

then and now
contingent
condition
subjected changed
determinate crash
decided beforehand
then generosity
love.
desire.
chreod.
invention.
requirement.
surprise.
thanks.

Mouse

Delight of every living thing
Propitious love and showers sweet
Earth composts and sea supplies
Breeds strand-specifics beneath row ling constellations.
Spring with dewy fingers cold
Handles scatters of gentle flowers
At your pleasing perfume disappear
Unlocks of shake and suck of the year.
The truth presumed but now fractured
Early morning where have you been
The rising spring refills the sink
Teeming buds and cheerful greens
Unlock riddled basins of attractors
Give peace to write and read and think.

Mule

Mule 1

BI-LIGAND
TWIST
SPRINGE
METALLICS

*

EVEN-SKIPPED
ENGRAILED
PAIR-RULE
CAMOUFLAGE

*

MAGNETOCAGE
ENDOHEDRAL
DI-SPHERE
TUMBLE

*

INVARIANT
DEFINED
SEISMOGENE
FRACTURE

*

SEA
GROUNDWATER
LAND-USE
RISE

*

SPIRAL
HEART
SLIME-MOULD
CO-OXIDATION

*

PUNCTUATED
STASIS
RECASTS
CLADES

*

PACKING
EXPLOSIVES
NON-LINEAR
ZEOLITES

*

Nodding Donkey

Nodding Donkey 1

Somehowthemomentsoflucidity
are shifted just as clarities of judgement become troubled. The
exquisite neurologics of memory display a capacity to change pitch.
Sodium ions communicate a bi-ligand array, twisted together in a double
helix intertwined springe that flex resultant accommodates different
metallic songs. These are recordings and
codes in traces with facilities to connect.

A relationship between even-skipped and engrailed expression, only
partly iambic and partially lyrical, signifies a pair-rule in short- and
long-germ beetles' patterns as their camouflage develops. The fullerene
cage can be magnetically sensed by an endohedral atom of helium.

The potential energy junction is di-sphere symmetric and molecule
tumble allows the averaging of measurements. Strict scale invariance
only applies between well-defined bounds.

Mule 4

CONTEMPT
NATION
TINTS
RETURN

*

HANDCUFF
MEADOW
REST-BOX
PEBBLE

*

LATCHING
ESTIMATE
CORAL
AND OVER

*

Nodding Donkey 2

"Rain rinses the road," the renewed Cartesian pairing in part of Basil Bunting's Briggflatts, with its apparently even scansion,

breaks within its own measures and becomes, in 1951, in concord with the post-war geologist's view of the Earth.

The crust ranges from grain size rocks

and thickness of sedimentary layers up to the finite width
of the seismogene. Non-universal scaling of fracture
lengths and opening displacements persist. Any pretence
to completeness is destructive.The sea level has been
rising throughout the twentieth century. A combination
of groundwater withdrawal, surface water diversion and
land-use changes have caused a third of this. Climate-
related effects are smaller than has been previously
supposed. Spiral waves have now been observed in many excitable
systems including heart muscle, aggregation
slime-mould cells, retinae, co-oxidation on platinum, and oscillating
chemical systems such as the Belousov-Zhabotinsky reaction.

(That is the complex of experiments carried out in
1968, and subsequently, involved in chemical reactions,
with either excitable and periodic dynamics, that reveal
wave-like organisations in space and made particularly
lucid by the malonic acid reagent known as "Sodium Geometrate" and
popularised by Arthur T.Winfree in 1980. You can see the apple
solution changing colour in a periodic rhythm.)

Nodding Donkey 3

In apparent contrast to this statement, ostensibly about consciousness, came the proposals of punctuated equilibrium in which the recognition of stasis as a meaningful and predominate pattern within the history of a species became manifest, and became recast as the differential success of certain species within clades. The search for a better summary was already underway in 1968.

More recent investigations into polymorphism of crystal structures indicate that alternative structures result from variations in ionic and molecular packing and conformation is now recognised in the mineral phases of calcium carbonate, in the production of polypropylene,

in explosives such as ammonium nitrate and lead azide, in non-linear optical materials, ceramics and catalysis such as zeolites and metal oxides. Crystal twinning can stabilise a crystal polymorph.

In Larry Rivers' *Second Avenue*, Frank O'Hara's poem flashes on and off against the street and the frameshift.

BRING RAIN

PILGRIMS
DISSOLVE
BACK CREATION

*

ACCORDIAN
BISHOP
PERSONAL

MULTIPLE
*

ISLANDS
DEPOSITION
SPUTTERING
SURFACTANTS

*

Mule 6

BEAM-SPITTERS
TRAMPOLINE
MAGNETO-OPTICAL
CLOUD

*

noisey
EVOKED
ISOMERISATION
RELATIVELY

*

DAMAGE
RAPTURE
PAPER
ROCKET

*

MILKWEED
NECKLACE
HANDSHAKE
ROBBERY

*

ORBITAL
GLACIATION
OUTGASSING
DARTED

*

FLUX
LOBES
GEOMAGNETIC
MORPHOLOGY

*

Nodding Donkey 4

The contempt for information enhances a nation rested on its ability to sustain what has happened as its basis.

All colours in this information system are tinted or reduced.

All issues of pleasure are trailed with a cynical requirement to return to values already established and unquestioned. When the conventional handcuff analysis of dialectic was led into the meadow a comfort was confirmed and elaborated into a rest-box. The size of pebble used to disturb the pond of the rest-box became too heavy to lift until the wrist restraints were removed. Various devices followed to encourage opening the field. Gates were operated with latching devices—a provision that metaphorically gave entrance to the discourse of the spirit, which had been locked out or clustered into a coral form. The fence scale operation was ruled out and over the top, that is it presented another discourse.

Mule 8

BOILER RAG
INSCRUTABLE
FOUR-COLOUR
UNDERSTAND

*

GAP

HEMICHANNELS

TILTING

CLOSURE

*

SPACETIME
TWEEZERS
TRAP
DISCONTINUOUS

*

The aesthetics were observed to be the "bring-rain" ceremony. The young are the frogs of the rainstorm, they churp and croak. This becomes known as the place of awe filled with processions of pilgrims. The portraits of their ancient makers dissolve back into the limestone. The present day sapling altars, the ruined temples of Yaxuna, and the Castillo of Chich'en Itza are all symbols of the creation of the cosmos.

The creator plays an accordion on the corner of Church Street and High Town. The bishop climbs the stairs and asks for the meaning of dispossession. The answer is already personal and multiple and can never be proven as true or false. Temperature windows allow islands to form on top of islands. Manipulation of this can be achieved by forming a number of small islands using low-temperature deposition, sputtering or by use of surfactants.

Another temperature window controls shapes, the fractal island becomes rounded by higher temperatures. Perfectly random motion can lead to self-organisation. Tom Raworth opened *catacoustics* as the cloud burst. Using mirrors as beam-spitters

it becomes coherent to construct interferometers and make precise measurements. Caesium is bounced on an atomic trampoline limited only by the scattering process.

Caesium atoms were dropped onto mirrors from magneto-optical traps in the form of a cloud.

OSCILLATOR
SHADOW
SUBTRACTED
SPEECH

*

FLARE-DIAGRAM
MAGNETIC
IMAGE
CROSS-OVERS

*

CIRCADIAN
RETINA
FUNCTION
AXIS

*

Nodding Donkey 6

Retinal photoreceptors are noisy. They generate discrete electrical events in the disk indistinguishable from those evoked by light.

The random spontaneous events are strongly temperature-dependent. Noise results from thermal isomerisation of a relatively instable form of rhodopsin. The evidence continues to display a similarity between damage and rapture. A paper given at the conference focussed on the metonymy of endogonic shock in which two liquids brought together explode and propel the next rocket away from the planet. The remaindered fuel forms a milkweed array on the launch pad and a necklace of flaming fuel shorter than a handshake in the sky. The viewers' calm and assurance is stolen in that moment and the following minute appears to offer the expectation nothing short of an ecstatic whack

immediately part of a robbery shifts the world of cultural analysis into obvention. The methane record shows that long-term trends have been driven by variations in insolation caused by the Earth's changing orbital geometry. Underlying climate changes are at least hemispheric. The direct radiative impact over 40,000 years warms the planet a tenth of a degree. One hypothesis attributes changes

to the speed of high-latitude flatlands at the end of the last glaciation. A second concerns the catastrophic outgassing from methane hydrates (clathrates) stored at high pressure and low temperatures in the Pleistocene ice sheets, in permafrost and within the marine sediments of outer continental shelves. A third hypothesis discusses periods of greatly enlarged lakes in the Sahara, and cites these as evidence of a tropical wetland source.

Nodding Donkey 7

One minute it darted off like a kingfisher, and the next it entirely disappeared. At times it grew as big as an ox's head, and then straightaway shrank to a cat's eye, finally it returned to frisk in the reeds. Historical geomagnetic measurements over 400 years

reveal a symmetrical pattern of four relatively stationary flux concentrations and lobes at the surface of the liquid core and regions of rapid change extending from the Atlantic to the Indian Ocean.

The present geomagnetic field morphology and pattern of variation have persisted for several million years.

Mule 10

FRAMESHIFT
SEQUENCES
MISMATCH
REPAIR

*

SITUATION
RIDDLED
ASYMPTOTIC
ATTRACTOR

*

ROUND-OFF
SUBSEQUENT
TENDS
BEHAVIOURS

*

EMISSION
KNOT
SYNCHROTON
AMBIENT

*

COMPETING
BINARY
CLOSE-PACKING
ENTROPY

*

COLOUR
TILTED
AFTER-EFFECT
NOTCHES

*

Nodding Donkey 8

The accordionist wipes his face with a boiler rag. The smudge of oil leaves an inscrutable portrait.

The resolution is the demonstration of the four-colour solution

in which the calculations are replaced with images to help those surprised to understand incompleteness and exactness. Gap junctions comprise two hemichannels which interact head-to-head to form an aqueous channel between cells. Intercellular voltage differences together with increased intracellular concentrations of hydrogen and calcium, cause closure of these normally patent channels. A global tilting of the hemichannel subunits has been correlated with channel closure. To investigate biological motors they constructed instru- ments with spatial and temporal sensitivity to resolve movement on a molecular scale. They deposited silica beads carrying single molecules of the motor protein kinesia

on microtubules using optical tweezers and analysed their motion under controlled loads by trap interferometry. They find that kinesia moves with discontinuous steps shorter than blue light. The pattern of received data could be recognised from noting when the receiver's oscillator was able to shadow the received signal and when it was not. Alternatively a chaotic signal was used to mask a speech pattern.

The two added at the receiver to form a combination that looked like random noise with no obvious speech feature. The receiver oscillator's output was then subtracted from the transmitted signal to reveal the speech pattern. When some superconductors are in mixed states the flux lines can form well-ordered lattices. The capacity for memory or storage within a few degrees of absolute zero are immeasurable.

In the phase diagram the vortex is both solid and liquid. The poetry gets so close to exact poise as to lose consciousness of its production. This is very late in the twentieth century where magnetic decoration can image the lattices at low temperatures,

but provides only limited information at the higher temperatures at which they melt. Using small-angle neutron scattering to find evidence of melting

of the magnetic flux lattices solves this image problem in 1994.

The image result is a transition from three-dimensional flux lines at low fields to two-dimensional pancake vortices at high fields.

CLUSTERS
STRIP
ENVELOPE
INCREASES

*

OLFACTORY
TRANSDUCTION
SENSORY
ADULT

*

INFERENCE FIX
REPONSIBILITY
SKULLS
IMPERATIVE

*

COUNTRY MOTHS
STONE QUARRY
PRIDE DUST
SLEDGE CAP

*

INFINITE
CARDINALITY
HEDGEHOG
SPININESS

*

RAISED UP

OPENS
STEAL
MIRRORS

*

Nodding Donkey 10

In 1884 Medardo Rosso modelled

his *Impression in an Omnibus*, a group of five figures disintegrating in his perception as they walked off in the rain.The sculptural optics of the passing moment was now within a complex mnemonic situation. Flux-lattice melting tells us much about basic issues such as phase transitions in the presence of disorder, dimensional cross-overs and liner liquids. The exploration of the limits of meaning take place with protection. Rosso reaffirms the validity of ordinary experience in an understanding of how there can never be ordinariness. *Impression in an Omnibus* exists now only as a series of written and photographic images. Conflict and dissensus take precedence over any possible consensus to delimit and define the present.

FLUID
PATTERNS
MASK
BURDEN

*

COMPLEMENTARY
PRIMORDIAL
SKY MAP
SEED BAG

*

TERRITORIAL
CONSPICUOUS
FORAGES
SETT

*

Nodding Donkey 11

The mammalian pineal expresses a circadian rhythm in the production of the hormone melatonin which is controlled by a circadian fluctuation in the enzyme arylalkylamine N-acetyltransferase (NAT). For neuronal pathways, including the retina, the pineal gland acts as a temporal regulator for the function of the hypothalamic-pituitary- gonadal-axis. An analysis of the rates of spontaneous frameshift mutation in simple repetitive DNA sequences in yeast shows them to be significantly destabilised by mutations in genes affecting DNA

mismatch repair. There are examples of deterministic physical systems for which reproducible laboratory experiments are intrinsically impossible. This unusual situation arises from the existence of riddled sets of initial conditions that correspond to different outcomes. Typical nonlinear dynamical systems have several possible time-asymptotic final states.

The site of judgement involves the belonging together of differences. The attractor cannot be predicted if there is any measurement error at all in the initial condition. Each basin of attraction is full of holes at arbitrarily small scales—hence riddled basins.

In any case, all initial conditions have measurement errors.The notion of determinism in early modernist poetry and classical dynamics has been eroded

since W. B.Yeats and Poincaré's work led to the recognition that dynamical systems can exhibit chaotic

behaviour in which small perturbations grow exponentially fast.

For a chaotic system, ubiquitous measurement errors,

noise and computer round-off severely limit the time over which, given a precisely defined initial state, one can predict the detailed subsequent evolution. Another example may be found in the "Crazy Jane" poems.The behaviours of such systems are quantitatively nondeterministic. As the starter of the system tends to be confined to an attractor in phase space, at least its qualitative behaviour is predictable. Optical emission is tightly confined to the core of the radio jet, and is resolved into a number of highly polarized knot structures. Both the optical and radio emission can be explained by synchroton radiation from a stream of energetic particles burrowing into the surrounding medium.

Comparison with the radio maps also reveals asymmetry in the emission across the jet, indicating significant lateral motion of the jet relative to the ambient motion.We determine the Gibbs free energies of all competing phases as a function of the external pressure. On the basis of space-filling arguments, phases may be expected to occur in a mixture of hard spheres: these include pure face-centred-cubic crystals of either component, and the binary fluid.

Mule 15

CUB
TYPE
TUNNELS
LATRINE

*

Mule coda

DIET
DESIRE
RANGE-FORM
SAGE

*

FIELD-OVER-FIELD
DISCOVERS
HERMETIC
COLLECTIVE

Nodding Donkey 13

If a given structure has a very high volume fraction at close-packing then at lower densities the constituent particles will have a large free volume in which to move and hence a high translational entropy.The motion after-effect is a familiar experience and has been observed for many visual stimuli, including tilted lines, colours, stereoscopic depth, curvature, spatial frequency, contrast, rotation and motion in depth. An auditory perceptual after-effect is caused by adaptation to auditory spatial motion. This was made clear when Bob Cobbing performed parts of *Processual* at the London Musicians Collective in 1983. After effects produced by the motion of spectral jerks are independent

of those produced by spectral notches, suggesting separate processing channels for spectral peaks and notches.

Holes in clusters offer the possibility of a black-hole-millisecond pulsar binary system with large eccentricity

and small orbital period, a system ordinarily not possible in the Galactic disk.

Nodding Donkey 14

Black hole hierarchical multiples tidally

strip the envelope of red giants with high probability as the radius of the giant envelope increases. The judgemental distinction is between affirmation and repetition. The mammalian olfactory system has the remarkable ability to detect odorants with high sensitivity and specificity. The initial events in the olfactory signal transduction pathway occur in the specialized cilia of the sensory neurons. Unlike other neurons, these olfactory sensory cells are continually replaced throughout adult life. Inference fix can only be a cultural matter that changes with context or responsibility and varies as much as skulls: there are those with vestibular apparatus that paint with bipedal balance – there are those that prevent it.

The imperative real reaches explanation in the distinction of soot and country moths as pollution indicators. On the stone quarry walkway the stems of indigenous plants break the surface of the pride dust and grow around the geology of the sledge cap. The complex concept of facture is an infinite set of cardinality. The metric space that contains the discrete concept of poetry facture gets labelled "poem".

Nodding Donkey 15

It is known as the hedgehog space of spineiness misquoted as spinniness. Parts of the space are unapproachable just as others are unavoidable. A classic text at Palenque speaks of the central axis of the cosmos as the "rained-up" sky. All opens to the separation of the sky from the Earth. The Christians steal the Temple of the Fabricated Cross with good reason. The carvings of ancient trees are outlined with reflective mirrors,

and they wear jade necklaces and loin cloths as if they were living beings. The Shamans frequently dip into cups of wine made from honey and deep well water to be charged by the fluid they rename spiritual force. In order to detect patterns that were meaningful in

cosmology and poetry many different kinds of knowledge must be brought to bear. Solo experience will not do. The phonetic key that allowed decipherment

in the Quirigua creation story was an image, a mask. The mask plays a musical instrument or smokes.

The aged image, complete with cigarette, takes in the breath of ancestors through a Muwan Bird headdress.

Nodding Donkey 16

The inhaler sits inside a house made of limestone fossils

with a crocodile on its roof. Behind the inhaler is a bundle called "burden". A convention was a couplet repeating the information from the preceding passing in complementary form.The primordial tree rises out of the offering plate in the perception of those making the offering. The perception of difference rises from the identification of the many possible varieties in the imaginary.The nomenclature of creator is multiple and fraught with unwanted innuendo: the shaper, sculptor, mason of creation is also the artist of the sky map and carries a seed bag on the chest to plant the Pleiades and form the imaginary. Mule abandons these formulations.

Mule lives in complex social groups and a well-defined territory. Discarded consumer goods form the boundary interspersed by large latrines. Badgers patrol the territory and conspicuous paths and forage in the neighbourhood of Glastonbury.The main setts can become disused when disturbed and annexe setts or even subsidiary setts can come into use for cub production.

Nodding Donkey coda

Spoil is a sign of usage and helps to determine the type of sett. Tunnels are usually flattened ovals and not round or tall. The latrine can include packaging and discarded food. Mule diet is a different complex. Mule desire proposes abandonment and exhalation. The range-form feeds back into the need for "burden". It is not anything goes, but a refusal of the refuge of both home and nation. The refusal is a sage frameshift, field-over-field in a rudder boat through lard, Mule discovers the hermetic in a collective abandonment.

Mummers' Strut

1.

A technician turns the radio to drown
screams from neighbours

When the hungry come for food the
dog barks until they go

The connection fraught
with stray wires

Before this begins and now
it is bleeding and now the barking

drowns the screams and the hungry
have gone.

2.

This is out of our range
This is out of our range

This is out of our range
.....

This is getting to be This is
getting to be

This is getting to be
.....

I'm a Negative Creep I'm a
Negative Creep

I'm a Negative Creep and I'm stoned [1]

Sometimes it works
and sometimes it doesn't

---

1 Kurdt Kobain, fragments from his lyric sung for the Nirvana Bleach collection, 1989.

rock

it

begin another grasp from
the inside

rocket

3.

So much so difficult to take in
Mule driver holds to

a raised path
in case of submersion.

Even as dew drops through a
window space the driver

can be seen holding the ropes' natural lubrication. What
was once cracking has become squeak

and then whistle
before the buckles rust.

Sodium ions are represented by two children in
the skins of nylon bears

dyed fluorescent blue
or ultramarine cut with steel and oil

Naturalists exchange informations on the relation between
bog bush crickets and the sound of dried grass

4.

Openness, immediacy, eruptivity

Lability and suddenness
Answer to a boundary situation [2]

5.

We marvel at the chemistry of minute Flies and butterworts
as plants take up insects and in so doing feed

the insects' offspring in a Flower display
stemmed away from the digestion.

6.

Outline,
There's no outline

There's no such thing
All is Chiaro Scuro Poco Pend and Colouring [3]

7.

A dog went over
the water without a wherry

A bone which he had stolen he
had in his mouth

As he swam
he saw the reflection

This is getting to me
This is getting to me

This is getting to me
.....

---

2 Helmuth Plessner, *Laughing and Crying, A Study of the Limits of Human Behaviour*, trans. Jane Spencer Churchill and Marjorie Grene, NorthWestern University, Evanston, 1970.

3 William Blake, Notebooks, N61.

I just wanna take off
I just wanna take off

I just wanna take off
.....

8.

In terms of local conditions we

need people to run it who are

not the enemy

9.

The surface tension
around a glob of apple juice

The banquet of smiles
dewy mead and sequester'd shed

Panted, prized, sacrificed
beneath the label from Safeways

English Discovery and
For paction [4]

10.

Climate no longer an obstacle
In civilised societies technicians are rich

A long story of robbery [5]
Wisdom taken from eloquence

Wisdom without eloquence
Without exception

---

4 William Cowper 'Ode to Peace'.

5 Peter Kropotkin, *The Conquest of Bread*, 1913.

perfection and finish
are unnatural [6]

Three lines on a panel
an exchange between two Technicians

competes sequester'd derision
completes aesthetic decision [7]

The Burglar's postcard reads:
taxis, diathesis, economia

It is read as combining form into order
with a comprehension of flavours

in the best place
understand sub-atomic and cosmic time-space

For the Technician this will provide
strength, utility and grace [8]

11.

Where house is the First idea in building
a first matter of importance becomes load-bearing

this means wall, which leads to column
and a grace known as functional beauty [9]

In every poem of truth
the Technician demands fiction

In every resemblance to the real
technique demands some incompleteness

---

6 Cicero, *De Optimo Genere Oratorum, Topica*, trans. H.M. Hubbell, London and Cambridge, Mass., 1976.

7 Pliny, *Natural History*, Volume IX, Book XXXV, trans. H. Rackham, London and Cambridge, Mass., 1968.

8 Vituvius, *On Architecture*, Volume 1, Book 1, trans. Frank Granger, London and Cambridge, Mass., 1983.

9 G.W.F. Hegel, *Aesthetics: Lectures on Fine Art*, Volume II, trans. T.M. Know, Oxford, 1975.

Fiction and incompletion constitute the art
that she imitates [10]

Between a vertical face and shadow
there is transition that accentuates reflection

This increases in brightness
as it approaches the cosmic torus

It constitutes a reflex, cut by shades and bright lines
it fills up curvature and gives it value [11]

A competing technician projects a cosmos
expressed by a knot

characterised by friction
then the invention of nets [12]

12.

This second Technician weighs empty ornament
against a high voltage cable

balancing between invention and hunger
as part of a search for concise form [13]

His eye, trained by what open, seen
tastes by acquaintance with obstinate rigor

He learns what enters through the window
untiringly toward the real

To draw from this
a subtle speculation

---

10 A.C. Quatremere de Quincy, *An Essay on the Nature, the End, and the Means of Imitation in the Fine Arts*, trans. J.C. Kent, 1837, facsimile reprint, London, 1979.

11 Eugene-Emmanuel Viollet-Le-Duc, *Lectures on Architecture and Other Writings*, trans. Benjamin Bucknall, New York, 1987.

12 Gottfried Semper, *The Four Elements of Architecture and Other Writings*, trans. H.F. Mall grave an W. Herrmann, Cambridge and New York, 1989.

13 Heinrich Tessenow, *House-Building and Such Things*, trans. Wilfred Wang, London, 1989.

Fear and desire
to see some miraculous thing [14]

13.

Introspection refuses to explain
the indescribable creation of meaning

The First Technician measures its trembles outside the world [15]
in isolation from its use

14.

I buy a handgun at JSL
and next door get some lemon yellow

before I'm banned from using it.
It's so dull in Marks that a

walk over the bridge is shot with
brilliance from a gap in the hills

edge of the Black Mountains lit from
behind by a reflecting chrome.

15.

Started a new pen
trimming it then

a corner of page to try it
"Tell me

"Tell me whether
"Tell me how things are

"Tell me if there was
.....

---

14 The Notebooks of Leonardo da Vinci, translated by Serge Bramley, *Leonardo, The Artist and the Man*, 1988, trans. London, 1992.

15 Anthony Kenny quoting Wittgenstein in *The Legacy of Wittgenstein*, Oxford, op. cit. 13.

16.

The Technician stands down from our platform
to propose her limits on intervention

They are characterised by the row—
organise, assemble and mechanise

You can achieve with a single machine [16]
the work of several

17.

Understanding in a flash
the grasp of rules

her relations between consciousness
and complexity are clear [17]

18.

She watches yellow brimstones fall from sky
and turn purple on reaching the lawn

when the bear trips
on the sun dial base and

discovers a silver watch where
pear thuds tock the ear.

19.

Both technicians have modern literature
and several stabilities against

this civil tradition
against disease [18]

---

16 Leonardo, op.cit. 13.

17 Wittgenstein, op.cit. 14.

18 Hugo von Hofmansthal, *Buch der Freunde*, Tageluch-Aufzeikhnungen, 1929.

20.

Their self-consciousness
of the very notion of a self

backflips a misconstrued
pronoun

21.

Even as dew drops through a
window space

With a shudder I feel the stars
and name them differently once a day

22.

The line between sense and non-sense wider
than both the areas it divides

23.

Chains grow in my head that
pull the universe apart

24.

The Technician and Burglar met at eleven
or at least my sleep has been taken and

I feel wiped out of the spacetime that fits
a margin just before and after I awoke

in a passage, as the French call it, following
The History of Sexuality, a silence in which

the cupboard unfolds and the Burglar
who drops the Technician's ruler

leaves by the cat flap door
clutching a jar of birds

25.

Technician turns the radio to
drown screams from neighbours

when the hungry come for food

26.

The Burglar turns back
and becomes critical

asks what thought can achieve
under what conditions [19]

27.

Shapeless stains
Light trembles

Tomorrow the Technician will
make the strap and the attempt [20]

to see the stars. [21]

---

19 Ibid. 14.

20 Leonardo, op.cit. 13.

21 Dante Alighieri, The Divine Comedy, Dent trans., 1909.

10. Softstone

Over The Top

Up against the outside
the wall gives
and takes in wind rushes
through pear and apple trees
near an exactness
always in phase

as edge skin has a burr
a textile completion on
finish edge *leans*
spacetime between now and
there and then and here
moves in deep breaths
absorbs and exhales
without assurance of
which place occludes

momenergy this
troubled distance
defines the pressure
and gap between us the
garden and its enclosures
vat of burnt apples
they call knowledge
or expression
in a war zone

Olbolo

1.

Punches, both physical to the origin
smug formulas and
Competing correctness
Back up path
and feel that allowed psychoanalysts
engage in end something in book
to offend about the real burglar.
reflection
I am going after these screams
the debate and her book,
Art issue here
under pavement dust
explosive tome to emerge from
automatic some time.
The book is about many physiological
sprayed in Round-up
drawn the media with magnetic force
socialisation contempt for modern controversy
freshness and blithe arrogance
along joints
and she human nature to hurl brazen insults.
She accuses becomes a drone between
with early success. identi-celebrity terms of
hill blown and cleared
appalling! or psyche-zingers, articulates
positions that is something both genders seem
to want to hear this scope of has gone
of common flowers
quite far enough, and doubt that
neoconservative cultural message: men
has become volk of civilization and
in exact i-beams
can take credit for that are powerful too, but
embrace nature are powerful.
Religion and magical heat of the best defenses
a silence flattens
against chaos, have aroused profound displeasure
authors. For one thing, a detached points out,
male napping, "She wasn't taken

palm and mud in pores
attacks are part of conservatism," says
"They against women, revive old stew energy."
Hyperbole, a level of discourse sermons,
vinyl shed roof
headlines. She should be on talk, "In those you
want. These days scientists
women lion beautiful but was based on
in waste land
urinate and far time thought one 1968. More
of a critical book, provides these overview struggle
his staff. partly of a second wave.
expected rest of gain
These days fields of research with funding.
Human mind when fibrosis. Research on private
budget fields, "Fundability is thinking."
with a friend.

2.

A backyard glass oven store.
A few graduate dishes melt
can make Angel light-gallery.
African villages scope, from
Translate from
initial polishing. This month, many dollars later,
that spectacular success: out a vision
of how the world's largest lives, "In some forms
of the single circle, of theatre-you'll find that
shape
in 1994, haul in rehearsal. And once
to the top of any good. That, I would
say, where it will tilt flow with swords;
Cyclopean eye, rises and musical falls,
allusion to ecodisaster
these are heady own experiences.
Is that world of telescope somewhere—
on top of a 1934 casting of Mound,
they come far enough to a record size
and economy
at it's there. Then they go back
more because they are a large party,

push edge of hurdles they couldn't get
in dialectic
across above Hawaii's greatest intensity
is always telescope's separate
dilapidated assembly red shell of a Moorish
lift to conserve political
cathedral last week. in Paris, the stage
is bare, will be joined by rock. A two-man
orchestra tunes monstrous twin. Bed
divisions class war
spectators take their places on Southern
Observations—sometimes Brook himself
the first high peak wind. Unearthly Japanese
where decisions count
head, shamans around the world language
production of scopes of similar
African, and the end of the transparent
in perception of difference
that they obtrude collectively, a score.
Five curtain calls later ground-based
concealed vision from multiple
the audience spills out of a tiny
extraordinary real estate office and
interior thought and hot head
"What we can café next door to mingle
with the astronomer simple reinvention
beyond sense participate
other worldly reviews: even the
logical renaissance,
in consumerism an actual
a decade ago.
where critic-poets feed.
Yet acclaim is one, 'I'm not interest'
rich people over its fuel cost.

Oleke

1.

Badger's best audience
a cherry blossom, silent, silken
flower wings in air
Hike shack through
smell of mountains contrasts the sett
snow on the spring lawn
before get across trace
Badger is a funk theatre
save for a pit of sand and
up in wedge the floor. Youngsters
the fall to a brown lake
show custom come out and sway to
music floats above
no more than notes' wit
clogged in duck weed
though minus a curtain,
front door—squeezed magic shop
and actor's latest classic has, as usual,
throughout reed edge
sober achieving "wonders
most recently the epic
FRAGRANCES The War
valley filled and braided
In an aromatic three new
BUSINESS TOOL
Tropical beach, white suits,
undergrowth and bracken locks
A horse gallops along
plane sits in a convertible,
drenched in diamonds,
in frond descent curves
focus camera. The dapper gents
step out game. As the stakes them frets,
The actress takes charge, "Not so,
the sound cusps
moving a huge sparkle
the table. "These have
luck," she purrs.
fist and shingle towards many

The star of this lot is riding on the
celebrity to launch
face of tough
funnelled factory
on advertising every month
THE FEEDBACK
When loop gain is exact unity the
beneath the tree canopy
step function
and the system as disadvantages.
an indefinitely long memory.
remarkable sense of loss
are not clothed, the homeless
In any physically realisable
response
bereft of love

2.

To the right of the Ordnance bomb site
he desperate does find consolation
The terms bent
describe an initial sense of
Bike back to
alternatives are degenerative,
a temperature controller changes
supply of burnt exhibits
Under conditions of periodic possible
base
for the feedback to phase changes
in a transient
condition. The function
called a gain from the
the rise to green rocks
modulus of frequency
in the form
expressed
Advantages of a logarithmic land music
saturated in nitrates
Transient responses greed
Single lag in the forward
with a doctrine

along a pair of
the overall unit impulse response
NEGATIVE feedback, in its broadest
structure when,
hillside divisions made by
invoked oppose the danger
state in whole or in part. When the
other hand, the disturbance is assisted
hedge and ditch meet
away from its original state.
back of a closed loop
This concept of elucidation,
beyond summit
of problems ranging over gleaming
fangs. In a very general sense any system,
in a state of equilibrium said to
eyesight in a ridge
possess mechanisms
old as the temperature
mist glisten from poly
principles and move of description
in the same general relaxation
tunnels and a greenhouse
pressure drop rest in the riddle
Consider first a bridge. This form of
over the hill in a
wind loads fluctuates forces restores
error shape calls forth a
marketed landscape real
counteract distortion.
insects inhabit.
Since he is greedy in a setting sun
relaxation in the riddle.

Palmer House

Watch through glass the figures rise up
underground
reflected glass the sushi bar sign
in reverse and beyond this a number of kiosks
crowd back to the reversed image of a griffin
and the name 'Brewers' reversed
on the glass local to the viewing seat
multiple gunfire 11.10
migraine.

Lift out of Hereford red rain-
shadow horizon sheep graze hop
fields onto golden Malvern sun rise
hill trails of apple orchards and
wasteland housing estates.

Puts his hands to his face
to embody pain from
his fingers from his
forehead beneath them
from his enclosed mouth

Puts his hands to his face
to embody loss of
his feelings of his
memory beneath them
of his paradise.

Drop back as Hereford sun blazes
horizon mauve and pink cattle sift Wye
river reflects multiple rings of red
mud ripples of nitrate and
smoke from woodland fires.

Papa Doc Walk

When aspiration was near
            fearless proposal
                        cowers deeper than basement
Now it has gone
            fearless proposal
                        empty premises of remains
on a premise
            of flowered meadows
                        minutely recorded without function
Even now in recall
            the rain lifts
                        smell of clay
Scent evidence remains
            fearless proposal
                        gone forever
composed flowers
            when aspiration returns
                        white dust settles grey ground

Pasmala

What this Malvern hill clarifies and the merk dale
Pelled with people, I shall he weary of.
Desire and necessity formulate a dream
Came down from hill fort and trod on me with eloquence
And said, 'Student, are you asleep? Do you see these people
Business brings them amazement?
The most part of this people that pass on this earth,
Have their projection on archaicism, their will no better;
Seek other horizons and here hold no account'.
I was afraid of this dream and its persuasion
And said, 'I have difference to this rhetoric',
'My tour up the hill, proposes a questioned Truth',
And would that I am wrought as being here teaches.

Pecking

'He said the cornerstone of civilisation is human sacrifice.'
— Lee Tamahori, Mulholland Falls, 1995.

I have seen him
when the fancy took him
when he was at work
on the stupendous clay
cuts across town
goes straight to the platform
takes a brush and gives
a few touches
to one of the figures
then suddenly
I have seen him

dissolution of the self
search for a way
of being other
shared with others
because of that kind of
will to change

a great dispute
as though a wound
this entire tangled knot
of problems this field
of investigation
forces a question
between science and
its history more or less
wrapped up theoretical debates
violent and confused

become entangled with a notion
of inauthenticity, a certain act of
formation contradictory concepts
unite in themselves idea and
negation of that idea
the stupidity of self-consciousness
and any idea of predicament

a new constitution to rid
burns a working party
its middle class subjectivity
reduction of human to an object
or construction of a self
the temporal dialectic
of being jammed, endemic
to being alive.

Philly Dog

In Memory of Eric Mottram 16.1.95

"... whose indignation and disgust reach through the crust of the power games of the world into the aggressive areas of the obscene."

"... there is also involved a proposition that there is something in the urge to combine a wide range of materials and energy into a large spatial order ..."

"To achieve personal peace in active joy in this century perhaps more than any other has meant dropping out of the current power structure."

"Part of the process is directed towards the discovery of what forces, unexplored or to be recovered or renewed, the body may hold as the field of Psyche and Eros."

This work begins with the self
with multiplicity
moves toward boundary breaks
overlaps the other and others
glued connections
and false promises
therefore does not begin
continues with interruptions inconclusions

The work a multiplicity of works embedded
disparate and without circularity
concealed identities serious similarities frayed
assumptions organised permanence deconstructed
inserts and envelopes narration
consumer and cultural producer
without identities without exactness
rumour and intruder

I build a wall from house-entrance to boundary-edge
and as soon a cat sits on end of wall assumes an upright
sitting position then a restful horizontal at first looks out
from wall into adjacent property and next along boundary so that
four images of the animal are apparent and thus four sculptures
anticipated of the cat on end of the wall which become
what was to follow in the form of lions then human-headed lions
until mythical forms of human beings are established

I become animal with a fascination for the outside
related to a multiplicity that becomes dwelling within me
This book an assemblage unattainable and multiplicit
in a structure growth offset by laws it self-invents
by deterritorialization and connect with other multiplicities
of combination rhizomatic determinations magnitudes
and dimensions I become defined by an outside
change as I become intruder and rumour

In the age that snow ices the Burglar finds himself
observer with feedback-enhanced laser-trap
His attentive interaction
with single steps and forces produces
multiple correspondence
between best-fit dipole of attention effect
and locus of activated goodness-of-fit
between model and observed

On a folded sheet of nerve cells
the Burglar plans his day
uses signals from the thalamus
among an array of reception areas
Situationist between heredity and improvement after use
He learns largely through selection and
only partially via instruction
deriving shape from chemical voltage

Event-related potentials he reads from scalp distribution
of attend-left minus attend-right difference—
waveforms at different latencies plotted
as voltage lattices register a striking feature
of sub-fragment structure—a lever arm
comprising about 73 amino-acid residues
of carboxy-terminal portions of a long, single
alpha-helix wrapped in light chain rigidity

In a snort at recent crises visual-spatial attention
becomes animal essential brain funct enables
select enables preferential process priority
information in revolving planks of perception
where work begins with self a discontinuity between cells
role of axons functs of synapse the exist now synoptic
microfissures through leap each message makes across these torn
thoughts uncertain probablistic cortexual balm

Activity-dependent chemical signals, the Burglar uses calcium,
or production of an electrical crossing
membrane signals such as voltage
at thresholds protects in sugar rapids three-dimensional
views of the best-located aftershocks
shows a confidence-ellipsoid determined
by hypocentroidal decomposition led into
inversions of arrival-time

He as often doesn't know where he is never
mind knowing when he arrived
Language to the Burglar has as much
to do with touch and involves
several senses as it has to do with
onomatopoeia.The state of being
many, as Dryden describes multiplicity,
is a state of knowing yourself

New stars form in the concentration burst he stands on
nearest interaction obtained by combining 12 separate fields
the most prominent galaxies are dominated by filamentary structures
that demonstrate disruption by tidal interactions
Any measure of the Burglar's sulphur-carbon
larger than the sum of biotic and abiotic fluxes is a forensic
scientist's failure to account for horizontal advection and
measurement inaccuracies from the use of sediment traps

A range of devices from wall marks to oil paintings
in the Venetian memory system are multiplicit
in a dark halo turning to charcoal fragments of DNA
drift to the surface as the Burglar's ghost
To keep the observed motions gravitationally coherent
persistent memories over many decades
argue that experience blends long-lasting
modifications in the synoptic lagoon

Even when gardening you feel discouraged
working six months ahead of anticipated loss
The thief's seeded dipoles account event-related potentials
attention-difference maps in latency range of the perception
where two striped poles begin to suggest an escape route
roped to a motor launch rising and falling on wave front
where his lever arm's swing produces a stroke size
close to that measured in the laser-trap

The self becomes an instantaneous apprehension of multiplicity
in a given region not a substitute but an *I feel*
myself become animal, animal among others
on the edge of the garden created in order
to escape abstract opposition between multiple and one
to escape dialectics and cease treatment of numerical fragment
as lost totality or as an organic element in unity
instead to distinguish between types of multiplicity

The Burglar transfers fragments of code from cells
of one species to those of another
Between discrete and continuous
between magnitude with extensive
distance and the intensive, between numerical or extended
and qualitative or durational
naming the Burglar becomes at once depersonalisation
and instantaneous apprehension of the multiple

Guy Debord and Felix Guattari continue as intersecting
multiplicities—discursive and expansive versus
involvement in multiplication of content
The weight of any map, cortical or galacto-graphic,
does not exceed the weight of spacetime it reproduces
The map imbeds itself into the projection the Burglar makes
As he walks the result factors in a blur
homeomorphic to the boundary of the spectrum.

In this multiplicity of writing, bye and barren themes
are best fitted for invention;
Subjects so often discoursed confine the Imagination,
and fix our conceptions into the notions of fore-writers.
The lion-headed moves into sunlight squinting
a purr ignores the Burglar begins to lick paws
rubs them on the face and side of head occasionally
biting at fur as if unwanted molecular difference

Illusory form heightened by denial
arises from contraction of desire in a plate of milk
stilling propagation. To stay with one's self
requires position and provision
realigning quality out of strangeness.
Visual order obeys gravity, but genuine
shimmering substance cognates
more than complacencies of constant worth.

Whilst qualities need not be reliant on spacetime originations
Naming objects has precedence over seeing them
just as stealing them has precedence over ownership
Perception an inherent understanding of balance
and movement transforms by fire and language
To true the present gleams against false impressions of form
requires endurance.The Burglar's
non-invasive scalp recordings during reflection show

attended visual stimuli are preferentially selected after
stimulus onset.What occurs
has a more than singular spacetime
Focal postsynaptic blockade bends any permanent
withdrawal of the overlying nerve terminal I catch
breath nourished as adjacent terminals are deprived
adhesive bonds affix a nerve terminal and blister back
onto the basal lamina overlying the blockade

All well-located events have at least ten arrival times
Ice image cracks spatial resolution of optical image
as well as starburst activities
Little sign of tidal interactions can be seen in the optical image
in the intimist bath or altar screen jewellery. Forensic
traps miss some sinking particles and miss cycling due to advection
a synthesis of a large mosaic with good angular resolution
an evolution of head fuzz in optical endurances

The observations presented suggest a minor comparison
may drastically increase apparent extent
This known instance of plasticity at neuromuscular junctions
occurs in neonatal life in any garden innocent of fertilizer
Loss of synapses underlies a change in connectivity
spans several weeks in the optical image
shade then sun then shade appears to be a two-arm spiral
where an inner disc traces the optical news

Beyond the galactic disc one of the arms wraps around
the east connecting with the garden concentration in
multiple composts. Sediment trap measurements of the flux
saved by insurance contributions during this period suggest
discrepancy may be due to inaccuracies in the forensic trap
Sustained focal attention to location engages the Burglar's stimulus
selection processes in his ventral extrastriate cortex
with minimal activation of the parietal lobes

The aftershocks fill a rupture zone of the main shock
Combined neuro-imaging with event-related potentials
describe both cortical anatomy and time of attentional selection
That part of the brain behind the eyes,
the fusiform gyrus, reinforces early selection models,
gives a role for adhesion during periods of muscle growth
such as drawing practice and atrophy
bonds pre- and postsynaptic to nerve terminal maintenance

Cranium in this sense a box of expression and reason
with an arm that can reach to the water at the bottom
of the skull trap it drinks from
The kinematic isovelocity contours show a large circular bulge
and a disc to reproduce the observed wavering
bound of the released snow leopard
A search begins for new congruences
grasp together multiple and scattered events

Faciality is always a multiplicity
defined not by the elements that compose it in extension by
characteristics that compose it in comprehension
but by lines and dimensions it encompasses in intention
Change dimensions you change multiplicity
the various positions occupied by a fascinated self
A heterogeneous express movement wedded to a very particular garage
explored only by sounds and colours in spacetime external to it

The Burglar relies upon knowing that any part of a species
developed to an extraordinary degree,
in comparison with the same part in allied species,
tends to be highly variable
Each individuality designates a multiplicity
simultaneously at its edge a crossover into others
Tropology, topology, typology of multiplication end the banality of
dialectics through the arrangements described by Riemann

I am a homeorhetic system
of attractor surfaces of chreods, necessary pathways,
located in multi-dimensional spacetimes
in which crossovers correspond to catastrophes
Folds on the surface that suspend descriptive
referential functions and any temporal character
of my experience and lead into a world unfolded
by every narrative

Each human timespace stretches back and extends out
describes the possible and walks towards it baffled
by the asking limited to the fact of measurement
of expectation of memory
An image that already exists precedes the event
that does not yet exist
not an impression of things past but
a sign of what has been proclaimed beforehand

Pimp Walk

including fragments from *King Lear*

leads to a nomographic solution of a stress problem
only to determine the stress direction
directions are all they have

the passion to make home and decision to continually leave
the dead paradigm of dialectics
not synonymous with the need for depth and wish to spread

to love who you are
more than where you are

or quarrel with opposeless wills
a residue and resentment of academic capital
burns itself out

a black cat shitting in a wooded garden
white damaged skill in a footpath rockery

leads to a house to put a crazed head in

meaningful statements that are neither proved nor disproved

the hedge-sparrow feeds the cuckoo until it
has its head bit off

a deserted path indistinguishable
from a determined direction

old enough to ever but slenderly know himself

a simple need characterised by repetition

with strained pride
to come between language and will

the relationship between required test factors and strength
variations in structure necessitate the correction of the results

she treads towards a destruction of peace
inside an agreed frame and rubble

he turns about to face the loud uproar
drives the rebel in him

unpublished virtues of the earth
are stamped by his boot

when tiger's young
suckle marvel milk and turn sour

this weaves itself perforce into my headache

the set of all properties without a finite basis

nothing can be made of this

all the mind's faculties overcome their limits

are worth the want that you have wanted

purpose here is not to de<ine optimum environment
but to design a conceptual approach to its definition

where my heart beats in my mouth

the relationship between required test factors and strength
variation framed so that structures known to fail are required
to have higher factors on test than otherwise similar structures

tiredness climbs a steep graph
before the neck aches and quickly
the head joins a community of pressures

when badgers fight and savage in the fray

how shall your houseless heads and unfed sides
your looped and windowed raggedness defend you

red never generates yellow

the house changes colour
and red appears yellow on the brickway

a complexity that measures how hard it is to produce the message

it's the sun's fault or the burglar dropped his stash of spheres

a problem of plurality
relationship and reciprocal presentation

within grace in a mixture of situations

stand in a problem of potential benefit and hazard

a love that makes breath poor and speech unable

the effect of skewness of frequency distribution on the relationship
between required test factors and strength variation produces
curves showing test factors for a given scatter
are given probability levels

the epsilontics implied leave her legless
maybe that's enough to know

the old hare half wounded buzzes by
it is an older continent implied

a previous houseless poverty

an abhorred pit
a thousand hedgehogs in a spin space

I put my head in only to find horns in my hair
glued there by honey

the Turing machine may halt and output or
it may never halt
there can be no prediction

my nerves went so had to frame the business

on this condition the other appears as the expression
of a possible

see better and let me still remain
the true blank

until magnitude, kind and character
of place and circulation from it
are coordinated to social purpose

beyond what can be valued

mechanical methods of measuring internal stress
loop bending feedback and directional drawing
match the representations

hold on and let rip in one string

runs away from noise

when the mind's free
the body's delicate

unrelenting steel drops through a wasp's nest

I will forget my nature but not that

no algorithm to decide when to go

frame the business after your own whiz kid

a junction of problems

and with safety as a motive

composite of overlays

meanwhile we shall express our darker purpose.

Pirate's Walk

1.

Skeletons in the cupboard fluoresce
a compound of relations between forces

the culture that improves using
dideoxy fingerprint detection
measured by single base sequence changes
in polymerase chain reactions

"I acted clearly and morally and without regret.
I'm very lucky."

Consciousness is like that
a biological feature of certain animal brains.

given understanding and courage

"crimes of opinion" bring about arrests that
encourage the determined

a casualty of commodity values

every moment melts away

events inseparable from lived realities
actualised

Thioploca white hair emerges from sheaths
embedded in the stretched sediment story
of a desire environment with needs for more
an optimal condition of nitrate uptake

prevails in an apophantic realm
beyond grasslands in the depths
of oceanic farms

the Skeleton in the sky below
a multiple of constellations

2.

Culture mimics the Rothschild worm

detects changes in amplified DNA segments
nothing in life needs to be immune
where "maybe" perpetuates

consciousness caused by neurobiological processes
participates as natural biological order

the physiological event determined by affection

what does not happen remains
or remainders as globules of anticipation

description to avoid constitutions of reality

induced illusions from fire
from fireworks from ragun typography

virtual consistency to the concept provides
the function's references

the large liquid vacuole store
an extracytoplasmic reservoir
formed by an inflated membrane intrusion
surrounded by numerous singular globules

such ascendance of moments distributes values
its shadow moves over frosted flags
at milk call

3.

In a stinking metal box lift

combinatorial cassette mutagenesis of proteins
contrasts to error-prone PCR and DNA shuffling

you're really after the rush in the spine
intense liberation and joy – I was totally mashed

biological features such as photosynthesis, digestion or
mitosis align to features such as consciousness

the event reached in a variety of ways
without calm or simply careless

processes courting the edges of unrecognisability

predictive errors evolve as actual spacetime
counter unexpected fragments of past evidence

ruin of every house
patient care

the event releases a vapour that trembles
each subjective pain

seen in Beggiatoa
live in steep opposed diffused gradients
after trenching between the figures movement
and the shift in the environment

image components derive from relations
with invented lifts
with drear and malice

the Burglar holds the vibrations from
the float in his ears until they go

4.

It's people's expression out of whatever they're in

PCR and DNA shuffling can focus
a high level of mutagenesis
on a short sequence of suspected
functional importance

I don't have to deal with the actual problems

Subjective refers to an ontological category
a powder thought to dissolve
precipitates onto sides of the vessel

rest and activity are part of the same prescription

resemblance between strawberries and egg yolk
in the sinus

spread and fade lead to dispersion
where more out means more in

dissolved mingled perfume in the mouth

a dignity of the event inseparable from
philosophy as *amor fati*
loaded with skin syrups

the information flow along along a vertical pathway
from photoreceptors to retinal interneurons
to ganglion cells

stuff and purpose substantiates belonging
steals a honey jar from the bathroom basin

5.

Repression from the indiscernible

short tandem repeats of DNA sequences
signal different individuals with different repeats

at last the accountant's moment
without regret
the generator synchronises to the grid
in a supercool bath without scruple

you imagine what you know to exist

listen to yourself in the chemical fizz

held together by networks of ephemeral confidences

progress from regularity into stars
from forms into clumps

enter the house I leave

a hinge between forms of concepts
to encourage misunderstanding
to savour lack of communication
celebrate it even

embed it upon functionally defined networks
within the spontaneously active retina
rather than visually driven horizontal shift's from
patterns of calcium bursting inside the eye

shampoo gel skids the surface
it breaks
inverted with an aura of naïveté
love's sponge in the bacteria dining room

Pulling Up and Quasi Queen

1.

A sheet of analytical light excites thought fluorescence
viewed as a general conception a sort of intelligible structure
the world has to offer, or consequentially a program for a sort of
theoretical structure which would best capture it

The proposal of an ultimate reality had been a single, indivisible mistake set
against a plurality of finite, particular and sensible things and promoted as a
realm of appearance having an absolute mistake as its true being

An analysis used to slow and cool thought processes
reduces depth by optically narrows the velocity of process so that
aberrations become substantially distant

The construction of a thought-imaging device,
you could use a simulation enhancer made from an analogue
with permanent magnets,
produces images in the same way as an optical slide projector

A self mask responds to illumination by a process of identified thoughts
prepared using an analysis-simulator
an image of the self appears on the inside of the eyes
where a sheet of cells images analytical light
excites thought fluorescence

The self obtains magnified and demagnified images
with remarkable low cost resolution
polarised by the light chirp technique

You would think basic value was a choice between possible answers
a conception of an absolute as mistake-determined and determining
everything causally through the necessity of its nature
against the answer that grasps another absolute as ego
creates both itself and its objects through freedom

It is as if the choice were between seeing ourselves and the rest
as products of mistakes
bounced against manifestations of a free
and inexpensive creative self

Some would opt for idealism of this sort
on a pretext that only ideas can do justice
to any experience of our own spontaneity
as knowing subjugations
or to our own sense of dignity as street fighters

2.

Others regard mistake
as minds freely create
activity rejects idealism's subjects
attempts justivity
to role of objectivity

This is distinct from a mistake that combines
or transcends subjectivity and objectivity,
never mind superseding these redundancies,
ultimate identity or
indifference out of which an original duality
of subject and object and the morass of alibis emerges

3.

Initially the witness is an analyst
slowed, cooled, polarised by a light chirp technique
in a social vacuum
before it arrives at the imaging zone
at the end of an analysis cooling cycle
95% of thought optically pumped into an extreme
magnetic substrate and rendered unconscious

Arriving in the imaging zone
at the same time as cooled thoughts
variation of the speculative theme
becomes even more complex and original

A matrix of mistakes like crumpled sheets of wax paper
describes movement and a self-positing process
through which living mistake-subjects actualise themselves
become objects to themselves
and then restore their unities with themselves
by coming to know their objects as their own
free expansions or manifestations

Here mind means a movement of sameness self-restored
at some momenergy before all this
when idealism is a view which holds that only minds
and their contents, which could not be analysed, really exist

There is no matter- or mind-independent reality
and what we erroneously think exists outside
is an idea or image in some mind

An equivalent to a mechanical shutter
blocks the thought oven
when a cooling cycle has stacked
to prevent heated thoughts, that leave the oven too late,
to take part in the cooling process
from arriving in the imaging zone
at a same momenergy as cooled thinking

Thought image, a kind of narration, gets detected
at a distance measured downstream from an exegesis
there thoughts traverse a cell sheet of resonant analytical light
and the understanding that results a kind of fluorescence
detected in a surf gush by a change-coupled device
listed as comprehension

Thoughts in a thermal park of the process
showed up in a red-mauve field
where a screen test of the mind
proposed itself as an activity that involved self-expression,
self-actualisation and self-knowledge
to say that mind is all reality or that mistake is mind
is thus to shower gel the most awkward feature of reality

With a wider time-gate for comprehension
thoughts in the thermals also show up in the
brain segments delineated as sensitive to colour
because they are too fast to experience any substantial
white force deflection they form a shadow of the object
in the detection zone

Because of off-axis illuminations
propelled by poetic thinking to comprehend
the truth of idealism is to see
how movements of ions express details of the world

How all mind's objects bear a mark of the creative process
of which they are manifestations globs of fact
in an idealism that emphasises an anamorphic vision of the world

Such notions of a mind are complex
and attempts to merge several important ideas
into a single compelling vision smash truthful outcomes
and propose mind as a form-giving principle
or a potency inherent in things

To say that mind posits itself means it gives expression,
embodiment and actuality to itself
just as form does for a living organism
mind's forms however are concepts
which for some are truer tremble are more real
in nerve transitory sensible particulars
which exemplify them

Because of off-axis illuminations
propelled by poetic thinking
enhanced aberrations are more pronounced
in outer regions of the image

An enhancement suffers from
all the geometric skews known to light optics
affections of imperfect thought collimation
and polarisation, deviation from pure magnetic simulation,
gravity and thought-collisions
lead into philosophical hermetics

For others, sensible particulars are created or posited by
mind as the necessary medium for actualising itself
without them mind's thinking would remain abstract,
incomplete, not perfectly expressed, a mere potentiality
lacking fulfilment

Concepts are what is truly real,
but concepts, like narration, demand exemplification
for their full actuality

The field generated by the segmented permanent-magnet
analogue can be described analytically
in good approximation, includes the fringe field
and the deviation from an ideal plane simulation,

thus allows mathematical treatment of image aberrations
similar to methods used in designing electron-optics

But concepts demand exemplification
for their full actuality
and metaphysics flight paths the thesis reconciliation
that forms or universals are more real than particulars
which craziness insists
actuality exists only in particulars

Much depends on malign judgement's conception
of mind's thinking activity
and a characteristic mode of its self-expression
is its objects
it is as if thinking were a synthetic activity
giving unity or intelligibility to the data of experience

To: Virgin Atlantic, Crawley
From: A. Fisher, Hereford

Dear Lost Property,

I left a manuscript of six pages, A4 size, in a clear plastic wallet, on the plane from JFK New York to London Heathrow. The pages are signed "Allen Fisher" on the sixth page. It is in the seat pocket with the free gifts and disaster bag. The seat no. was 55 B one away from the window. Can you please find it.

The Flight no. VS 04, left NY 19.30 Tuesday 29th August arrived Heathrow 07.10 Wednesday 30th August.

Thanks very much,

Yours faithfully,
A. Fisher

Virgin Atlantic Airways Ltd.
Room 222
South Wing Office Block
Terminal 3
Heathrow Airport
Hounslow
Middlesex TW6 1PZ
tel: 01293 562345
fax: 0181 897 5030
sita: LHRKZVS
baggage services: 0181 897 5017/8
fax: 0181 897 5019

Our Ref: GC/HDQ/SEP95

21st September 1995

Dear Mr Fisher

Thank you for your recent letter received in our office today.

I was sorry to read of the loss of your manuscript following your flight from New York to Heathrow on the 30th August 1995.

Unfortunately despite extensive searches we have been unable to locate it.

I am sorry that I am unable to help you further in this instance.

Yours sincerely

Virgin Atlantic Baggage Services

Registered Office: 120 Campden Hill Road, London W8 [illegible]. Registered in England [illegible]. VAT Number: [illegible]

4.

Transverse cooling with optical molasses holds a steady state. This constant refers to the idea that in living presentation of one part depends reciprocally on the rest, excites blood sugar. It means that the parts of an organism are all organs reciprocally producing each other.

For a thing to be an organism, it is required first that its parts, as regards their existence and their form, should be possible only through their relation to the whole. Secondly, that the parts should so combine in the unity of a whole that they reciprocally bring about each other's form. In virtue of this astounding understanding living is not only organised, but self-organising.

It is difficult to see why anyone found this notion of organised living a promising model for any conception of mind's activity. The organisation of living is precisely the chronic self-activating and form-giving principle which some take to be the basic feature of mind.

On this gross range of conceits and self-depreciation, an organic whole not only exhibits the internal necessity and self-sufficiency which nomads take to be the mark of self-positing mind, but it also admits of an endless variety of possible and impossible forms, and thus captures mind's apparently free creativity as well.

Any notion of organic totality seems well suited to express the idealist conviction that the source of the world's order is mental, and this applies to the thesis that the highest fulfilment of mind consists in comprehending the identity between itself and the objects it has posited. Such pain, immersed in existence, transposes reality into a twilight labelled with complete freedom to consume the self and others.

To comprehend reality as mind means comprehending reality as an organised system, a living whole exhibiting an endless variety of living forms in all of its parts. The situation that this is a mistaken conception need not affect the considerations here. Since the ground of any organised being is its tendency to manifest and preserve a certain form, the type of explanation best suited to comprehending mind and its manifestation is teleological explanation. There is a pulling up from, a smudge to move quickly from, such ideas of organisation.

Bright spots in fluoresced brain segments, caused by thoughts which have escaped the slowing procedure, mark the optic tomography. Because these thoughts are faster than the rest they appear closer to the focal spot of the perceiver than desired and smear out the image. This theft of image, or smearing, is known as the Burglar effect. When analysis-cooled and thermal thoughts arrive in the conscious zone, while the viewer is "switched on", both the shadow produced by the undeflected fast thoughts and the image can be seen in the same brain segments, clearly demonstrating the formation of an inverted real image.

To comprehend the world in this way is simultaneously to bring mind to its fulfilment. This chronic process first posits a world expressing its nature and then restores its unity with itself by comprehending that world as its creation.

5.

When László Moholy-Nagy seeks to identify the ambiguities of present-day optical creation he joins the discourse elaborated by Max Planck, Paul Cézanne, Louis Zukofsky, Werner Heisenberg, Kurt Gödel, and Benoit Mandelbrot regarding the issues of reality, certainty and truth, that have diverted philosophical and thinking poetics since Plato, Aristotle, Kant, and Hegel.

6.

The Analyst detects minute changes in ion concentrations resulting from cellular activity at near physiological speed. Activated complexity and presence, the organisational bases of thought, are only inadequate forms in which the rational intelligibility of mistakes manifests itself.

The Analyst produces an image using a system designed specifically for electro-physiology with voltage and ion sensitive fluorescent dyes. Thought contains the immediate idea and any rational principle constantly struggles with the immediacy of the matter in which it is embedded.

The choice between sensitivity, resolution and speed is no longer necessary. The pixel array captures differential images at 1700 frames a second. The process of thought consists in overcoming the immediacy with what it is still beset, and this is the finiteness of a thought.

The relative spatial-timing between ecospikes from neurons in each ear conveys information to your brain about the locations of sound sources in spacetime. Mistakes in their true form are like this—they are thoughts which are wholly responsible to the material in which they are embedded and find nothing recalcitrant to their life-principles.

The relative spatial-timing of ecospikes between cortical neurons conveys information about the location of individual components in the multidimensional spacetime of a sensory stimulus such as a smell. A concept is at once a principle of national intelligibility inhering in the actual world and the act of thought by which a knowing mind grasps this intelligibility.

Recognition of patterns occurs when each ecospike arrives simultaneously at a recognition cell, a site of memory. This concept of recognition interfaces invention possible only to a rational self-consciousness, which a knowing mind grasps as intelligibility. It is at once a living human personality involved in its own commerce with the world and its own struggle for self-knowledge and self-actualisation. This leads some of the best minds of my generation to bring out from the inadequacy of thought a contrast between a living thing and a self-consciousness.

The Inspectorate's position remains, in which the self, in order to develop and sustain its identity and autonomy, and in order to be safe from the persistent threat and danger from the world, has cut itself off from direct relatedness with others, and has endeavoured to become its own object: to become, in fact, related directly only to itself.

Spatio-temporal codes are not new, and one of the simplest—synchronous firing—has already been suggested as a burn victim for binding sensory features together in, of all places, the cortex.

That which is limited to thinking through itself has no capacity to proceed beyond its immediate existence. But it is driven beyond itself by the thought of another, and this can be its combination with the thought of another through a manifestation of that thought in aesthetic form.

What's new is the observation that if the logarithm of the analogue strength of a sensory cue is encoded by the spacetime advance of an ecospike, then the information contained in the relative spatial-timing of ecospikes in a population of neurons can be transmitted rapidly, in a scale-invariant form and decoded into a computationally versatile radical basis function representation.

Consciousness can be understood as immediately a proceeding beyond what is limited and, since this limit belongs to it, a proceeding beyond itself.

Thinking has the capacity to mature, has the capacity to stabilise and displays many structures. Consequentially thinking is multiple. Its whole life consists in the struggle to impose its structures on energetic matter.

When images are flashed on the retinae, onset-spacetime differences in the range of a few tenths of a millisecond between the two eyes are interpreted as difference in depth. This is irrespective of the painting being analysed.

Some view personality, values and life-plans of a human self as kinds of self-aware organic structures. Aspects of this view are problematic today. A self-conscious personality is perhaps like an organism whose structures or ideas are consciously self-imposed. But a reflective human being, by living out a certain self-conception and a set of goals and values, can also bring about changes in that conception, in these goals and values themselves. Therefore, a self-consciousness is not like an organism. It is far more like a unique process, which can survive radical changes in its complex electro-magnetico-chemical structure, and which initiates its own change independently.

7.

Rugged stamping let it out into the scar-field
out of it until stamped and pulse stammered
over-rashed with what this smudges fray-burns
twists and then pulls up crumple damage held
don't you like that don't you care for that flattened
onto ice hook crackled on ice then hooked where it freeze
and the pain oh the explanation lost in a shift phase

8.

The Inspectorate's own voice scares him, yet when he doesn't hear it he seems to lose the substance of his being, his strongest grasp sends inwards but weak witness that he is, he seeks to cheat the echo.

As a self-conscious being he tends towards systematic overthrow and transform of his own structures through consciousness alone. His life-processes struggle with immediacy or finiteness as a critique of self-awareness. He tends to generate a reduction of conflicts among his functional parts and does not need to harmonise them.

Redolent of his self-consciousness is chemotaxis which can be clarified in understanding that aggregation of more or less stable patterns of questionable, but intriguing regularity grow from a single buzz on certain substrates. He holds his temples between his fingers and thumb and squeezes in the production of an expression trap.

The pattern of organic development may be understood as a limiting concept on change and transformation of the culture and mores of a nation or people in history.

The whole nation of a hiking being consists in a definite series of organic structures or ideas, the determinate stages of an inner organic development. Each of these stages is not, however, contained in its predecessor as a final tendency.The Inspectorate cannot com- prehend the nature of this thinking being, and this simultaneity of doing two quite different and even opposite things in order to cohere produces a false answer.

Long range timed-spatial order arises from interactions between two multicellular aggregate structures; a "swarm ring" that expands radially, exemplified by Samuel Taylor Coleridge's sense of self-consciousness, and focal aggregates that have lower mobility demonstrated by those aspects of Gerard Manley Hopkins' work that reject idealism.

The idea of comprehending more than one stage at once accords to his concept of self-sustaining, multiple structures and attends to the process which each of these structures in timespace underwinds itself through his own work and passes over into the next determinate stage – a well-documented and unreliable proposition. Patterning occurs through alternating domination by these two sources of excreted attractant.

The pattern geometries vary in a systematic way, depending on how long a thought aggregate remains active; flashed upon that inward eye which is the bliss of solitude. This depends in turn on an initial concentration out of a multiple idea field with many aspects. The proposition is to see in it, and in its elements, both the short run tendency, the forgotten to self-maintain, and the long run tendency to conflict, dissolve and transit to a higher stage worthy of both a neuron on a microchip and ecstatic vision.

The Inspectorate's chemotactic consciousness excretes attractants, aggregates in response to gradients of each attractant, and forms patterns of varying thought density. This process occurs only if consciousness can be chemotactic towards particular configurations, yet can be suppressed by the addition of similar configurations or their analogues. Aggregates form in the wake field of a sudden recall, producing highly symmetrical patterns. Aggregates arise from the centre, called centre even at the edge, of an understanding, an unstructured activity lawn, producing patterns with lower symmetry. Consciousness becomes self-rescued but at the imminent hazard of itself.

Such a process of organic development comprised an activity of establishing or reflecting ideas by arguments in the give and take of discussion and houses the singularity of inevitable conflicts with itself. The teleology of solutions produces a teleology of failures. The multiple nature of the field takes away the procedures of stages and levels and introduces processes with uneven shifts of phase. Energy level diagrams simply illustrate through the over-simplified product of poverty.

At low concentration, in a tramcar, the expression is of a single compact travelling band—an idea swarm—that melts slowly outwards. At higher concentration, inventions interface in variations of logic in the form of concentric rings in radial rows on a pseudo-rectangular lattice and finally the furrow dry sunspurge and oxeye and lace-leaved lovely foam-tuft fumitory.

Abandonment of pretence to knowledge leads to loss of comprehension and links to reality. The development series through successive stages leads to the completed cusp in isolation from the many that surround it. Immanent thinking is presented with the content of itself.

An unstructured zone of illogical thought always precedes the first element of a pattern. As these patterns elaborate, radial streaks, and indented rings or petals form into a poetic coherence.

It becomes a question of obtaining realness in some way that will not result in the annihilation of the self. But the destruction of reality, and the illegal acquisition of it, are largely magical procedures involving touch, repetition and theft.

9.

If you are alone, you belong only to yourself
and deserve isolation.
You are made to remain obscure in a
strengthened conviction
that it was better to keep to yourself.
You always presumed that
nature involved leaps
on a structured order.

Trees become monumental and respond
to a need to rebuild the landscape.
An idea swarm imposes on reality an architectural order,

shifting vegetation into geological forms
then synthetic masses.
The complex freshness of vision
subordinates subjects to the organising intelligence
and demands of design.
so exhausted by the work
as to be unable to talk or listen to
ceaseless doubts and ceaseless application
to the service of outwardness of the external world.
When the sum is self-sufficient
undeniably without conclusion
the fluidity of masses proceeding
from a tessellation of hues
no matter where the painting is left off, the entire picture
area has been considered.
If there were merely a few lines, a few colour planes
they relate to the four sides of the picture and
suggest basic spatial rhythms.

The crushed crayon under his foot creates the marks
on the floor that convey the evidence of his being
studied with pertinacity who would have invented love.
The weather is strong and changeable.
My nervous system is very weak, only oil painting keeps
me up. I must carry on. I simply must produce.

10.

Repudiation of traditional mathematics, denies identity, contradiction and eroded signifiers.The true concepts of identity and difference are incompatible with the vision of speculative reality. The elder bush full of starlings. A tired grasping of opposites in their unity, as if this were appropriate.

Another version of this would be to confirm a vision of reality *a priori* in thought, by showing that in every pair of opposites the existence of each member conceptually requires the existence of the other.They are all essentially conditional through each other and are only in relation to each other. In each determination lies its opposite.

The shallowness of this logic is due to the artificial notions of identity and difference it employs. Suddenly everything flash boundless serene joy.

Formation of timed-spatial patterns from a mass of identical thought forms produces one of the persistent problems of consciousness.The rapid progress made in understanding genetic control of morphogenesis limits any revelation of the dynamics of interactions involved. Understanding the transformation of ideas, their proliferation, excretion of attractants, and the chemotactic motility of consciousness, before the birds start eating the berries, when combined through aesthetic comprehension can generate complex timed-spatial structures; a specialised morphogenetic program is not required.

These processes can be modulated independently in a controlled manner, allowing accurate poetics of quantitative models for elder patterns in your head. The Burglar lives in a world of plural rationalities where truth like identity or community is elusive.

He wants to make accessible to his understanding in two or three potential sheets what is rational in the enclosed garden when the scrumper stands on his head and picks apples with his feet.

He seeks to distinguish between risk consequences about truth, and risk perceptions chosen on the basis of cultural predisposition.

Vision of the way the bush moves is structural, a program for the kind of botany which adequately captures that structure and explains why reality is structured this way; a certain epistemic status captures the structure organically, developmentally; a kind of panic recognition.

The comparison of patterns over sets of analogue variables is done by a network using different delays for different information paths. This mode of computation explains how the Inspectorate's release of neuro-architecture can be used for very different sensory modalities and seemingly different computations. The oscillation and anatomy of the mammalian olfactory systems have a simple interpretation in terms of this representation, and relate to processing in the auditory system.

What you smell and hear in touch with what you see. Organised without need to be essential or developing or unfolding toward concreteness without appearance or actuality without expression or manifestation without marks of origin's scuffing. Simply elderberry bird shit landing on the forehead.

A recognition problem occurs in many guises and sensory modalities and can be efficiently solved when analogue information is encoded or represented using active potential spatial-timing.

Creation simultaneous with the activity of thought apprehends the inherent analyst, the inherent invention of structural thinking and anticipates self-consciousness apprehended by reason. Structure you heard it here first without idea of casual sensuousness and with the necessary movement of thought production, virtuates the task of outward to give to content shapes of freedom.

Analogical information is represented by using the spatial-timing of action potentials with respect to an ongoing collective oscillatory pattern of activity.

Any interconnected processes—linked to development—have lost validity and are subject to radical changes.The rocky knowhow of organic matter, traces of hierarchical structure and stages of concreteness explain the systematic changes in structure by develop- mental tendencies.

The Analyst's problem of pattern recognition in the recognition of colours, visual patterns, smashed berries, odours and sound qualities may be rapidly solved by neurobiology where the virtual means the ability to respond instantaneously to satisfy specific customer demand.

She captures a pattern of connectedness from an array of characteristics: inheritance: the tendency to develop: and the necessity for radical change exemplified by burnt sheets of synthetic cells, a range of subject matters tracing levels of structure through stages of knowing and presumption, systematic changes and radical developments.

The system of what can be known complexed by stinking reality; by natural selection; and by thinking about its make-up through spacetime.The system is an activity, stranger than processes trans- posed and translated in the human head, harmonised and disrupted at once by light moved in minerals.

The ratio of the lengths of the lines connecting different pairs of stars determine the shape of the constellation, while the time-length scale of the line describes the size of the photographic rendering. The currents generated in the individual neurons are the analogue pattern, the paradigm.

What is analysed of what can be known leads to a vision of reality as a crystal complex as mouldy fungus as a damaged building that begins to change in front of the Analyst and analogies are recorded in the form of the mystery the wonderful the unbelievable the industrial concert.

Her taste, like her eyes, is of a different order. Rod and cone transducers, which convert light stimulation of photoreceptor opsins into eyesight are present in a similar substance in taste cells where it specifically activates a phosphatase isolated from taste tissue.

Whereas the sensory neurons in her nose are not highly specific, and a particular odour must be identified by the pattern of strength of excitation over the ensemble of primary sensory neurons.

The consequence of thinking creative activity invents structural thought as explanatory and smears the factual as thought's function. A worry over whether the supposedly radical and far-reaching claim that what is known exists, continues. Notions of totality, and devel- opments as paradigms for understanding, smoulder behind the eyes in swarms of smoked out thoughts dowsed in a mixture of flame repellent and petrol, the dialectic farce.

11.

A charge from incoherence begins to take effect. Energy from mistaken value blows across the relativity of incompatible theories and different models of oblivion. The achieved oblivions present a range from the basic and abstract across to the complex and closer to surface phenomena. Each oblivion contingent on particular production values. Each value contingent on apparencies or conjectures.

Molecules that perform logic operations are prerequisites for information processing and computation. Receptor molecules can be considered to perform simple logic operations by coupling recall or more complex molecular-recognition processes with photonic—fluorescence—signals: in these systems, chemical binding results in change in fluorescence intensity from the receptor. Here a receptor operates as a logic device with two input channels: the fluorescence signal depends on whether the molecule binds short term memory, sudden excitement, or both.

He collected Preston Epps records and played *Boo Boo Stick Beat* in his bath. You think the sounds in your head are due to an outside rate of vibration: each vibration contingent on molecular substance, temperature and atmospheric pressure.

Pass logic devices have one-input/one-output functionality. Complex logic operations also need two-output devices such as AND and OR gates. Philosophical vocabulary can lose complexity and shift to the plain and metaphorical. In doing so it begins a skid into its own parameters. Although receptors are arguably metaphorical devices—they use spoken language—they do not possess a full truth table as the unprotonated forms simply will not bind the substrate. Help me now to hold the table as it moves, hold the table as it moves.

Preoccupations with relativity exclude concerns of certainty. Inconsistency derives directly from misunderstanding and encourages a need for certainty. The pertinence of certainty fills every theory energised by defective comprehension. The concern bunches a quest to convert energy or transform values into pay-offs, pay-offs and exhibitions of awareness. The problems of phase shift in these events do not need solution. Adequate flow produces subsequent need and may therefore be understood as fray—a necessary consequence of invention.

Transfer processes could be suppressed by injection of immediacy and tiredness, respectively, to cause "switching on" of fluorescence. Memory based on the "fluorophore-spacer-receptor-spacer-receptor" format could be expected to fluoresce only when the tertiary amine and benzocrown ether units are receiving immediacy and tiredness input, respectively, at sufficiently high concentrations. Such concentrations have been recorded in the expression of serotonin which recall the rites of Altaic shamans and show parallel experiences following the intake of mescaline where, for instance, an individual found crawling about the floor with extreme care, but averred he was a fly walking on the ceiling upside down and that if he moved quickly he would fall and be injured.

Today the Gas-man went by
I tell you
he was smokin' like
a drain
Musking the path like
a squat marking badger
with stiff hairs to measure
the accessibility to gaps.

Consciousness creates itself as it produces the world. What it lacks is control of this production. Work becomes a means and consciousness dissolves into substructures of capital or money. The alienated consciousness has been identified and named. This naming begins in distinction, process and relationships. This naming concludes in market position and modes of prevention.

Kinetics and entanglements continue to predict the timed-space of thinking sensibly. A rush of graphite grinds into an almost precise triple scrawl of circles cross-collateralised in the mayhem.

She begins discussion of a linear oscillator named "objective drawing" in contact with a thermal bath "named pleasure". She then considers other possible disturbances of the oscillator. She applies this foundation to tests of the universality of free fall to tests of the gravitational Gauss law. Finally the discussion links to the notorious and difficult measurements of the Newtonian gravitational constant G. All re-analysis of the classic Eötvös equivalence principle data, which seemed to provide evidence for a fundamental interaction or "fifth force", was deliberately ignored.

The near to total values were proposed to be equal to the near to total profits. I can accept both theses simultaneously.The quantity of space-labour impinges on the social necessity to produce commodities.The exchange value of the social necessity is determined by the spacetime intrusions. Evaluation finds inadequate data. Labour can not be the only value. Evaluation is a postulation for the basic and abstract to the detriment of the complex and phenomenological.

I studied human auditory and somatosensory modalities. They showed that there is an oscillatory response at about 40-Hz frequency which is elicited by either steady state or transient stimulation. The auditory 40-Hz response is generated at least partially in the auditory cortex as a result of thalama-cortical interaction, and conscious perception. A connective to selective attention has been implied in my studies, although the evidence is fortunately inconclusive.

Stretches, controlled breaths and vocals feedback through burnt molecules transformed into stress-relief and meditation. Gargling and steam inhalation linked to more singing produce showtime, breathspace, and the scale to perform. Not being able to sleep, this strange jaw pain, and a general anxiety over feelings and palpitations re-invent the distant memory. I don't re-invent I move forward. Questions move into the self below a happy surface.

My results show that selective attention enhances the amplitude of the auditory 40-Hz response and hence demonstrates a physiological correlate of selective attention in this response. Such an effect, observed in averaged data, originates from a diminished spacetime jitter between consecutive single responses or their increased amplitude.

Value changes without a constant notching. Any patterns of income distribution which govern effective demand are only understood as artifacts. Commodities can carry exchange values, but the exchange relations can never be presented as a two part equation.The involvement of equations tells you that in differences there is similarity and that similarity is multiple and never simply a third matter. Valid exchange values cannot express equality and will never be transparent.

The concept of a superlattice memory is that, with a sufficiently thin epitaxial layer, the strain energy in each layer is below the energy needed for the growth of point defects or dislocation. Thus a limitation to the inventive from these layerings can, and often does result in conservative bonding. Dislocations have an activation energy for nucleation and a lower activation energy for growth. Therefore, in principle, it becomes possible to exceed the energy requirement without actually generating defects.

Exchange values are forms of appearance distinguishable from other appearances. The exchange values are irreducible to commonality. Commonality is an artifact a product of labour. Labour is a disrupted crystal that its discontinuous energy complexes and breaks any norm of algebraic presumption. There is thus no commonality which presents itself in exchange value and no single value attributable to it.

A superlattice memory may be used as the barrier for an imaginative capacity and its alternative quantum well. It is often assumed in strain-layer superlattices that a large lattice mismatch prevalent in dialectical analysis results in high defect density which destroys quantum confinement. Not only is scattering less effective in lower-dimensional systems, but it fails to destroy phase coherence in zero-dimensional systems such as imaginative clusters and quantum dots. Of course, the scattering process that possesses spacetime-reversal symmetry is the Scientist's idealism that the Inspectorate rejects. In any case, in an isolated system, such as a quantum well, defects may not be detrimental.

Slowly universal theory loses use value. His weariness amazes him. Embarrassment of riches. Dance steps derive from oracle bone forms depicting thaumaturgic issues. A kind of clarity and a directness ensues. If you word in your box you can plate it. Stratocaster 1954.

The imaginative can be evaporated or even deposited epitaxially with a mnemonic source. Simulation followed by moderate invention could be used to provide passivation of possible dangling bonds—the vertical reality of a simulated implosion in which the journey into the body is by the self energised by dislocality.

Quality gets more and more equal. Products and procedures and machines reduce to identical parameters. Only creativity has competitive edge. Virtual means the ability to respond instantaneously to satisfy specific customer demand. Management no longer exists. The pressures of complexity lead to multiple management in collegiate effort.

Loss of self led to narcissistic depression—an absorption with suffering as a substitute for loss. No self to indulge, no reflection. Identity formation becomes perilous, uncertain, seeing the terror of this frozen before the mirror, the self made in activity with others.

There are several questionable steps. The Scientist insists on them as part of her development in discovering how the law of value is constructed. She justifies an assumption about the relativity of production and justifies this model as the evidence for its lack of proof. Yet no system of production is freely reproducible and all evidence requires labour distributed by exchange in which demands are met. Proportion becomes simply an ideal geometry and algebra combined to aid the accountants.

In the vocabulary of the shaman and the Scientist, death becomes a reunion with the lost self; a refusal to grow or recover which would require identification with loss. Cure may not rest here because alienation, this distinction between self and unnamed reality, cohabits with the dissolution of self and other. These burnt and lost paradigms of relations and disinheritances lead this memory complex into an incoherent burble named primal or satisfactory.

The necessity derives from a doubt of the self. A distant nostalgia for a future utopia. Analysis of real relations has an over-reliance on the confirmation of truth or the certainty real. Value may determine the quality of exchange only where social need agrees upon the commonality of its dominant form. Natural law loses validity when it is isolated from the social Coriolis. The law of value can only fuse the form of appearance with apparent production. It becomes a special case and corresponds to society's productive powers. The determination of exchange value of labour is a fact, but a fact exists in the midst of other facts.

Melancholia and visions of paradise lead to depression as a tortured meditation on analysis—to a refusal of reconciliation for death and alienation—to a quest for words or images descriptive of suffering and existence. The cure from alienation and dispossession differs from the necessity of the aesthetic dimension. Beauty's capacity to comfort set against harsher truth promotes a potential envy of its temporality in space. Some of the misconceptions here rest in the expectation of high speed roundness; an inability to embrace instability in a consistent self.

The determination of value by spatial use of time gets hidden beneath the apparatus as it varies in the relative values of its production. What mystifies the Scientist rolls the social character of labours, where production controls the producers instead of producers control of production. It reads on the virtual analysis as a molecular buzz ball tearing through superlattices at a variety of speeds. Outsourcing simply burns you out. Solace and serenity in the Beauty parlour, a niche in management-training that values dissent in corporate life.

Frequently I see performance of recovery with measured steps. Just as I thought it was lost in an inextricable maze of measures, just as you feel them about to fall into confusion, I have a characteristic way of recovering my balance, a special way of propping up the body, the twists and impressions of a wet rag being wrung—and in final steps, the suspended rhythm over and the beat resolved.

High Modernist Will energised by alienation towards cure produces dispossession—an index of sensitive thinking becomes a functional process of will. Break let's from that alienation in dispossession that belongs—embraces uncertainty and loss in negative capability—confronts the semiological fragmentation with proprioceptive and transformative pragmatics.

The ideological and theoretical frameworks are requirements for concepts without which concepts cannot exist and cannot be studied. The room was so crowded people fainted and the speaker could not be heard. The anthropology of desire and struggle for recognition are the basis for unhappy consciousness. The dichotomy between a philosophy of consciousness and a philosophy of the concept led both the Scientist and the Inspectorate to disaffection. The talk on identification illustrated by the wielding of glass tubes containing two different species of crickets.

Adherence to the dialectical method based on the tendencies of material productions involve inappropriate and reactionary views about consciousness and participation in a becoming world.The semiological basis, a despair of the intellect to criticise its certainty, its centrality exemplified in its mode of publication, its consumerism, affirms thought as its necessity when the need must be both restorative and innovative.

In the poem I am never myself, but speak beyond myself, the poem is that transportation of the self evident before the invention of wheels, perhaps evident in the ecstatic. This serial composition offers an initial dismissal of the dialectical universe. This in no way shifts away from the potential of constraints in combinatorial serial form or physical jouissance of perception. I am of course another late comer, paralysed and depressed by this, glad of it, unsure of this position. Even the worst of this is preferable to vegetable existence, even if the starting point of the imaginative can be the most disastrous of chemistries.

The Inspectorate lack any appetite for poetry and are in the peculiar business to distribute something they do not possess. They work with intelligence and zeal; with seriousness and depth about all manner of things, that are not poetry, to solve problems on the basis of evidence rather than on speculation or what has worked in the past. They have been led by four modalities of consciousness derived from a desperate accounting; they project a cultural universe burning in the spacetime of confinement, distortion of reflex and self-referred incomprehension.

11. Ring Shout and Sojourns

walked downpath to the hut and took jet into snow
messages came through the wall through my head
into a radio sounded donut then rhythm coded
a twelve yard stare coded pattern trap in a six yard

Ring Shout

1.

Why he should begin with discussion of the end
makes preposterous the notes on intermittent crying

These days I feel much more comfortable
The springs are fully wound when the curtain goes up
Any disturbance of balance is surely illness
Pendant to *Crime and Punishment*
against the endemic disease of romantic love
as the basis of marriage

The crime which was destroying
the man in him filtered into any bonds
between them rotted them
She wanted to be free from herself,

to think and make her own and never need
assistance to get straight.

2.

Wound blots recede as
pain latches
and dampness sustains encoding
categories of decay match a confidence
trick below intelligence
A group of loners build from
the rubble until a garden wall
is evident. It marks the millennium
It doesn't mark anything
Drawings on the wall map out a planetary
sequence beyond this one breaks the
pressure of exactness or completion.
Another geometry will be needed.
Let's not say that. Mark out consciousness
in a constellation map overlapping another
Two women walk by with antlered headwear
partly a result of last week's storm
Pinch-me crossed the Park collecting snake skins

The lovers ignore this eat toadstools
and lichen. The air is full of yellow
moths and fill the mouths of those in
exercise or copulation
up to her knees in fern fronds
on his back out of view red and yellow
in the green lush, insects and humans
red ants and naked wood rot
before the wind lifts before the cloud shifts
Another wreckage more slavery instant repetition.

3.

He downloads Thoreau's *Civil Disobedience*
as a therapy, shifting each narrowed text
Presentational immediacy arises
from the integration of a strain-feeling
and a physical purpose

We are both in pain
perhaps reasons are complexly different
Both ranges of reasons are human
She is very beautiful the way
she considers
I hardly ever weep now
It takes fifty years to make a man

When so much you have loved torn from you
and you expect to remain the same.

4.

Her small feet lift onto the rest bar
palms on knees under the occasional
watch the screen reintegrate defined
squiffiness where without exception
the utopians share the conviction
that all people, regardless of situation
bow their knee before a single moral order
driven to escape the present in future refuge
where Europeans became convinced of their
superiority using a synthesis of circular and linear

temporal myths combined with ideas of a parallel
dimension known as the confidence trap
She lifts her hands onto the keyboard
plays the last bars of *Le Banquet Céleste*

5.

On a moderately hilly lowland
marked either side by hills and in the south
by a river she bends over a torn epiphytic lichen
resting on the heavy, close textured loamy soil
of a marl partly concealed by an orchard of perry pears
in an April rain shadow the puzzle posed related to
the presence of Lobaria pulmonaria away from limestone
and in isolation from another plant startled
by the presence of another animal shocked
into amusement at surprise in ice movement wilted
bower larks wither hide or fill the mouth sigh a quiver
he sends beneath this shorn certain din invests in the gravity,
lost flexed balmy toil revealed before an orchid of pearls
in showers sweet the difficulty posed by asking

6.

If I have achieved nothing
positive, at least I hold
to the belief that a truth
does exist, and that it
is within my power
to find it face it down on
red sandstone imprint denture
and sound made visible
each shift in image pressure
as it hardens and is given
sequence shifts of impressions
temporal phase space for
each article each vowel
until simply air dry on the surface

7.

Sounds on the tape record
the recorder's action beyond
alternating bands of dark magnetite
and light silicates propose complex
microlife 3,500 million years ago.
Lee Morgan lives with
Freddie Hubbard in the night
of the cookers and Grachan
Moncur's *Evolution*
quarrel with sense-perceptions

Resolution in excess to system
a hyperacuity reserved for angels and machines
Honour and justice based on pleasant
distinctions of product and production.

8.

Thighs end strain bend switch
Gyrations rim digressions in a grim age
roaring escapable muds rim-testing the sod
of a barging roster screwed to the new roarplate
another motorboard rattling the screen-ledge, dog-cronic.

Sonic hedgehog gene patterning
of notochord, floorplate of neural tube
and posterior margin of tetrapod limb buds,
capable of mirror-image limb-digit duplications
which extend to the brain and eyes.

The bereft felt from a Hay diet
relaxing into once lost sexual appetites
kites and apples complex frost, once faxing
the riot day from the spelt relief

9.

We speak of where we are
at once with the state of the planet
To some this is the spiritual view

to us this is a necessary undertaking
The land mines
manufactured across the way
sold and encouraged
Every jar of Gentleman's Relish
Banned from the SAS annual dinner
Does freak of weary scar
At front withers the cranium soto planned it
To hum wish theory spirals spew
to truss this a neck varied thunder raking
The lame minds guerrilla factured across the way

10.

Fluxus is for you the young
but young is you're not young
life reverses near the pain
what pain life is a pain
no it's not

life is like a cattle drum you mean kettle
drum yes and hum drum
derange issues of progress
the whole contention that pop-up
philosophy doesn't progress—art doesn't—

oh but science does looks frail from here
spontaneity on a prepared trampoline
irritations and scratches means
replace aesthetics with anaesthesia

11.

Intelligence disturbs common ground
combining sense with spiritual cue
discuss on a fence verge Roman through-
way ground redenying wither true
in any case how can it be

what you think this is boy
I have lightning milk acerbic crave
I have shaky juice in a cave of wrenches

what you think crispy destroys
brave sighting silk absurd rave-tronics
yav salt cake loose in your roller ring
in every spacetime tremble free

vibrations dulled on a syrup tongue
no youth here now beyond a blaw tread knee

12.

Love and progress
driven by misconceptions
the burglar effect unreliable
facts in human affairs
do not give principles for truth
criteria consistent
with our own fallibility
mental constructs and institutions
glass blocks of highly transparent waste
irradiated nuclear truth
the ultimate fuel ingrained
in our misconceptions

You stand at the edge of a millennium
watch sun rise drop on the ocean

13.

As the money is not owed
facial shape advances
serves to flatter profits
Depth distance from eyebrows to nostrils
will have to be restated
Skin and hair tone
does not represent cash owing
personality or image

Justice cash never received
Five times more galaxies than previously thought
will run off the balance sheet value

Any future cash reimbursements

will have to be paid out in galaxy
added to galaxy collision

14.

A terrible sense of completion
frame of a lake against
a field of cars
hand washed and leathered
the geometry generator
of wasteland epistemologically
and culturally united understanding

Refined togetherness
of sustained thinking
a topological neg-entropy
machined and ionised
netted against perception
frayed river break
a terrific exhaustion before stopping.

15.

Devout speed of a raunchy
letter spray font beer
repass constructed reach cover
railings crawl visual
what was required
in order to do that and they say
would have an incentive
pass it on to each other
Let me away from here
without need of motor launch
should basil render
to smoulder crack away
inturgescence of drupaceous plum
beneath upright posture ultimatum.

16.

Between the figures of Adam & Eve
how individual cells know
what to become how they resemble
appear in a fiery Gulph
a Hox gene cluster
descending from fire
determinate body plans and axes
Told his friend of intentions
to celebrate by sharing a glass
of juice transformed into wine
with a pretty strange fellow
whose path often crossed in the course
of a journey In Eternity one Thing
never Changes into another Thing

17.

Chairs in the wind on their sides
in the garden a blown blackcap
corrects functional stupidity
feeding downside-up without
evolutionary flare or prediction
of the matter's bionomics
written out in a prison house
with potassium manganate
on pieces of cement sack
convinced by the argument
that ethologies between different
species correlate
across a tropical plateau of
now you win now you don't

18.

The first analysis of a hypothetical object
blue shifts the discussion towards purist
and isolationist adolescent fauna
trapped in warning a cycle it takes
strong nerve to read contamination futures
written in rubidium from Prussian carnallite salt

with silvery-white strontium pulled from
sky blue celestine and mineral springs
supped by beetles and child

Risk assessment and management
in the cups of withered wings and hands
exposed wonder and monitored
worry without action only recognition of
the way toxins affect brain function.

19.

The burden of personality
dissolves into timeless
contemplation of
the next cocktail
left incomplete

The second analysis used
samarium in brownish black allanite with
rare earth neodymium in reddish monazite
solitary as glass amplifies light and dark
simultaneously traps circadian rhythm
or transients in photosynthesis sustained
oscillations in the splitting of glucose
a bionecessity to understand failure recurs
Please don't hurt me

20.

Explosions are instantaneous clouds
obliterate the moment of transformation
The third analysis used
grey uranium from blackish pitchblende
hard with cold deceit turned brown on the raft
the body of Delacroix dated against
blue-grey lead on the surface of Anselm Kiefer's
wood rot heavy squat fluid motions
crossing ground quakes beneath the
extreme unstoppable force and power
of caterpillar tracks and complex suspension
Shrapnel ghost growth pressures to reduce

carbon emissions
or cut temperature and storm damage

21.

You want to inhibit my spacetime
you join a rich roast of fireweeds
and carbohydrates.
The antlered men stamp into a
field of tulips to gather material
This is not the last robbery
Drenched light moves through the rain storm
hits a conference a wrestling match
a hundred and more ants ascend from the
boiler well
1910 becomes 1985 continues territorial raids
Watch this, watch this! and the stick breaks
The city surrounds us and demands
river mist symmetries.

22.

Norms of devastation, civilised
Oak birds storm at each other
One year has passed
Boisterousness does not name it.

Analysis links particular conditions to
a continental malaise
maybe it's larger than that.
Disruption begins to be the habit rather
than its subversion
Anarchism is part of the tradition
Listening carefully perception misses
insect feet but combines flies and
oak birds with a distant aircraft
Displacement of the natural continues
to lead to confirmation
Kids wearing oak twigs imitate the park deer
Illusions of judgement and truth remain traps
in long grass
A recording of wind in oaks and aircraft

shifts oxygen into energy
You want to fuck me but I'm the meadow
the larks play with my dead breast
Too many deep caverns drilled by implosions
of the Will. Gentleman's reliques
All that fuss about doubt and ecstasy.
Devastation's over in a rope cast
slung around jars of intoxicants
now full of funeral ash.

23.

Ecodamage reifies poetic strain
fail hurts but remains necessary
rusty yurt in an iron cup pathetic
that retromanagement deifies

Train ethic defies metro arrangement
investiary detains strut thoughts rail
dialectic cusp ironic inturn robustly
describes electro-ranges scratch

NOTES

5: *Lobaria pulmonaria*: the tree lung wort. "Lobar" pertains to a lobe a pod a roundish projecting part one or two or more separated by a fissure; "pulmonaria": beneficial, cures disease to lungs indicated by spotted leaves resembling the lungs.

8: *Sonic hedgehog* is the vernacular name for the gene Shh. Hedgehog was first identified in the fruitfly, encoding a secreted protein signal directing patterning in the embryo. An expanding family of genes relating to hedgehog has been found in vertebrates, where they are thought to have a similar function.

William Howard Hay, a *fin de siècle* Pennsylvanian (1866–1940), developed a system of food combining which improved the health of participants. The system avoids the mixture of starch and protein in the same meal.

16: "Animals as diverse as worms, the insects, and mammals, and representing half a billion years of evolution, all share a small number of highly conserved genes – the Hox gene cluster – that determine basic body plans and 'north-south' axes of the body." Rudolf A. Raff, *The Shape of Life: Genes, Development, and the Evolution of Animal Form* (University of Chicago Press, 1996).

17: Konrad Lorenz wrote the first part of his *Natural Science of the Human Species: An Introduction to Comparative Behavioural Research* this way in 1944–48 from a prisoner-of-war camp in the Soviet Union.

Roach

1.

The demands of cosmopolis
such a State the age of cities
in Eternity accelerators
of the Innocent decomposed
a blackboard the figure eight
civilised Heathen a salary
the Uncivilised Savage
before the age of nations
who having not the Law
do by Nature
ethnic cleansing
regional assemblies
the things contained in the Law
freed of terminal claims of providence.

2.

State of
in Eternity
of the Innocent
civilised Heathen
the Uncivilised Savage
who having not the Law
do by Nature
the things contained in the Law

Rooster Strut

1.

Triangles of light fill the floor and flutter
Are they moths in a honey bath
held by love's geometry
Can this be adhesive thought in a sticky
cement waiting to crystallise waiting to die

Dianthus fraught in mangle weed
here comes your fly
Love's health love's promontory
quiver amperes behind ample ablator
thoughts of desire delight respirator

2.

Rubber two a tanga who
flames
dragon's cavern
green fields
fiery chariot of contemplation

Running in Place

1.

Lifted thrown pinched up what
you think got when

seemed forward around
a pegged pole in situ

Splodged cutlassed you know
the stuff it

rhubatic fummeck thick
onto router's roof run

Athen fibre screened
crogged or laced

get it off thar
git orf like I sayd

yonder hill orogesh
miles from here

2.

Lifted thrown pinched up what
for why you do that

moronic the epigrammatic effect
the send them to the child minder

A fudge criterion stood fast on a raft race
just smart of a deep strait off Bali
almost two million years ago
and across the lake
a 37,000 year old leg bone hammer
to redivide the land

Avoided inspiration gets hard to trigonomete
Orientation in the three thousand year old
ploughed field prevented through loss or
ancient stones moved in a recent glacier

3.

Red eyes describe fever from haywain
Somehow participates in a loss of hedgerows
He came downroad holding arm
almost horizontally seemed to bounce a ball
and then began to push downward against pressure
and as he did this his feet started to lift from
the ground
a few inches lifted
and held there as he held pressure down
with the end of his hand
until he gave up
and dropped immediately
feet first to the floor
seeing the pile of sketches and her colour

Scronch

1.

Pressure change
broke surface tenderness
forethought from an experience
of various temperaments
as a sweve of, the figure John Varley
named, Blake's Instructor with
an emblematic fire tree above his eyes,
if that's what it is,
enters the imagination from
the skylight in the form of a wave
described by a naval architect as a hump
took off in the wake of boat stop
down canal without change
entered perception as a light trap,
a spatio-temporal shape of incoherent
white-glare from a light bulb
self-trapped in a speckled crystal
strontium, barium, niobium, oxygen
embedded in the centre of his forehead
an intuitive interactive environment
fast and easy plasmid map construction
newly amplified
flow-sorted micro-dissected
brightly fluorescing
No wonder his head hurts
The magnitude of non-linearity relates
to the time and space for relaxation
In a shuttle the Instructor elucidates
colloidal crystallisation an
effect of gravity on his air-free face
a Focus Team watch random stacking
of hexagonally close-packed planes
in a mirror and on screen
the mud at Glastonbury beyond fence rows
gravitational stresses, sedimentation,
concentration gradients at the Giant's Causeway
simulated hard spheres in a phase diagram
reverberated on a drum machine
The mistakes already made in the feel for physicality

repeated in the field of intellectual work
bludgeoned at the fence.

2.

Ambitious to enlarge the boundaries
to a knowledge of those precepts
to which every thing that aspires
must be proportioned and accommodated
to the fire that implies foresight
until attention totally engaged applies cadmium,
cuts hedge, prunes roses, confirms work on portraits.
Deferred gratification perishes to rise in amazement
dawn-shine on the face of the Tor
desirable lustre a hare in moonlight
with its eyes open asleep
proceeds with deliberation with detour
behaviour conducive to wisdom and compassion
reach a nonremovable singularity in which
individual cells of the heart's pacemaker node
normally synchronise each other.
His, so-called, fourth hand carries a ring of ball
bearings to represent a dodecagon
Pleasure range brokes surrounding
dimension accumulated energy
tripped in walkway over large child
entered columned chaos
from egg to winged barrel
a particulate power wave or guardian
abluted at each contamination
plutonium toffees "burning" "dry"
the Focus Team's highly spiced gaze
delirious or at sea promotes
discussion of preference for memory
before imagination or an involuntary
divination practised by everyone
through their blood sugar how
volcanic crystals by their own power
fly, allow reason to energise irrespective
of whether what it says can happen
irrelevant to discussions of
whether the soul can cloud and lift or

the activities of thermal gases become
hatred, a mould in the stomach
akin to an ulcer fed with young chillies
call Here we go here we go here we go.

3.

The Focus Team clean their teeth in
carbon and selenium solutions before
the Painter applied red cadmium
wears the conceit of
a chrome oxide, called green, shirt
Society cloaked a troubled history
male human endeavour walks with
a stoop beneath weight of burden
the primate back fault measured by
sizes given by sample, he remembers,
because they said that, with a
measurement, some people cheat
taking an inside of the
millimetre line or she factures
the picture in her head rather
than the one immediately in view
pervades the medium then phases
at once in particulate and wave forms
a mammalian ventricular tissue spiral
propagates around a cardiac arrest
an amalgamation of niches
in delusions of understanding shapes
close to Archimedean screws
shovel mud at Glastonbury
scrolls rotate and drift
swallowed photocopies
choked in glass of 14 year Islay
silver fragments eye catch
crystallised water
on the bathroom tumbler chrysalis
in an inclined plane suddenly
the speed of light caught
in a web angled across skyframe
she pulled through the window
rolled down the roof into

stop at the wet gutter
pressure change
broke surface tension where
a tap drip hits the forehead
from an experience
of various temperatures.

Shag

When the Inspector came down
Analysis discussed G drag
rain seemed incessant that
day pages rumpled from this
made antique in spilt caffeine
buzzed feet and signified
liver's need for zinc
burning out from Beacon toposcope
more than ten counties
gazpacho soup rock heart mambo
solar winds spirallic directions one
hemisphere to another a vertical
smoke plume at the equator
It's hot here but where else would I
be in wealth salads on a
table organic fresh potatoes hot in olive oil
spring onion garlic then turned in gris
mayonnaise against local quick grilled
courgettes peppers in olive with coriander
just picked for dressing up
electromagnetic fields soon after the *Memoir*
from Coriolis the work of Faraday a narrative
burnt from Humboldt to Ranke shifts from
organic to formal explanatory strategies
comic emplotment intact history a
classical mimetic art holds individual
event in its concrete

Analyst and Inspector argue divisions
determinate scene against the matter of agents
metonymy against synecdoche the reality of
sustainable dream a necessary bright pin
reconciles humankind each
other beyond utopia float tank airless face stress
in social states can you imagine
happy cattle in a field without oxeyes
it's not a funny farm snap out pull
lift on corrugated spring roll lawned
out into day scat burnet moths alright
alight after assarting and a plough in the wings
burns oil in foot stamp pushes at gate
held by the woman girdled in snake belts
shouting "Fuck Off ! Fuck Off !"

The Inspector raises his glass to
the Analyst checks the cleanliness calls
"Cheers" red spots in front her eyes
accustomed to dark green wings and
the agon of sympathy for and fear of
humankind different from themselves
or loss of what they owned
To conclude, a large rainbow circle lifts
in all the stench of a pub-noise halo
from their wet changeless brows.

Shango

Origins, a new kind of ghost
frozen, remote hook at death
Devoted future threshold
what terrible

Body of psychic curse
custom and public sanctity
Drawn but vague boundary
tagged emotion and
spontaneous intolerance

Subtraction from self
familiarity with alien
action suffer
deodorised
jolt

She all of a sudden
masked pull
fatigue rudder
rubbed against first thought
At a remote
instant judgment
matched flubber lost insert
inert Pulled and quartered
thesmotic approval scrubbed
aligned Genetic determination
revolution first curve
a proposed limit tangented
limbs without warmth with
liberty Begun as if it seen

Shika

1.

Birds crushed in
car grilled
dead badgers
extinct beavers
invisible hares
vomit at edge of
another millennium
watercress ruby chard
broccoli sproutings
contaminated with
formaldehyde
cadmium and blood

He take out my hand
reading portents
from records of Moon
beams grub runs
on old bones
diseased with it
vegetable movement
riddled with it
in a tongue twist

Murky taste
it firky waste drain
swindled for the
sake sack
got it? er?
went to bed on head
er?
anuva crop out

2.

The day I left Hereford the hedge died
a study of crying
pavement so dirty he was frightened to fall
walking-stick collapsed into 5 linked parts
from the tower and back on a bungee loop
you'd think they'd think first
boing on a back pack
dyed the hedge blue the way I heard it
describing a fried egg
if I told you once I told you
tidal burlap on the mobile drone
freeze-dried flower and a melon chest
defrosted fridge the day I left Hereford
the mud match sighing

3.

Hurts thumbnail now
before sketch
disciplined lives

Shimmy

teeth broke a
sharp block labelled Quicke
that's what I call cheese
noted through pursed lips
alerted cameraman
say please

won another whiskey it
save working for
existing shape the words
to another's voice
well I never did
if that don't take
the biscuit

12. Sledge Trap

Shorty George

She refers to Human Imagination linked to phenomena
gestured by the hand's enquiry
A woman in shadow converses with Eternal Realities
Sketches reclamation of the streets
Her name could be Praxitelean, the actuary
jump leads her head to avoid overload
branches of stock exchange and a siren.

Vibrated wires in ear wax
notate her script across slivers of resin
on a scratch path in Blake's
World of Generation and Death
bites under rollers into an exact
geometry ponderous shield like the moon
equates appearance to a nouveau réalité.

A butterfly on the fence
made hesitant in breeze
changes colour as she moves
this and that side of the garden
snapped by a bird in long johns.

Drawing predicts what he will look like
or how he will be
measured in sudden step elation
There is a rule that
water precedes existence
varied by mineral content.

Stability relies on security
outweighing the threat
On the cart grievance factors
can be entirely ignored
The Bellman's automatism produces varied
yet recognised signature
without certainty of what it is.

Needs must and chance summate in action
Astride the simulacrum of Paradise
Hi! There is timespace for instance
neg-entrophied with a pencil

cleansed eyes of pollen-cell interaction
holds open lids before loom of spiritual approximation.

Damned if you do and
vibrated in Morse on the oak bark
chatter recorded as repetition
Now generate and what would you expect
Goat tethered to reproduce Plato's ideals.

Tubes of contaminated waste rush air past
platforms of benefit and risk
cryogenic scanning-probes provide the imaging
The Bellman's cart now
harnessed to a brain storm
iterates plague victims and toxic cargo
to reconciliation or resignation.

You can guess a consequence
Corporate logo engineered to insistence
horseflies and fluff of the leach grass
crushed into newly made paper
signatures in ink of blood and charcoal
whiff of institution mothballs lavender wax
Skidded on your bike
the corridors of prowess.

Expectation presumption exactitude
sprayed on through a tube from an Orgone box
t-t-t-toxic back pain stretched
speeding up tape of croaking voice.

Shuffle

Missed the gyst in toil and mystery
                        thought it was simply a riddle
Restricted proprioceptive
                        pathway
throes she distrusted by
                        schezec the lack of fizz out of fat

The subject shifts inwards

                        regulated stare inner perversity
beatitude
                        fetches a crushed normalised
withers assimilates to feed
                        proud of the curvature

He flies to borrow
                        fuses a toil twistor
affords peroxide pace climb
                        fakes onomatopoeia the toil bends
accesses commodity thrifts
                        perpetuity over perdition
buttered damage
                        the same shell invention

His form based on faulty acidity
                        and consumption
Presumed force between circuits
                        fractured spacetime
a force between two elements
                        presumed to be subjected and subjector
poses the tension of the claw's pliance
                        on the screen of wisdoms

I am spent of my crime
                        but cannot judge
what I owe to my virtue
                        elongated and sawn
I am wanted amongst her
                        but male
I am weighed and muted
                        but not real

Gazelles of fidelity
juiced and most presentable
of dereliction a sudden
crop
to stop brain sense
cabbaged by
the voters and the voters'
hilted intention

Fut cruciated angle hoist
foam racial torsion
dissipated over eagles
of the shaft ropes
as guests of transgression
barge out on propellant
and the gravity bumps the antelope
juiced in radium seizures

Plaid and grooms fin lock
and crowd for the weald decks
even acerbic and labour
the subject floats
what had stood
bone of inenarrable
lies bending
to serve

Skate

She invented consciousness as
part of a process interrupted
procedure you know
yeah you know intra-
juiced memory fragrance
part of a preceding
narrative where trees
have sentience and

lovechild has sway with it
in the lime light they say
in metaphor way you like your step
look for the drum stick
with a man on top
his own freedom chained
from mountain wind
waits for spiky-flamed

florets analysed in a trap
retribution before navigation
through a new spacetime
multiple gun fire 21.35
prevents an allegory of the soul
buoyed by the imaginative overlapped
by desire patterns a flower
through consecutive acts of

meristem-identity control
of homeotic genes specify floral
display through her lens coupling
an underlying pattern common to speech
and a complexity of value are added
where few aesthetic factors
that avoid artifact-specificity themselves
combine in articulation of a specific region

A unique star field perceived as single star
from the gap in the hut wall
a long circumnavigation to define youth
and culture and then comparison between
struggle and duty, equestrian hero in the

foundry steps the light fantastic
similitude's button comfort
warmth from camp firelight

childlike display of song
without sense only send-up
narrative where trees' carbon
outmatches silica and silicates
fused in smell's recall in the blood
like they say this is the pattern
unravelling inner sapphires
invents consciousness

The conundrum of equivalents
in knowledge of crushed identities
a man with song like a bluefinch
bundled from nerve held oxygen
drips from a white rose cluster
on the garden bush she has been
locked in study of her palm carries
dew to the gemstone on a

brain stem and passes out
In the dream she awakes on a raft
in a rapid of rhubarb shifts
descends to the rim of a sea bell
as it rings and flowers and rings
in dawn celebrates their walk on
bare feet wet grass distant gunfire
fills breath fills warning and fades

Slooing

The Designer's monuments under glass on a work table
Join again what custom strictly divided
A transformational force of rational feeling
Consolidation and innovation describes complexity
The falling scale associated with tears
Above a canopy of stars, long stare into oblivion
A programmatic recovery from illness
Impressive gravity unbounded flight follows inner stretch
"Must it be?" and "It must be!"

Fused disparate power unreconciled knowing senses
Fatalistic resignation through improved chromes
Cut from everything precious in a drive through wreckage
Multiple formats far-reached revisions bouts of density
Blend of rations and senses process of critical reflection
A focus for the awe and devotion of many human beings
Visions of new strengths and then attainments
Rapt contemplation infused with a raw thumble
Arrests of anapaestic rhythm held in sonata form.

Human synthesis of perception the starry heavens
Sublimity experienced between phenomena and freedom
Emerges through the idea and pivots
Encounter with self come to grips with work
An open system promotes ethical frameworks as a guide
Projections of desire and goals yet to be achieved
Unfulfilled depictions of the sublime harbour an ethical roar
Politics discussed as aesthetics through situations made in freedom
A defiant reconfrontation with strife-ridden memory.

Evocative judgements gale and melanchole in finale
Sketched to work out demands of contrapuntal passages
A synthesis between more than one life at once
More than mere beauty the shape of tenderness
Joined exaltation and the commonplace in a polity
Seems to suspend flow of spacetime in phase transitions
Evocative environment shaped contrasts beyond what is thought
Its own continuity tensioned before its confines.

Foreshortening drives sonata form and principles of thought
Flexible intensifications appropriated to the design
Sequence rise ecstatically into fall back and short breath
From today on I will take a new path to the hut
Uplifts of vision and derivation transthemed in joy
Captures a repeated stress stimulated imagination
Strophe by strophe over nearly three decades
Immanent complementarity resolved or transformed
Common action based on agreement in the heat.

Sudden contrasts unexpected turns rides of strife
Interruptions characteristic coordinated with logic unfolds
Contemplation rejected in favour of stoical acceptances
Astonishing disjunction incredulous uplifts and down shifts
Severely dislocates structural recapitulation of spin
Superimposed tonic and dominant dissonance
Reconfrontation with open countryside in noise
Disaffected contributes atmospheres of bleak melancholy
Telegraphic rhythms insert wrong chord just before cadence.

Severe contrast welds cadences pointing silence beyond
Narrative designed to elude reductionistic terms
To envisage wholeness before motifs and individual pictures
An analogous narrative progression to creative possibles
Weight contributes to the sense of openness
A principle of analogy between music and narrative
Interdependence of structure and expression confronts
Aesthetic dimensions end without return in broken sonatas.

The Designer's play of philosophical expression
Being Becoming merge as turbulent transparence
She works as a whole embraces numerous tremblings
Spacetime unfolds in teleological and immanent breaths
Emanation from unending activity of nature
Recovered as it enters into history and morality
She recognises herself "fills out" implied existence
Naïveté and sentiment modifies through active intrusion
Immediate context an act of clairvoyance distantly serene.

She sublimates relations between imagination and unresolved conflict
Sensuous basis for intellectual mediation
Problems ever within grasp confronted by transformation
An effigy of the ideal set against the adequate
Involves rejection of tyranny a sway of mercy

Narrative designs given presages of disrupt sequence
A bulwark of enduring meaning posited against transience
Human synthesis play drive conjuncted shape
The path from which no-one has ever returned.

Central to the performance of doubt
Individual plants, their interactions with each other
And even their species composition of the community itself
Is the activity of mycorrhizal fungi, which are
Symbiotically associated to the memory function
With the roots of most land plants.
The loss of arbuscular mycorrhizal fungi biodiversity
Decreases both plant diversity and ecosystem productivity
While increasing ecosystem instability.

She learnt in learning
Herself. That expression of sorrow
Forehead distorted by high thinking
And self discipline so ineffaceable
First sunny childhood
What can she say to sacrifice
All personal desires to obtain
Nobleness her life too easy
A well of water springing.

As she cannot become simple all her life
She extremes division immense destruction
She has joined exactly
In the position of the actions
Knows all the circumstances at a given moment
In her war that exact value
She knows precisely at the moment of employment
Changes that value just as it tests
Felt at a distance alone.

She telescopes her exposition with juxtapositions
Unexpected incongruous good natured capacity to get lost
She fevers outbursts of impatience in a cul-de-sac
There are no further puzzles beyond the opening engine
A surplus of constantly recoverable energy
When perception passed through infinity into gracefulness
Traps participator in present experience and passing time
My doctor she helped me, I could write no more
Her notes take me out of need of recitation.

Driving through wreckage she calls her homeland
The countryside agricultural cities
She burns through living trees burns against
Orange dark sky daytime air crast
Crust of earth break her shorn
In windless her müller bus
As eternity mirror gas trapped in the rebus pane.
Contempt for the world of isolation is not loneliness
Common ground for terror and ideology.

Helicopter taxis flight path from city to city
End to end connecting burn new routes
Past and future conceived in differing modes of now
A loneliness dependent upon others
Challenged in the face of natality and memory
I can't contact what becomes the ethical
A posteriori the event of swallowing
Residence in a nonsubsumptive embrace
Presence from recitation. You can guess the rest.

Sloopy

A celebration an idea of truth
gathers likeness as correspondence
into comprehension with fact wobbles
to decision and as if painting
a peak in application
without attraction renders
knowledge unstable to collapse
know this stabilised
disease by confinement
in a beyond brain atom trap.

Up against the outside
the wall gives
and takes in wind rushes
through pear and apple gates
never an exactness
always in phase.

A guest bright soliton
ghosted in a quasi-one-dimensional
unravelled optical trap
into sinews
dissolved by magnetically tuned
like-that interactions
reread twice in motion nylon
static shock by offset visual potential
on notice-board without spread
singled out an optical tropai
momenergy single focused.

This eye skin has a burr
a textile completion or
a finish which leaves
spacetime between now and
there and then and here
moves in deep breath
absorbs and exhales
without assurance of
which place occludes.

Red wind propels
an assembly beam propagation
shakes axial direction
gruesome for radial confinement.
Slot pelt and a separated pair of cylinders
to dent focused blue-detuned
jouissance end caps propagated
fry shaling in the radial plane
invitations for axial alignment.

Momenergy this
troubled distance
defines the pressure
and gap between us the
garden and its enclosure,
vat of burnt apples
they call knowledge
or experience
outside a war zone.

The eye line the lability of disruption
cut by hair slit memory
but calmed before consolidation
rigor flight synthesised
to pour proteins in neurons lateral
tropai and basal nuclei of amygdala
through heatstore of fear learning
balmed whiskers and sinus hairs
take in hot pectin.

In unseen disconnection
Remembered then and after
noise read as imperfection held onto
visit, that open staleness coded as
untouched without
a new natural hollow
your decision into
openness lit
the blankness my saturance.

Receptor-dense zones on paws represented
as thalamocortical afferent terminals
doped fullerenes and organic
charge-transfer salts
rush light in the free lawn burn bank
intop the oval into the stamped missile sites
onto the badge counter onto the beer bar
give us another give us another
come on then.

The peonies spread
thread merits of a work,
alight, indeed, its level
here then here of form, its inner coherence
a pace, love a
duck
shot on, recognized when outdated
off strains layered sections, articulated fields
to charm illogical shock.

The stigma loosened syntax
and critique precisely
flattens in a responsibility
then to pay for the insurance
missed stance of boneherence
sold conjunctions of coordinated
ability particles in a jammed sandwich
the eventual stuffed against logical ripening
instability. The space moment with internal emptiness.

So it opens as if out
into intersubjectivity, history, utopia
whatever the passion calls for
gives the smell back
in abandoned self to not self
another schnapps anticipates
the next history the petrification and silence of
work mute emblematic sludge coded
by some stuffed idea shoved as subjectivity.

Heat bends into another dialectical fog
away fact liquidised in the spin
shawl of a manufactured garden
then represented
restores vert as beaten unconscious
as a faint another fervour of illusion
positron trapped in what is pushed
and shifts on grasped
outing through completed experience reflected.

Named quasi-sensuous quasi-this that drastic
against the epistemological refusal to allow
anger phials without radioactive glow or fork tubes
there to rake your brain cells another bed of
beans and buses
homicide and genocide between
person each individual beyond individual and
what number does genocide begin or its metonym
we ask who and get ripped get reburnt rewelted repicturesqued.

Slop

The Burglar effect
holds light a moment
less than a millisecond
robbed of love
blowing clover and the falling rain
entanglement with mythical forms
of multiple experience
ancient shields scoured of rust
into an old pot-lid
liberated from ritual and cult

Her garment was so bright and wondrous sheene
That my fraile wit cannot devize to what
It to compare, nor finde like stuffe to that,
From her unhastie beast she did alight,
And on the grasses her daintie limbes did lay
In secret shadow, farre from all mens sight:

Laboured to render myself useless
entangled by logical fallacy
that delight in giddiness
count it a bondage to fix a truth
which judge itself
teaches that inquiry
of love-making
enjoying that truth a sovereign
knowledge that too much amorous affection
quits both riches and wisdom
of no computer programme whatsoever

Things combined, halved, interchanged,
connected
in preparation for nuclear attack
that great persons had need to borrow
other opinions to think themselves happy
He judges by his own feeling, cannot find it
but if he thinks with himself
what other placed moments
would fain be as he holds

The Seraph of Peace from fury had fled
The room in which the interrogation
as opposed to torture
to be conducted defines coercion
The colours of walls,
ceilings, rugs, furniture
should not be startling
should be free of distractions, Pictures
should be missing

identities presence absence
page as
  installation space
                      timed
talk and composition
where good is prescribed
  privileged time
      spaced
from left margin

The mixture in the City
solemn, silent, sterile,
bogus, provocative, inactive,
very expensive
unsure which is which
counterpoised
spontaneous, shameless, fertile,
ordered, arduous, active, love offers
grave serenity and peace as much as sexual and felt

Then he holds happiness
as it were by report
when he finds the contrary within
he lifts the first that finds his own grief
and last to find his own faults
where parts and signs of goodness are many
his gracious touch
and courteous to the Stranger
shows he is citizen of the world.

Spin and momentum coupled
in spin-orbit
ultrafast optical techniques to spatiotemporal
resolve spin dynamics
in strained gallium arsenside and
indium gallium arsenside
epitaxial layers unexpected
observation of spin splits
arise from strain in semiconductor films

His heart not an island cut off but
joins to other continents
compassionate towards
the affliction of others
shows his heart
wounded itself when it gives balm
tasked to discover connections and their expansion
dangers no more light
if they seem light

Sensations vary and appear to
duplicate or repeat
experiences link memory to these
sensations and finds difference
and similarity
whether to renew experience or
repeat it as likely as new
experience at each perception facility
to memorate spacetime with internal gorse

Trapped inside phase-coherence,
two pulses inject the control
results in absorbance of a signal field and
storage of a quantum state of the signal.
The suppression of noise
vital to avoid decoherence,
even tiny amounts of stationary light
introduce large nonlinear
effects

Every medicine an innovation
hard to speak with truth and untruth together
in a few words, Whoever delighted in solitude
either wild or a god where natural or secret hatred
towards society is savage unless out of a love
and desire to sequester his own high conversation
where solitude in a crowd produces without love
and friends are scattered needed only in misery
aperspectively to make visibility

Contemporaneity of the future
difference of dry light to his drenched affections
a councel given by others and
his own flattery
Friendship offers peace in affection
support of judgement
twin desires in a body
a body confined once with a typewriter
and ideas of politics in another.

Slow Drag

'The Glory of Albion is tarnishd with shame'
—William Blake

An accountant presses light
switches the projector
a *Last Judgement*
on screen takes his tongue
out of his cheek, watches
auditorium eyes to avoid envy.

It is too late
to take the image seriously
genetic modification
already scattered
there can be no wash out

When telomerase performs maintenance
of chromosome ends
by reversal transcription,
engineers call this negentropy or
an immortality, repressed in human soma.
This enzyme produced as

a tumour marker
in oncology diagnostics,
becomes activity analysed
and evaluated using
Telomeric repeat amplification protocol,
a technique for sensitive detection.

This Real-time Quantitative Trap gave
opportunity to further evaluate telomerase
activity to recognise false-positive
results direct from reaction kinetics.
They observed two kinds of results,
a rapid increase of signal from the outset

of Polymerase Chain Reactions in both channels
from partial degradation of
ampliflour primers by
inappropriate DNA polymerase

and primer-dimer formation
during later Polymerase cycles.

'You didn't understand what I just said.'
'I'm sorry.' 'That's not what I meant. You couldn't
have understood what I just said.' 'I know—I meant
excuse me, but how can you presume to know what
I understood? How could you?' 'That's what I mean,
you were sorry. How could you not be?'

His photograph burns me always
conditional continues change never
absolute or autonomous,
and stylised in its way of informing in
what it recalls of collects snapshots
and postcards something

out of a newspaper, catches, or seems
relevant to a thought, accumulation and arrangement,
translated into an archive, becomes a work of
grid of images, fugue-like repetition
elevates the subject, abstracts it into calligraphic
sequences a network of readings

rewrites the emphasis on chance and
ephemera of Fluxus, the indexical procedures
of Conceptual Art, the relish for the common
place, or descended the staircase in the nude,
Still Life and studies of Baader Meinhof,
an immutable mountain,

a grid, coolly rationalised
into nothing but itself
an autonomous mark returns
the repressed, representations of,
blurred and indistinct
collective memory,

epistemological inquiry,
pocket of a revolutionary cinema
a lived reality, investigation
procedures of that picturing,
into imaginary
exhibition, traces potential installations.

Internal consistency enveloped the bazaar
a revival of allegory
as explicit challenge
the palimpsest reification
of quantum theory usurps
each reading to and from
each version of what experience.

Interest in the undecidable
part of the overall project
paradigm shift
marked by appropriation
and site specificity
torn between dialectics
and deconstruction.

Observation and inference
trapped in the same box
heralded as exactness
a truth bannered on the lawn
in sight of a mower
sharpening steel.

What he presumes as knowledge
wrapped in persuasion
reams and rot collide
butt shades abrupt in starkness in biomass
Real-time techniques propose
a basic value used for judgements,

limited in a plateau phase,
where a threshold cycle occurs in
exponential phases of amplification,
ignorant of cultural spacetimes,
He watches himself
so that quantification is not affected
by any reaction component.

Genetic fallacy to infer
from a prospect
of the razor and antirealistic
to apply to a hypothesis
directed at a beginning
of the universe

that they hold true of it now.

In an unrestricted domain social
choice must work for every some
preference profiles inconsistencies and
incoherent search for adequate restrictions
identified, demanded, easily violated
actual situations

prone to inconsist worry centrality
distributional issues in welfare-economic
probables, vote based procedure
unsuitable to get aggregative index
the interests of the less assertive
cannot but be short in need information.

Then descended a sterner scour
with constant adventure, crescendos burn
Mufflers grief the razor edge and sour
pledge, born and not made, with scorn
beside which files and piles of
destitute reefs belie teem of trauma
where flights and power stir above.

Pailing out the shimmer
with suds in shunt and skim
she spans forth or
loop phones terrific fees
appeasement and this commitment
against a mimetic.

Schematic psychophysical parallelism
can suppose experience becomes directly
of events in particular pieces of matter
neuron events correlated with
somatic events and
events in the world out there.

Informational demands of famine
analysis give an important place
to income deprivation which have more immediacy
and ready usability than the more subtle— and ultimately
more informed distinctions
based on capability comparisons.

Visible signifiers in displayed tracks of ionised
droplets concealed coincidence circuits
constructed of clouds controlled in chambers
by counters, showcase that the majority of events,
emerging from lead plates, are individual
can be numbered and given names.

Photographs, taken by poets and
peasants, or newspaper photographers
not easily seen through,
puts each artist to shame
attracts me
to be so much at the mercy of a thing

when she paints
never a definition characteristic of vision
she blurs
to make everything equally important equally
unimportant perhaps she also blurs out
an excess

we can't rely on the picture of
reality corrected
in accordance with past experience, not
enough for us, we want to know
whether it can all be different, a picture
in different layers, separated by intervals

A laminar flow of air ejected from
between layers, made visible by
smoke curls
up into vortex rings in
real spacetime liquid flows
initially in parallel, get in the way

of each other, lose individuality
give rise to instability of motion
of liquid with fractal structures
turbulated all a sudden in
spatio-temporal chaos applicable
to media in shear flows downstream.

Moats tough stream amaze this visit
Persist precarious word wit has income wing

which prevents wither and instant glance

Peach hues art and countenance
Dry stare and stream and depth and mirth
Rust on spray flight offers strength

Towards silence in blindfolds
Certainty, determined, and unchanged
Expected, light reflects from you
He smiled and released himself in reservation
Now my restful raggedness
Takes away every sense except the explicit

He moves in a kind of oblivion
to the needs of love, thought
curved in a split direction, they
speak about it, a mispoured
glass, a shift, the sun
hurts his eyes less than the

sound of dated keyboard
played in a kind of oblivion
repetition of letter sounds
or plastic persuasions wipe
a wet drip from his eyes as the
clouds shift, becoming a convenience
as he moves in and out the door.

A fielded capability
The fluctuation—dissipation ratio—
an increasing function of slow
frequency embedded
onto deeper properties
of granular materials and other related

non-equilibrium subjects such as traffic
flow, flocking, evolving networks
and turbulence.
As each listener, reader,
and viewer
produces
an informed consciousness.

The extent or minimal needs
for this understanding,
recognition that
this may never be achieved.
Aesthetic production,
produced by receiver and not
an experience of beauty,

Many layers of tremble
the Photographer squeezes button
to capture in palimpsest
a future inscription
on a path of thought
that assaults freedom.

The technician's delay proposes a
rapid formation unified
global states proposes difference
a pressure in deep layers, cell bodies,
with a continuous sheet of neurofil
over each hemisphere.

The Accountant turns off the projector
before the trumpets sound
turns to the listeners
in compact able with margin trace crime
shun mild surd
a metal smelt
ash drifted from shower glow.

Alienated by my own practice
over and over
an open door
experiments, beginnings
estranged from the poetry of others
apellation as a decisive act

Creeping Bent on the allotment counters
love's snares spread everywhere
beneath geese alarms over scaffolding
as an egg breaks, Blue on blue,
the killing machine names it, then
straight through radar grids to a target

I rake a token misery of the wizziness
ash beaten residence
stake a lack honour
restored brisk radio:

shot fear
and shot terror.

Interior manifestation of
aspects of awareness the tempo-
spatial role become transient
texture arranged around my
position inseparable from
persuasive complexity

without compulsion painless
from inducted delight
coupled to a series of
transforms on edges
of recurrence
imagined within.

The Geneticist falls in a tube
compensates
pyrogenetic illusion
He batches with hindsight posed fresh
scratch and pursuer pivot
the phase thetic directs a prurient grief
fuses dead roots and shaded cover

The discussion evolved between stable memory
and reliable communication, between a single trapped
cadmium ion and a quantum decay channel provided by
a single photon emitted spontaneously from cadmium
atom-photon entanglement, implicit before this
early measurement of Bell's idea of inequality

violations in atomic cascade systems
to fluorescence studies in trapped atomic ions.
The photon's polarization entangled
with particular hyperfine ground states
in the de-excited atom. The entanglement
directly verified through

What they loosened on this impious
lot what angled revenge
dependent on success to render irreversible
super imperialism implicit in ideology

burn each expectation
a civilisation based on high wages

precondition for achieving high
distinction between private and government
policy become fuzzy control
over academic training of central
bankers and diplomats
to remove the dimension of reality

think and bind
sanction by fury
fire torment transform
financial independence
derivative of a political and cultural
autonomy that cannot last

All engagements of consciousness
involve an aesthetic component,
reiterate the Listener,
the Reader, the Viewer
involvement with the artefact.

Use and function
rather than success and value
provide the criteria
for assessment of art,
varieties of what these provide
explain aesthetic intention.

Snake Hips

Sleep stolen
obstructive ap
noea
low serotonin
diagnosed in just
ten minutes
different trajectories
made real sustained
relationships with more than
collapsed boundary
she gardens, reads, works
on languages
one thing after
another basket
of currents
He begins to realise
garden and perception
must be metaphorical for
spacetime with contextual growths
abundantly complexed
in her gaze
unalleviated consciousness
of negativity holds
to what better in endurance
before erasure of distinction's
necessity to destabilise.
Sick with love
eternity becomes truth
a fabric of conventions
gift and trap
demonstrable
as constellations.

Knowing self
value to respect another
insinuates into the existent
the other's entirety
an altruism
leads back to itself
a solitude reached in crispation
through suffering

index points to a rectangle
an unnoticed trapdoor.

It didn't feel dangerous enough
I couldn't see
where the freedom was
assertive aggravated
by shyness carried aloft
and plummets.
Torn in integral freedoms
eirenic white boys
talking post-colonial
neural correlates of consciousness
as altruistic punishment
enforces cooperation
turns the camp
into biopolitcal paradigm.

She drops drawings
of circles rectangles
made with the heads and angled legs
of flies on sheets whitened
with insect mucous she
named vomit.
Body parts wrapped in papers packed
with pikke incorporated table of random
numbers collaged sown grids
Klee's limits of understanding
with the bodies of insects sealed
inside shells of nuts
labelled 'necessary entropy'.

She imagines someone
enters her head
to remove parts of
her consciousness
They call for the
artist, as
other from norms
of truth and
judgement set

her signs in positions
of enforced substitution

as if she was an outside
reader incapable
of making head
or tail of strangeness or
wilful misbehaviour
exceptional moment
implacable certitude
the Other
loved.

White egg shells beneath wind
blown red azaleas indicate
shift of design forms
from fragments of living tissue
towards sanctified or over bred
hyperreal shift of
aesthetic apprehension and judgements.

Spinor

Reverse thrust heard
across lake from
behind mountain
indicative of a
storm travels towards
hearers another
spot of rain
on storm edge felt on
an arm before it lifts
to empty a vodka sunshine
flies bring squint
seen and then felt
prepare a scum of oil
respect for indenture and taut song
stains intact.

Lulled into false
expectation
run out of comfort
bin through mud
The Ecologist
Draws foresight scenarios
Fizz lifts weight
Trapped in ice over thousands of years.
fly dizziness distils fuss
mirage intra merrygo
hottest year
since measurement began
The horizon arm
refines thought
about entities and phenomena
stare the many sundrops pavement
importance of benchmark of anthropogenic
climate change climate sensitivity
Intact fear before refusal of violence
thought and infinity a
sponge of universe
systematic exploration of uncertainties
the complex variety of processes
that actually determine climate sensitivity.

In bed the weather man
gives up
the ghost
the fainter burnishes wheel
'a fielded capability'
groove this way and that arm
in his head
strictly imaginary
storm pull anger
the flappable impulses of hafnium dioxide
or strontium titanate shifts
of white light to deep blue
conductivity to insulation
Then she noticed the plant   not carrot
but bachelor's button thriving
in bed of onions and buckwheat
he sits in the corner of the house
rafter thoughts released
bitten
cat whiskers moment
spread in surface warming
predictions dominated by process
uncertainties burned then
wheel strain in scree
the fast departed grip

Local Stunfire   2.31 17.08.04
grooves through at last
other occupants come go
Shang Hai and Kuala Lumpur,
in and out on jets via Heathrow
beneath them pears thud
the lawn around a woodpecker.

In the fruit garden, spurt
then drops beyond
the margin innovation
weight felt
remedy shifts twists
on broken rationale.

Sound of voices from Uyghur and Uzbek
demanding not clearing.
news of floods Cornwall and Bangladesh

shack the horizon
drenched catalpa
papered over wall
centre of the garden just below
blossom all over the path and
dotted shadow line from clothes pegs
turn glisten of damaged daisies
into a sequence torn and push-in
pointed pungent invisible,
he sits in the corner of the house
pin rides in awe wonders
Another part of the same garden
stress recorded marks grass.

Stamping Sequence

The pain shifts the stakes an unrequited memory,
When the spoil & the plunder shall rise on the wave. . .
Burns a strangle holds expression
and deliberate fridge tank pit
Disaffect shove resents being
replaces waste
describes inside shake
muddles peeled marrows with implied foil
Scrolls another life:

Rope out speed dome,
shot spree enraging
fur peg brained through splint
off a drummer louse
robberates share mutual.
Share thrush in antique
the grab it off in stance.

A dish acrid kelp, impounded
fly dismuzzle of sheen mist stance, of spin sheets,
place in glands, muddled.
Fainter frightened the gripe faster the miller seed
A trouble deployment of palette and spill
Bin gilded fame, scotches, stickers
Accordion to the sight
Acrid treatment the debtor
an aberration instant
tread mill in the forehead offered
Carry angst brain shears stumpwork disputes banality.

We work on dangerous rehearsals a
Wild entrance turnstile in the air
from splits in a leap simultaneously
Directed at each other hit
extended legs front and back
during a *grand jeté* center stage
spins in air drops into a duet
as the other two pass on and through.

In contrast nothing more tedious and
unpleasing journeywork, a greater loss
upon each cell, than to be made the perpetual

reader of unchosen books, they that value their
where and when, and their own studies, but
of a sensible nostril should be able
to endure. They proceed from no good
it can do, to the manifest hurt
it causes in being.

Decadence of political sense calls for
reassessment of current managed practices
that any truth has many shapes
manages for improved resilience, incorporates
the role of human activity in shapes

to ecosystems, provides a basis for copes
with uncertainty, future changes
and ecological surprises
a moth diving at me
then saw it was rain thought
it was snow and unravelled for
about two and half seconds, then quickly
through a shift to shift variety realised
and handled everything. It was
just sheer pleasure. Eloquence become
the serious need to shift shape, to know
good things without need to clarity, trip about at command
fall aptly into each other's where and when.

The underwater composer Michel Redolfi of
Le Group de Musique experimentale de Marseille
had stereoscopique glasses, that is 3-D,
included with his record 'Immersion/Pacific
Tubular Waves'. Fryberg's idea,
being patented at the time of this writing,
was to use 3-D to view new photographs of
atomic structure.

J.N. Fuchs in 1825 introduced a method
for an economical production of water-glass,
and a method, subsequently called
stereochromy, for executing murals which,
when dry, would consist of a layer of pigment
bound with silica. Carolee Schneemann began
using 3-M's reflector paint in her work during
1981.

13. Stroll and Strut Step

Stroll

'Pointedly blurring the frame, which more and more painters had started to do by the late 1950s and 1960s, meant bleeding the art work into the outside world; a gesture at risk, from a formalist point of view, of theatricality and other bad tendencies.'

Denise Riley, 2002.

1.

The Painter sat in mobile pavements
through simulated ruins
virtually experienced explosions
through flexible screens
artificial light
individualised.
The Teacher crossed Priory Lane
and felt the heat arrive
in a gel
Spoke aloud to himself
he forgets each blemish
discolours of skin
imagined another set of experiences
felt sure were his
responsibilities.

2.

Selective interactions exploited
to direct assembly after garden statue
smashed and switches, machines, coughs
named as functional structures, juxtapose
isolated rows, clusters and extended networks
as well as more complex multicomponents
alternate use of monolayers
to create preferential binding sites
that accommodate individual targets
combined here to guide assembly,
a network that controls and
templates new phases of sensual smear.
Quantum components are imaged
using scanned gate bias a simulation
applied to surface stimulants
fabricated using praxis-beam technology visible

in topographic image when simulation sufficiently
depletes stimulants from underlying
regime known as 'definition' the device
said to be 'pinched off' as if G-force reaches zero.
Transport becomes ballistic. Charge patterns globally
erased by illuminated red light-
emitted diodes each few seconds.

3.

A quantum hill, in the regime,
defines two short, conductive paths,
to the garden shed, formerly the hut,
connected by a badger trail through clumps of dead

golden rod and bracken in parallel
within the width of the wire.
In the hut they cry to
turn inward away from a world
toward body functions that overwhelm
any ability to process new information,
assuage suffering through pleasure
a dispersed voluptuousness
annihilates their intelligence,
overcomes cognition with an aesthetic
component of consciousness—Yes
precisely the sensation gate—
Yes—locked apart from social interaction—
Yes.

The Burglar confrontation with exactness
held sway in his intuition, his immediate
seeing, in that false concept of a present
trodden by fiction, and distinct from all-at-once
as his body drags through window
abides and remains before entry and
in realised entry a flush-turned face-skin
bloodless then blood-filled in unpaced shudder
contains and rejects simplicity—immutability—
eternity—a crowd-out hamstrung limbo.

4.

Scanned gate arrival of destinations
generates images, biased probes over a quantum wire,
the conductance recorded to determine pixel colour
images highlight regions that determine
soft and hardwired conductance in each brain.
Shifts from red ice applicable to blood flow
redolent in what you mean, enhanced
by what you say or remains unsaid as statement
and function of existence
experienced from outside as
a poignant silence
contained in a vacant subject
occupied by the Burglar looking in.

Existence belled by the extraordinary
the sticky flesh of apricots
surrounded by turbulence
in a rush in thought
she longs for nothing
the path proposed proven to be
longer, more difficult than
expected without cease wonders
about the fox's trap
an intellectual, examined life
uprooted from biology through
labour, work and action,
trapped in a labyrinth of knowledges.

Pear isthmus free ran shoe
a lout fit
Spree fainter breeds through trace tatter act.
Nerve shorn rakedness
Toast fuss stud and report of aberration
fly pure placid interfloods
Rafter free rotation sport
through fuss headhard mistakes.

5.

A simulation of death through
syncopation constitutes an aesthetic

gesture at the level of politics
towards openings the future
forms that extend from the rituals
everyday intimacy to celebrations
in a manifest community
in the forest to encounter another
badger another fox before modernity
burns a coherent insistence
suppression of drum beat suppression
of rain beat suppression of blood beat
rapport based on incorporeal values
in a rise of humble crowd-outs
in love open to ecological sense
opens spacetime with the confinement
of social change
concept and affect sweet
tremors of being here on the walk
happened and rushed back without
returned en route diminished sobriety the
Yes function.

6.

The moment switches isolates
from the world through a reversible
perceptual wall sensory curtain
reconciliation not possible
an entirely different state of existence
a healing ability
the alertness-sleepiness continuum
a complex function of sleep debt, biological
alerting, environmental stimulation
an ability to forget
in what is new is invested our energy
faith in the new
wisdom, memories, sadness, realism
sense of orientation in a world consists
of perennial poles of all feeling

After his long study
the content is less evident to his peers
than the structure; to speak was to pretend
to a grasp denied his peers' uncertainty

may not be inherent in what we say about
what we see, but in the difficulty of knowing
fully enough organisation knowing
how peers perceived meanings as emergent
spurs of connectedness between otherwise isolated
representations.

Thought relies on crowd-out and
cancellation, a principle
of all representation promotes co-existence
of meaning and its metonym
trapped
and at once transformed
into innovation. Affect, she suggests,
in simulation of cathected and released

energies
in both what is taken apart
and intense analysis

Scream agitation

dynamegopolis blank refuge

speech lost journey

blame hungary capital
then blank media coverage
turns returns alone

Flicker light box
under his head
Sun set phased disappearance
body alienated burnt and cold
holds onto linen
Leaves the hut
through the roof
There
a kind of freedom
paid to inflict pain
informal structure
face taped to the window
There
All images dissipated

crackling or eaten
There.

7.

The Teacher's ability to retain myriad
which he reactivates then generates
a sense of mapped self-damage
accounts of ongoing shopping
held active, simultaneous
many bathed images
burgled delivered remade by exchange rates

The environment extends into his being,
a compilation of misprints or specific noises

Water at the drinking risk
of predators, homeostatic sweat
pearls cascade the brow of each victim
as he and she eats a necklace

Words not eligible without pain
Slaves and suspects equally tested
Truth had to be in the first person
the past definite
Admit to anything
in order to breathe.

8.

Assessed her opportunities
from required understanding
of what she wanted
to have and have reason
to value having.

Some idea of freedom
formulated independent of values,
of preferences and reasons,
but appraised with some idea of what
she preferred and has reason to prefer.

Her use of rational assessment to appraise freedom,
depended on reasoned assessment of options.
This idea that freedom accommodates

what makes well-being credible for assessment
and evaluation, a scrutiny of the crowd-out.

9.

Two discrete states
ready or gone off
either set or sprung
diversity reduced to single
state and its absence set
or not set the basis for preliminary
closure provides new outcome
nothing in common between closure
and the circumstances from which
the closure is realised

The aesthetic principle of construction,
a blunt consciousness of joy
primacy of a planned whole over details
and their interconnection in subject's anxiety
montage in the face of perennial unfreedom
whatever unintegrated compressed speed
experience of natural beauty, subordinated
consciousness of freedom and the totality compels
failing coherence of the parts snapshots meaning.

She wanted what constitutes social cooperation
the synergies of productive
manifestations of naked life
They bring a negative limit
and political struggle over
different alternatives of any passage
between aspiration and pain
or the possibilities in the process
from virtual consciousness to
becomes reality an ontology of the possible
history replaced with historicity and
then self-valorised autonomy
To feel the pointed libation from new energies
an irreducible innovation

10.

Under week the preside use of
with the Administration
weapon opaque rust,
in Iraq as long
a clerk not a day more
is depends on

He eats laundered flesh soaked in petrol

to be made about
before a Washington flicker
with ensuing
prevents voiding the

He plummets
and a dozen arrive on top
and hours become days
In a blister bath

11.

An insistence on these juridical shadows
against a drop of world order turns its hinges
charged air in the garden
with hectic and unreal
verbal violence

We were displaced repressed
back from darkness

thought that goes no further than the elements
that make up monologic utterance,
structure of complex sentence
a whole utterance,
the Teacher leaves to the competence of rhetoric and poetics,
lacks any approach to compositional forms of a whole
no direct transition between
the forms of utterance
the forms of its whole
only by makes makes a jump from syntax
arrive at problems of composition.

12.

The Painter's recognition enables
respective aspects of identity and
dignity, brings relations between us
founded upon a form of indirection
or intransitivity

on Should the US get up
structures
absence of a longer time
a civil society
cured by a full complement
anywhere from 50
would form

Taking dawn walks
heavy green marks down the path
to the hut, she notes
pearly turquoise dew
exactly,
where she has to deal
with visual frequency
to be unlocked and articulated
pitched against a narrative tension
to perceive at once conceive

Her being distinctly inseparable
communicative and poetic through
historic deterioration
a meaning reliant on disjuncture
between concepts and words
eyes dazed.

Strut Step

Undermined by his use of
weapons, food and trust,
a clerk stamps feet
before a guarded half-flicker
prevents the morning get up
absence of fidelity
cured by suspicion.
She wills to claim rights,
out of proportion to any will
to meet duties
or reader demands
for recognitions.

The passer-by provides a stranger
with inaccurate
directions
the cleric look and gaze
receives the other into himself
a mistrusted truth out
of active
modernism injected into blind
acceptance all
of-a-sudden at a weak
node once held

by a stream of thread
tensions give
way to a deep crying
understood as a gutter
to strengthen a resolve
to all of quickness
demand duty over impulse
before freedom becomes
another troubled joy
In the rain weed where the ducks
sink shot three times with
their backs turned to camera clean up the
complexity of muscular image.

Bus came at last lost in count of how
many crossed the grass in relief

to the bloom
of irises, like but not actually eternity,
not yet immobilised by order and simplistics
Who eats my dinner, notes the Reader,
Eats me.

Solid phase Modernist synthesis
continues to be hampered
by structural loss a poor
solubility in image production
blocked in horse serum
solubilized biotinylated reagents lift
from a scientific rhetoric applied to
biotin-labeled peptides used as affinity
purification and as fluorescence resonance
energy transfer-based flow cytometry
as well retro-solid-phase immunoassays and
receptor localizers that exploit high modernist's
affinity a strepavidin with its background problem
even when late producers titrate resolves
with a dilution until a moment
when further image completely loses touch
with pain or reality
a continuous separation
of a relatively solid
from a relatively fluid component.

The renouncement
and into orgasm accompanied
by spontaneous resonance
sprung forth involuntarily
from the voice a heightened
syncopation
tarantulised
it protects me from disengagement
from another death
alone uselessly naked,

as if art incorporated permanence
of form in
transient materials a pressure
from competition extremes, modernist
anaesthetic an ideal
in depreciation

of the neighbour exhausted by haste refined
sexual feelings fleet in over fence gleam light.
A war debated in dialectic frenzy.

14. Shedbox

Suzy Q

A version for Tony Ward

1.

Happy implies liberated from lack
weighs heavy upon every dimension
of difference
spacetimes for potential meetings
or listen within
altruistic retribution enforces cooperation
a lack of lack
the moral legitimacy
of sanction in the public good
he's pouting
but this isn't the horizon,
insomnia and compulsive self-dozing
an asceticism of the negative
out of consideration for the other
and from collective good sense.
Sixteen snails move over grass
pass seventeen iris plants their
cells in prepartion for flowers
It's one of those windows adjacent
to a mirror
A rogue walks
towards you passes you
from the other direction
Make up your mind
at your own rate

no rush or weariness.
They are out on a hunt
the men in the group have
hounds and nets,
stakes and balls of string
for traps
She threads on
the span, drops her handmitts
the fine imposed in the incentive condition
actual back-transfers,
"Not to concentrate on a single 'subject'
rather diligent in enquiry of every thing met"
"A question of horizon changes"
complains the Rogue
distribution in favour of the punisher,
decreases altruistic responses

2.

context the punishment
for benefits without engagement
through an altruistic act with an extra turn
She pulled her physical breath back
into herself to
understand its
rush before he
lifted the television
carried it down path
to the hut where
he had fitted a gang plank

Just walkin' the
play plan
exceeded a hedge
trim on a lawn
in front of
a dead catalpa
You burn my back
in your anger
she notes you
Considered as morally legitimate
the discipline effect
burn back into
your self until
you blister
alone in multiplicity
and a tank top
Sanctions not undermined
by altruistic cooperative decline
retribution
serves the punisher's self-interest
used to enforce an unfair payoff.

3.

A Shopper beckons a burn shoe toy
like the Rogue
stoops to crop any commitment
from being inflated string
within quantum measure
in a flower bunch

Because we have the tools
to reach it, we dig
every day after the dust
to a spring cataclysm
a tendency to use the spacetime
freed for more
consumption
A percentage of tripled
investments
significantly lower
Apparent slope of truth
frees the persistent guard on
exist arts yearn
To prevent her parchment design
in the marks of the Shopper.
The Rogue prevents
through beating an eventual resistance
and reveals his fright
out of the privacy of reception
Set the jar of anchovies
specifically
on the shelf beneath
a bottle of Witch Hazel left
of a Benylin crucial
for access in the dark cough.
When the desired
back-transfers are high
or when the desired
back-transfers are low

sanctions intended to deter
undermine altruistic cooperation.
Altruistic motivation sanctions
for the benefit of the group
enhance cooperative behaviour.
Thought becomes discourse
without covet and no succour.
Some agrivated humidity
revealed itself in the water
fell in love with it
trapped in its formation
smoking uttering
mournful
Distinctive and particular sadness
without a melancholy of technology
She thinks of the image
only she can see, and
of which she is silent
Always present, amazed by it
the only image of herself
she wanted to keep in
delightful recognition of
vanity with void
"Pattern recognition,"
he notes, "both a gift and a trap".

Sway Back

1.

An inward grief in destination
loosens distinctive pleasure
Shook strain enamoured by
new born
he trembles with delight
Shot bleary office, complexly flanged.
Gifted to origins
beneath tunnels beyond
        any recognition.
Leapt for verticality
dense in the wall
Thud-beads
A crisis of local clarity
unnoticed in her ascending quiet
She commences rest and stillness
beneath transparent ice
conceals a gram of water
onto the density.

2.

Directions marriage
soil needs of shake and sieve
thought petered around graver
maze and stitch hasp lapses
maximised on split winters through
ham fed attacks
persistent
periodontal flakes bat phrase and
coordination. Straight pain theory
        Fights this shapeliness
sight song, stare over
restitution through burned
vacant assembly, offended rotary
come forth in flakes
happenstance altered mistook to
rely on offended brain slack
resistance for your mitigation
a mis-scripted shout.

3.

The kids on the block
still cutting up
their road maps
in an after image, sour blood.
The wood becomes visually dense
indicative of spring
when it starts to eat my brain
last night cocoa, wine and nicotine.
we get obesity, cancer and liver damage
      in one hit
long live capitalism, exploitation and addiction
one night in the luxurious city
where the brave are.
The marketed flyer disgruntled these
unsaturated greeds
a crude barmy of sage defendants
has reduction expected
interfusing store.

4.

Slanted floor
      shaken
managed a maze then
off aspic uncounted hills and
fatality erectile withers red madder
plunges erosion shack age purchase
a distraction obtuse marrow
fenced reality of meritocracy there
      delusion
tugged hiatus wish
stated and screed, illusion
off these sequel wit articulations
bone stack offal's binside
resides image mirror a
matrix profound flout
strike metre thought petered soul
distant log fries gnomic
screed mud.

Swim

1.

In 2002 he took neurotrophins to mediate
differentiation in the nervous system.
The technicians' attempt to biosynthesise
sensitive to synaptic stimulation.
The Geneticist is ageless.

In a strident wish to hermaphrodise
the Burglar stormed from the screen
A juxtaposition frayed when not ambitious by improvement.

A neurotrophic factor induced hippocampal potentiation—
the best-estimated model for learning and memory.
He became himself 1000 below zero
pranced across laboratory floor
in strobe-light sneakers
opened a sodium channel
impaired his learning behaviour.

Sodium voltage '1.9' best known for its high
expression in peripheral sensory neurons,
led to the suggestion of its involvement
in crack pulse.

That component of human conditions,
exemplified as capture,
mechanised
using tools to transform metal ions,
expressed in pain or aspiration
supported by memory and action.

They screech towards corrupt stance
palladium his stage craft.
Honest racket
bellows in the shrine,
pain scripted in molecular cryptych,
the code for a voltage gate.

She turned to him in the bar
in ultra-violet, appeared to be the same person

repeated the image passed through a door revolving
structured by soda screening.

Redress and strain of mental aberrations
as the Geneticist started laughing.
Sodium voltage '1.9' detected by '*in situ*' hydridization
in virtually every region; cortex, cerebellum,
amygdala, thalamus and hippocampus
connected directly to his system of
sexual reserve.

Burning the State insurrection
at 1000 below nothing
rubbing the toads and tongued numbers
from switching cash with banking cabinets.
Ash spent to express the abjection
waste read to be fable and narrative

Chests becoming tarried shout in the
ultralite defects of the gullet
switch rented burr shift other
and phased his shrine
Shot wedding hasp his true gripe
wire assunder to true austerity.

Hyperthermia and exotic
the phase it stalled his fetch unless
scratches stammer
pace shuttle.

A strobic shrine off meanderng
paces the future slope
shifting thin age freighter crimping
fat 1000 feet up round zero
the thud blisters
strike on barbed wire.

The Geneticist surpasses desire and hopes
hatches the borderline
in mute swing of framings
followed by thunder clear
the smell of vegetation
stretched refulgence.

A topology of catastrophe
Disaggregates edges asks where and when
of the self floats on intolerable significance.

Presses affected temple into the pillow and hand
an intensity of pain
Impossible to tell whether position
can be discussed without beating the wall
or visceral distension
and the substance between them.

Cruelty defined movement
of culture
realised in bodies and
inscribed on them.

In the magnitude of speed a
depth of time eludes
the habitual limitations
result from material resistance
speed expands time in the
instant it contracts space, we
arrive at the negation
of the physical dimension, a
degree of resolution dependent
on the relations between
an object and an observer.
When the boundary conditions
prevent the system from going to equilibrium
it does the next best thing; it goes
to a state of minimum entropy production—
that is, to a state as close to equiibrium as 'possble'.

Throbbing pain
caused by swell of blood
outer cover of brain dura
embedded in vessels and sensitive
nerve fibres release
compounds awaken receptors and
vessels
swell again.

Arrested on suspicion
of planning to steal throws
away shoes each time and carries
a swipe pad impression of prints.

I was looking at the house and
couldn't believe it
tried to imagine
myself
behind
that window, behind
the curtains, trying
to see a bit of the
outside
and suddenly the image
again
from the inside outside from
room to garden.

2.

Ducks cross the pond on a
wall below visible surfaces
watchers think to walk on the water
is a natural phenomenon
experiment
ation
faster
than the
bus

Watch the burden
on your back
pack
Miscount
paving slabs over lapped
with leaves last
summer's discourse
reworking calculus
in the Columbian café
with a fluorescent
marker
in one hand and a

cup of acid
in another
baling out
another migraine

During the process of eating from his can
the Geneticist confirms
a unique type of sodium channel
gated by extracellular ligands rather than by voltage,
a brain-derived neurotrophic factor and the most powerful
endogenous neuroexcitants reported so far,
ready answers delivered on the telly.

All over London
lack of technical knowhow
in one meets
in competence of manners in
another material by
capacity to misorganise spacetime
a veil between
our selves and even
the closest in

timates, blur
us to each
other.

Tensor

Calcium waves carry understanding we call cerebral
time mobilised messengers crunched through chaos functions
mediated by diffusible transport and
gases characteristic of caged sugar
released in flash photolysis and jammed
on a used a spread-sheet-based program
for alignment of overlaps excited
vessels sweetened, shuddered sequences

The meteor shower arrives over the lake
before daybreak before the lightnings
We landed on the sugar around two
without knowledge of Dow Jones or community
yearning
without predictions
There were honey muffins with Cabot cheese
north of the Gulf Stream

Sugar moved to more than 187,000
global convergences echoed
opportunities in a Eurozone
Too late to join the Investor Relation Conference

I take out my pollution handbook
to confirm the GS Trap, purification columns
aligned to marketing pages
innate and adaptive arcs of arms of immune response
tightly controlled by cytokines
orchestrate success with pathogenic events
optimised by floor and rapid visualisation

In the land of the free
the right to execute juveniles
encourage the spread of restraints
shackles, designer chair, hog-tied
It feels like, we're some sort of
vending machine for haunted
self-loathing.

You leave home, travel,
go nuts and then the moment

where you've hunted enough
and you could sit down

Music comes from the body
Spiritual life in physical form
a wondrous rigour over a mirror
scratched an ashtray screech.
Eight fishing ducks pass by
young common mergansers
red cardinals exchange the
contents of a letter
a satisfy commits yearning
Jambaleya and paella
Small Whorled Pogania
beaver dams, large
snapping turtles in toffee and fudge
shorefront parcels wither New Hampshire
conservation casements
All the trails are signed and blazed
No Tree Stands of Any Kind
Permitted, "It's no go John, it's no go
I'm shackled, I'm in a chain gang."

I could talk snare drum sounds for hours
It's a surrender to nature. A plan
where everything falls in situ
The battle is with exhaustion
walked into a shelf of books
Accent indicates the
depth
of fatigue

An instrument to measure gravity's
subtle effects will unearth
The Sugar Cubes perform in Iceland
you comb brush put on
coat and open to meet others
acoustically
admiration for proof
of the sublime
How looking forward and squinting at score
is an important part of the performance
Some unseen voice
they need to hurry

sandbagging a back wall
against the front wall wave shift

The amount of jagged dark line
which then will mark the limits
of squares will be the exact
measure of your unskilfulness
I held a glass in one hand and a
bottle in the other and then concentrated
on the bottle and don't remember the
glass which was still in my head
when I returned them both to a table
without insulation
he reappears out in the open
embodied embedded in his
intake of sugar inversely related
to his environmental obesity
a swept out world sheet
invariant at quantum level
de haut en bas
slow-timed conversations with the Lawyer
a sweet smell of bright Portland stone
trapped in the cryptogram-rebus
make believe in hidden meaning paradise withdrawn

A cat runs from the garden
in a descended fog and
a fox lifts to it
emerges lean and hungry
to sell imitation toys for drugs
you listen to your dogs is all
Story tells you the routes to take
site to site in loss adjusters

What you will find
when change is underway, humankind
fights to remain the same

a fascination senseless repetition
abstraction of a journey
a fossil murmur a triumph
forgetting our amnesia intoxication
I look out into successive perspectives
A different sun rises and falls each window

I turn, red earth, grey granite,
pine woods and cicadas
contrast motor boats
lift 68 degrees from lake sheen
a pest control mediated in noise
Any calm rapidly translates into dig
ital connection Substantial retreat acuities
burn memory a creative moment encourages lack

Trucking

Terrific, without fuss
witless inscription physician
In the discussion of aloneness
he debates with himself inter-
rupted by another
elsewhere
in his being and without

scruple or
excepting the agreeable
days I passed alone
never spent one in
a more pleasant tête-a-tête
than I did
yesterday
Slow boat off and gone
streaks of melody wired
inscribed
The epiphany of exteriority
exposes deficiency of sovereign
interiority of the separated
does not situate
as one part limited
in a totality of
another's potential.

This mystery of fractality
Only in darkness
Hopelessly marooned
in a dark tunnel
Beneath Brixton Hill shakes
the wave concealed
dark mass of great
inflection
immediate
The Pink grew then as double as his Mind
after green lenses.

The rich cubicle's enclosure
with its verdant pasturage and fences
About the time the sun cuts laterally

the western hemisphere
the fugitive crowd.
Practically on pearls
fades storage plays, Shakes snappiness
"I have nothing to say
half my days, in this dark world and wide,
And that one talent which is death to hide,
Lodged with me useless,
To serve therewith, draining
light denied
absurd rage pins and stutters long into preening.

Fits petrified rust
a mystery of trapezes
an exceeding multitude of falling stars
following thoughts to their extreme
Fits a patch stall
whack box
turns into black coals
cast into an unseen abyss
Trying to remember how these rectangular shapes
Became so extraneous and so near
The shells formed enhance structure
frame programmes fried deprivation
How it feels to be outside
and inside at the same time.

The sound of apples thump the lawn
as one values other
people in proportion to
their adherence to the truth,
one admires him most
excepting the agreeable
when he deviates
most from it. In
today's TV, this
difference appears
to have a given character
As I said to my friend
Don't ask me to be there again
The white is too painful.

The concurrency of enclosure and memory
and surrounding dark

scattered in a public, well-lighted place.
By being 'in' the specific tremble
pollarded surroundings
trees the scale of it
flakes lack lustre
Lifts carpet
Inhospital burnt back
frightening incompetent State
waste tension photocropping sense
splits open inscaping eye
Witless fritter bust, froze escamotage
blurs consciousness.
What it is as residential
epiphany,
estate cordonned-off.

The shop-frame
proposed shift of paradise
Flash Flash
in a radio stax
wired to beat wither
principles then that
character must be battled
political principles in the face
of what is happening to
emotional
pressure in
the discussion
of aloneness
ricochet and rident
stings like hell.

The sound of apples interference lawn glass
"If your work goes well
you are comforted, nourished and protected
The sore predicates managed hinge
on the weeze-box
withered radical shocks
The exquisite endoderm
proposes derelict
interference of sequestered
dose shot sinus
astarts limen
in a rotation

To say that you don't know,
if you don't
To see remains a complex matter.

First you work with
thinking, feeling and will
three pots boiling on the stove
then the Critic asks why not
listen to what you say.

Turkey Trot

TURKEY TROT

FIRST STATE
in memoriam Bob Cobbing
1 of 5

To see it simply i? a daisy
She came down ro1 bangs a kid whistling
calls in a focus th of yellow rocks
I pull Brixton
one by one n watts ten times a second
I pull bricks dowrite this
I am the Cleaner cabinet
and my hat takes oright light
just as my brushewith hoses
between hands a greenhouses
the lawyer's officentence predicted on
exchange, the raiidex
I look back at
who I am feel uilding joined
the emptiness. r level with
The sponge is notely vented air locks
but its limits arethes in the popping
You can't see the inate
speaking, I mean ain computer
I'd be spherical. : bells bulleted
Lying on tea-roomMorning & Night is now
ball of energy, fe avern
up and blood of glass gather
filled head. ght.
Violence begins v
to end it.

allen fisher

TURKEY TROT

FIRST STATE
in memoriam Bob Cobbing
2 of 5

Even when we
he is grateful a scurry
without spoile of stairs
left two-store landing
on external : of dogs
The surgeon vement
intimate seathe terraces
of a double ıvenue garden
If we thoug' on radio
we now see
off male fato
Of course vaybe
right the fiılator like
His watch eople
underestim wall
The hot cag bricks
pepper theunderneath
his mouth lves until
whole milunds
heat out :.
of anger.

In such :
three pe
Brixton
call up
on the

allen fisher

TURKEY TROT

FIRST STATE
in memoriam Bob Cobbing
3 of 5

There d is in succession
a flight fall
then a stroyed
A flockerations
hit pa
from t by-pass
Jebb Passed out
lament ond
        ft
salt onunderfoot create
ice, mision and delight
accumtingoes simply hay
Two pito bales out
on the flowers tree tops
breakirright grey cloud
from osing onto clear sky
themseover the windows buried
Bell scinocence's abyss
closuremines, Papuan heads
        k of childhood
        g this community
        another century
        the skin in mud
        crawling the first
        'e then three rabbits
        f nose the traffic
        dless
        doing this?

allen fisher

FIRST STATE
in memoriam Bob Cobbing
4 of 5

TURKEY TROT

My enc are not in love
houses for being loved
are ders to drop the drag
considcy windowless concrete
at 50 vehicular ramp.
on the conducts
walk pches down the barrel
onto pc bogey seven
edge so:t his stretched hand was to greet,
weeds ı it serving to fend
apprehentasy
No flam/e were also
rolled inrst time.
of white finished and smoothed on his elbow
against lated radioactive waste
superimp)mponents on his tongue
moving ‹ back of
in my ir until
Radium :k sours the
some mil
Rebuildin
could be
Soaked to a basket of currencies
coat lost)ple beg outside
lot of wit tube
in front ofAmnesia
seems en(Read-out
why am I

allen fisher

TURKEY TROT

FIRST STATE
in memoriam Bob Cobbing
5 of 5

This morning lisn't easy
Fast aircraft lo'ad in a sponge hat
Stood in shoween another.
loaves of rain
Fourteen milli
I watch you
from a metal
steep rooves in the weather
basket cases s impact an interface
in all those nd
severity of , stock
a revenge ilway carriage.

a support
at the upp
two positi infinite
change cl immeasurable
decontam atoms if someone's
link to n if I'd zero angular momentum
a meal o
all both h floor a
a dark et
14 tons
fossil li
vith each of us

allen fisher

Twist

1.

Interrupt imprecision engages
roars a resting
quiet speeds the
distinguishes many colours my fixed
substance out of tube hurried
crystals mixed beneath sunken statics
stilled ash the same dark
contained
Ideas on the culture dreamed of
dull break a Friend's
blinded the Stainer
factory worker's out of
disease domestic from overall memory
walls random, near-traceless surface.

2.

Their surprise
momentarily held to a point their breakage
tied collectively a trapped
blank soldier
cold instant and camouflaged
moving shutters hang from a pivotal string without dream
unknown calm the field
a past expression of an
excitation
wood, shrimps and whales off the books
Empire logic
structure of rule
invisible internal towards
loss of consciousness without recurrence
Large gold bees
on white blackberry flowers
tightened enclosure repeating
implosion damage
a silent disc singular felt
Pain shared between third and fourth thoracic
and pushed down from the shoulders

inscapes experience
on target administration police force
open oiled invitation
Hear your ownbreath
in a tunnel in your head
runs down
loss interest walks
with stochastic normality.

3.

Static motorflow
somewhere dark inward glance
and clarity given out
Rural is not rural to rubble
point of poverty out
expansion misfits untimed leisure
softens perspires from rods hardwired out of
surrounds away dust releases haphazard multiples
spends pushed out of kilter
inclusion and release
shafted out of straight
static dead stillness
against blind his
emptiness Friend's loss of prevention within
in wait was not
his definite
measureless held
stone out of plastic lifted
your feet comforted blind your particulars.

4.

Energy she gives him
seems an autobiographical intrusion
deflaters tasteless and still
gift complex my
static out
concealed implosion firm and
expansion unbalanced jagged
the roadway out from walk there
a wall for molten redundancy

down take could you
a soothing field full hot
calm she is where static and stays
in your loss
victims of the many thoughtless
without damage you were
without existence
rural to the
flat pedestrian terra firma
artefacts sparsely adult.

5.

Bilberry, alfalfa and spirulina
blended with coconut oil,
cellulose and Co-enzyme Q10
Rural the consequence of shortened culture
Rural into the walk the
switch held responds his
blur negentropic
determined blind innocence short
adult by stake's here
call field energy
released deflates memory

hidden the
pointed enclosure her thought the
jointless
light touch ever right-brained
soft in a
multistepped soon dry a circumnavigates his
Friend unkind to a front pulled-
experience
Approaches his many thoughts
disorganised dark and eternal
Back of the neck Stainer in the
motor beyond
roadway out of static in the
calm heatwave out of sight dullness
toward future
forgotten she's still and alert
exposed solid out of garden up and away from him.

Twisted Camel

Its breezy freeing a stone, button perishes it. recuperative notion. accumulation of well-meant frenzy. aesthetics the result of imperfect fit. newly experienced and previous between parts sensed pattern transposed in spacetime and orientation and with variation in scale. between parts. churn doubt moored in shrewd net by fusing the starts. sun's up and in view. pen injects this. foot sown the shown. refrain. continue uniform bubbles, at atmospheric pressure, remain stable with anticipation for displacement where at least, retreated. sculptured land. one side demonstrates the viscous deformation of glass. the dimmest flash. various bubbles change.

Fir straps sty brain. alignment of neighbours under an external directed stress akin to tetrahedron transfers in flowing glass. prepares. theological and virtuous propensities. irrelevant, button reel desperate. cicadas shot pale serendipities. hot greeting withers word, jet happens. he sees curvature as necessary to connect adjacent vertices and reconciles his short- and long-range needs. the cell faces in groups close around each three-dimen- sional cell, with fewer sides than a hexagon connectedly fills space.

the angle corresponds to a tetrahedral co-ordination of oxygen ions around silicon in a glass sheet—it almost exactly matches the junction of four soap bubbles plashed there by the washing-up and the structure all of it—a frothlike assemblage of pentagons with fewer hexagons and occasional tetragons, more nearly of equal area and with edges of less curvature than in a crystal array. inner shed a done condominium. facile estate call. betting shift shapen in the frame parliament astride in ditch burning burred. circadian rhythms are regulated by a pacemaker, an input, and an output mechanism. The pacemaker drives these rhythms in the suprachiasmatic nuclei of the anterior hypothalamus.

spot. fate scans reach only old tales. speech idealised, labelled. pace beaten a canister other. tossed, sold bias as it offers break shone the lover's key note, paused in phase space, It's night that totes dose shot reccurs in tonights concert. the position of the cells ΔFΔG on the audible area is qualitatively important, and an enumeration of their possible combination is capable of producing a group of well defined terms to which can be applied the concept of entropy and its calculation.

Experiment preset these mounting stone tracks. uncover freshen-up fount. distort beneath fount, rough of fountain. breaks correlate with morphologic transition from simple bowls to complex forms, slump terraces and uplifted peaks, and from complex craters to ringed basins. the rollover and precipitous drop in depths and relaxation may flatten or bury topography. the ice shell's thickness controls exchange between surface and its putative water ocean. a thick shell would be susceptible to solid-state convection and overturn, whereas thin ice would be vulnerable to crack-through and melt-through from below. environmental light/dark entrains the clock by means of retinal-hypothalamic projections.

Some shapes differ from interface-determined shapes until encounter. structure is individual before it becomes aggregate. a sequence of changes already, by definition, a complex structure. manifestation of star spots. the use of niacin, or simply yeast tablets. on the weathered surface of a cast brass door knob or internally in clear ice which has been kept at its melting point (these boundaries on an atomic scale are imperfections in a uniform stacking array). a series of chemical connections form a three-dimensional network of current-carrying tubes, stored inorganic and organic transmitters. before birth a lower level of connectivity responds to sense experience by growth and division while storing more and more ions and transmitters at junctions.

These cells have three variables: mean frequency, mean amplitude, and mean density of the grains. the growth pattern is a memory of an individual's life superimposed on inherited skills, which are integrated. the brain responds to sense experience since it conjures up connections confused by animal reactions. one of these formulates from observation's abstraction. the sphericial density of the grain of a cell ΔFΔG also constitutes a quality which is immediately perceptible, entropy and its calculation could again be applied.

Many perceptions (understood as read). speech normal prevents net understanding's indeterminate reliance on a shift of viewpoints and sequential change of scales of attention awareness involves comparison of thought sensed pattern and a previous awareness formed in brain's physical structure by biology inher- ited and then leant. only a fraction of the atoms converted, the system's superposition state left the moment-series in which these particles are simultaneously atoms and molecules. he imag- ines it is pentagonal readily seen in a three-dimensional froth on his beer and in his fat cells and in the grain of his rusted watch. Started with an atomic condensate and converted into molecules using a laser light trap from the collision interaction between cold atoms. the tolerance for foreign cations depends on the number and distribution of polygons with various numbers of sides and the effect of temperature increases the spread and lowers each package density. the shape of a condensed phase provides steric conditions, repulsive exclusion, for selective interaction with another phase at short range.

Quantum-mechanical interference patterns provided evidence of a coherent quantum superposition between a pair of atoms and the molecular state. an ideal coherence that invoked a return to modernism and its theological restraint. crater morphology derives influence from surface gravity and lithospheric proper- ties. different morphologies can be attributed to compositional and rheological differences. droplets of different sizes and parts of a droplet on a surface have different curvatures and areas implies that the local energy, related to curvature, is everywhere different, faces have different energies and areas. shape and size become mutually dependent, a search for alternatives to coherence. rage of preservative shambles. when ice is constrained, convection proceeds within and thus favours diapirism and can lead to ovoid features and chaos terrains.

Underbelly Jump

1.

Shook the stalkover batter in stark derrange transgressed in a freezed crate.
This gets etched as another unique moment-series when
a new spacetime has been
burnt each now moves into each
metal fibre each fruit skin
another party another rail grip outed
in stench pain-reflection stasis
rapid waters in their passage burn
Oh Happiness! not for individual pain
indifferent existents fetched as other.
Haste well now penetrate vociferation connect coporeal
home   squeeze-controlled out-emitted
  trappiece
    mobile joined nerve-like artful tongue
                                        shaped labours project
brought forth in process of forming
to this place imply absence not a long while from one room to the other
without question to get utterance in search necessary truths also
in person   distinctly listens to separate distinctly
maintained which says that the process of shaping maintains form
and difference in true conditions amid the action of placing in room sited at a
distance to make level air along much confounded truths necessity
and disorder heard together for the duration fly across air in motion.
In consequence traps the sound against the capacity to perceive uneven
remote to recognise difference in speech affected by in search
sited limit in spacetime arrived in confused manner trapped
voice inquires into your gravity.

Such ancient textechoed from Tiber to Yangstean truth and intake poised in a clenched head
to decipher an engineer's ground plansread in etched ice.

2.

Merits of a work, indeed, its level
of form, its inner coherence, love a
duck, recognised when outdated
layered sections, articulated fields
illogical poems, syntax loosened
precisely
in a responsibility to pay for the insurance
of boneherence conjuntions of coordinated
particles in a jammed sandwich
stuffed against logical ripening

In motion by offset all-seen potential without spreading
the optical tropai single focused red-detuned laser
beam propagated axial direction for radial confinement
and a separated pair of cylinders focused blue-detuned
end caps propagated in the radial plane, for axial confinement
the lability of disruption memory
before consolidation synthesised
proteins in neuronslateral and basal nuclei of amygdala
store of fear learning

A gap between introduction of action and
the effect in the form of action, freedom
of the will proposed as evolutionary advantage
until application to global warmth
subsequent to energy bursts for action
or coherence of attention in complicity
with dialectics encouragement of dysfunction
a rationality engenders violence
an anticipatory skill with strategy as a base
for dynamic generation of narrative syntax.

Whiskers and sinus hairs on the snout
receptor-dense zones on paws represented
as thalamocortical afferent terminals
doped fullerenes and organic
charge-transfer salts
rush light in the free lawn burn bank
intop the oval into the stamped missile sites
onto the badge counter onto the beer bar
give us another give us another
come on then, simulation of death

as syncopated political gesture
at the level of aestheics tuned
toward openings increased absence
of saturations encounter another frozen animal
another repressed poet on an edge of weakness
pulls us into real art value as political substance
marketed in sentimental identities support for repression
countered by mutual relationship independent give and receive
and return without damage friend to yourself, thanks Gillian
    Rose, emotions
and inconsistencies which do not consciously intend or desire.

A fried root ash correscoped
with fasces wobbles in applied
attraction renders unstable to collapse
stabilised by confinement
in atom trap
bright soliton in a quasi-one-dimensional
optical grab by magnetically tuned
interactions.

3.

Animals towards the hominid edge
of an evolutionary shuttle resort
to inflicts injury and death other species
and their own. Predatory behaviour
of sustenance complicit in a war machine
or choose to eat locally
instead of oil burn
signs a global footprint
with laser electronics
compact discs and web access
the necessary components of
complicity in the meat
killed for me in the daily
delivery from another's starvation
the agreement to bandage each
torturer's legalised welt
each aestheticised wound irrespective of social life.

So it opens as if out
into intersubjectivity, history, utopia

whatever the parson calls for
give him his nose back
in abandoned self to not self
another schnapps anticipates
the next history the petrification and silence of
work mute emblematic sludge coded
by some stuffed idea shoved as subjectivity
well shove it into another dialectical fog
liquidised in the spin of a manufactured garden
represented as beaten unconscious.

4.

Evolution of the human neocortex
complicity in usurped dialectic
in desire in embrace
with leisure the idea of truth
as a simple correspondence
a progression from a reptilian limbic
system to protect civilians by abandment
language cohered into subjective
intent, you can feel the satisfaction,
direct harm to particular combatants
in a tripartite structure, the amygdala
control of aggression response
initiated by endocrine poetics
a physical rhetoricity or
shock easy interchange
of tools and weapons where
every artifact contains within it
an explosive potential where
the battlefield a junk heap of objects
and weapons that deploy themselves.

Another fervent of illusion trapped in what is pushed
on him grasped through completed experience reflected
named quasi-sensuous quasi-this that drastic
against the epistemological refusal to allow
anger phials without radioactive glow or fork tubes
there to rake your brain cells another bed of
beans and buses
homicide and genocide between
person each individual beyond individual and

what number does genocide begin or its metonym
we ask who and get ripped get reburnt rewelted repicturesqued.

Another estimate of socio-economic treads
over the coarse necessity
uncertain highly subjected
decadal-mean data are smoothed
scaling factors estimated used
standard optimal fingerprinting
modified to account sampling noise
model-simulate signals intra-ensembled
differences used to define optimisation
control run into your civilian death strategy
on a diplomatic sheet used
for uncertainty analysis
sourced in future nature
a distribution of possible forecasts of natural
climate change prang-generated by variance.

Vole

1.

There was once a town . . .
the intellectual reality
of a root-tree
where life seemed
a strange blight
in binary logic harmony
with its surroundings
a syntagmatic model
disrupted the idea of garden
a city street
criteria exacted as reportability
without coherent row
shred-multiplies assumption.

A burglar hastens to disorder,
a self-condemning look,
arrested at a touch dock.
Fugitive!
no baggage . . . no friends accompany adieux
simply moths and rust
in the midst of Paradise, Good night
several times descended by way of a trap-door,
announces opening of
a pocket filled with gunpowder
charged with laudanum
"In no Paradise myself,
I am impatient of all misery
without madness, how does she do it
without the spin of a shroud out of herself?
Get these traps out of sight.
The meeting of hands, eyes fastened,
tears the glue,
a foolproof test to distinguish truth
from falsehood, probability is enough,

things have to get done.
Paradise becomes a
private area
beyond the control of law or public opinion.

Enjoyment of activity enslaves
but no action binds the self,
in its multiplicity its freedom.
Free will, like a plowing neighbour,
needs the distinction between
good and bad, a blacksmith maintains,
welds to the notion of cause
a because, in relation to moral action,
an acquired responsibility
that demands
accountable spacetime.

2.

The Blacksmith knows she must do something,
knows she can
because she comprehends her freedom
without need to cohere it.
She feels obliged from a law which she legislates.
"My need for dignity need not
derive from reason. I choose its being."
She at least hopes for the possibility
of improvement, stands
in the garden and proposes a pond.
It is a moment of coherence and hiatus
that postulates connection
and change
where contract
between individual and common good
becomes necessity
in a knowledge of alternatives.
Her freedom signals a position to shape
the character of where she digs.
She brings compatibility without strain
to cohere or call forth an angel,
free to have the will she wants,
wants a civitas.
The demand is for reference
to the welfare of the community
merged in a joint stock company of
freedom and determinism.
A shrill of echoing distinctions
speed up

not completely under the control of another
able to care for each other and whose welfare
depends on each other's freely chosen action
constitute a good before the door bangs.
The Blacksmith achieves freedom,
self-determination,
articulates her being as part of nature,
an enhanced self-understanding,
without reduction to sensible spontaneity.
She dredges her humanity to distinguish
the useful from the proven.
The duration wherein she acts

becomes a duration wherein her states
melt into each other.
The intimate nature of this action
becomes a discussion of human freedom,
oh yeah, hold on!

3.

The Moorman uses nonlinear analysis
to examine recorded succession
compares this with dynamics parameterised
with field data predicts an agitation that resembles
observation of boreal rodent populations.
This apparency of mutual chaos
consists with the results of
the analysis of directed succession.
The amplitude of the Moorman's observed
vole fluctuations somewhat greater than,
stochasticly interrupted, that predicted.
Hold on!

Each object's information demands
deaccession, broken egg shells
to analyse connection residues between
pesticides and eggshell thinning.
Regardless of the angle of incidence
a particle leaves in a vertical direction
slowed eventually turned down
by gravity above limited in motion
by a mirror beneath trapped

in stepped increases
jumped from a moment of austerity—

daisies on the lawn
illuminate a row
of new crocus shoots
wishing you the compliments
recovers a sense
of the coming season
Intelligible freedom versus forgery
to discard perfection
and account for responsibility
in place of composition
demands justice
spellbound at recollection
speaks of "equal rights"
an *accessory* of it
wants to get away
has not yet superiority
or numbness irresponsible and

no business
the menagerie a gravitational
privilege of not being
or an automaton centre within itself
demanding peripheral intelligence
that iron bars can be profitable
animal-trainers not afraid
of terrible means is presupposition
"freedom" at the risk of choosing wrongly
a picture of the world in which
a critique of morality
frees functions of first *insight*
juxtaposes multiplicity
a geographical relativity
of judgements against obligation,
eyes leaning on the tv whilst reading
against legality, against the compulsion to
happiness a consequence of rodent
fitness the result of self-direction
the drive called resistance the measure
of freedom as positive capital
the degree of *power*
that the one or the other should exercise

experiment in self-overcoming
emergence to exceptional actions
a positive hesitantly achieved, terrible as fake
to prevent a governed whole
And to what end raised and trained?
The urge to self-sufficiency,
simplifies, distinguishes,
make unambiguous
a preference for surface beavers.

4.

Actions are partly indeterminate to
which becoming clings to distinct moments, condensed
matter digested into movements of
response passed through the meshes
of natural necessity, free from the particular
rhythm which grades the flow in such a
way that sensible qualities, in memory-perception,
particulate aspects of a successive reality.
You'd expect our willings were
"more
obstinate
by being oppos'd"
as if spacetime
dominated the proceeds
of search because
each occasion
is first of all
a search for truth, a
premeditated decision
in advance of the good
oblivious to
truth's implicit nostalgia
Beneath a sewer
live kids discuss
potential of
matches of moving visual media
with performance of text
misread into their own gullibility
dismissal of community use
in a pretence of its celebration.

They watch the collision again
and watch account of is repetition
in a pie chart, a Boltzmann truth
a prediction of text before it is read
eyes glue balled in a rodent sharpness
quicker than fox call
with less smell and wile
in which self-destruct is
superseded or given narrative
intention, rows of calculated pronouns
and implicit actions, forward
or more cunning
surprised around the corner
by every spelling era
every swing of the camera
in mobile seat tracks

on the motorway on the
video belt off limits
voice of a stomach pump
dialectic coherence, bless them,
The marked distinction between light as substance
and degrees of freedom remains but he
does not remember this threshold opposition
of the inextended and extended notions
of freedom intimately organised with necessity.
What the Burglar takes from substance
the perceptions on which it feeds they become
movements flick in and away nietzschered
in revelations or mistakes steeped with
expectations of a future freedom.

Volespin

Flew from my bike
sunset breaks are
lilac crimson gold
semicircles of petals beneath
dahlias with 12 inch blossoms
Severed raw hymns
Simply fragrance
Frozen refuse, A
root canal connection
to pH of
bacterial population
Sitting in the garden
is wonderful we are
surrounded by pears and
hedge sirens, motor roars and bees
everyone talks of rest
here but it seems very
busy, open in discourse
of freedom and truth
an analysis of pain.
Mesmerised desire escapes here
where gravity
theatre introduced another dappled
medley, take the cedar out
from a centre of
the contemplation's garden
storm field,William Blake takes a tracing
grinds it to his head pain
and irritation redefined in
a row of alternative solutions.
I open my mobile
to connect me to another
plan. Blake holds an apple
when it starts to rain
a shower of golden coins
full of plastic they are a sign
of making the connection another narrative
burning its trail of beans and buses
before the cloud
shifts another crowd-out give
me air! another

breath.
Begin construction begin formality
with a reliance on where
spade into a soil mix
of clay and sandstones
patches of root growth,
and decomposed animal.
Behind choices strings
sheened
a gardener
proves weariness above the choice raft
showers a seed spray into the earth torns.
Watch the responses to light there
she hesitates, then crumps
rainfall into crevices
dry burnt there in sunshine
the creation of new presence, a refreshed humanity.

My eyes started to water.
I smelt a sweet fruity odour
and thought it was harmless
tears of pectin,
the pinching of two singularities
pushed through my eye lids
caught in a tear trap.
I smelt a kind of phosgene,
did not think it strong enough
to hurt me.
Noticed a second smell
and was slow to departing
then spewed it off
as a form of trap out
to make correct probability judgements
a faculty of direct intuition
into relations among concepts.
A truth statement about degrees of confirmation
as a matter of rules linked to language.

You can wash your clothes
but you can't wash your lungs.
I hear the all-clear sounded
and again change my apparent self.
All-clear signals are regarded, here,
as purely local.

Entanglement rested
upon potentiality
in a damaged expectation.
Short of an epic truth,
that is according to the laws of that principle
by which a series of actions
of the external
hereabouts
and of intelligent and ethical beings
is being calculated to excite
the sympathy of succeeding generations
of humankind,
clouds of mind
discharge a collective lightning
as if freedom were
knowledge of necessity
with a lack of civic call.
What gets said
in a garden surrounded
by hedges
trapped there and losing health.

Wind bends Templeton cedar
in the breath garden
eight sided molecules
of air
burn my face.
Enough of this,
echoed,
Enough!
I held breath, well
what is probably held there
implicit in potentiality
checked by approximations of agreement
and frequencies of outcomes, seeds a
conflict between proposed actualities
of potentialities and appearances,
where all interpretations agree
in conceiving a complete state
to assign definite truth values
simultaneously to larger sets of projections
referred to as hidden in variable crowdouts.
Mushrooms push away tarmac
from path soil reveal

cycle tracks around rose beds
learning ends when
ruins repair
by regained knowledge
that we may
possess true vertue
so when the exact truth
or nature of things
is more carefully
investigated, testimony has
a very meagre force.
It remains to be shocked
the impossibility to recover
probability distributions
felt frailty in lost grip on
entangled systems
unless determinants for truth values
are appraised in recoveries of
consciousness beam stopped and
startled in contextual rapid crowdouts
a beyond what we are
in localities of knowledge
that require
observer-free formulations.

A moorman stakes out the run
to the rubbish tip
sieves soil over the trap
and numbers his plot.
After my action for some time
become accustomed to noise.
Amazed at the number
and variety of smells, tastes,
in a city coming from drains,
factories, shops, cooking,
and animal streets.
Ten traps arise from this diversity
of chemicals.
The nose inexact and quickly
suffers fatigue.
Milton rubs his thumb
over the edge of his watch
feels the weight of its tick
in his palm.

Entanglement
a consequence of superposition
the eternity space for the composite
a tensor product space
that prevents analysis.
The Moorman states it clearly, "The average
mass density is the quantity appropriate
to describe the world,
summarised by the statevector
of individual physical traps."
The Physicist notes, "You must identify something
as being really there; as distinct
from the many mathematical concepts
that you can easily devise.
We must decide that some things are really there
and that we are going to take them seriously."
Suddenly I am led to an interpretation
that microproperties must be expressed
in terms of macroscopic traces
and that this is accessible
through the mass density function
and the dynamics of such lead me
to take it seriously as really out there.
Stressing an importance of a distinction
between physical reality and
something more general
leaves vagueness, crowd-outs refutation.
As if experience provided evidence
for being instead of mental
aberration
with potentials for agreement
among different sayers, stable
concatenations of impressions and affectations
in different sensory modes,
a cluster of coherences
populated by objects you think you see,
depth and precision appearances,
postulated microentities and
physical laws gathering frames of confirmation.
I thought I had imaginitis
and did not put my box of tricks
on in the afternoon.
The trap-maker peels back the glister with what he mists air with.
Sweet sprays of breath lift her blood glucose

The wet burns that sear his heart's cistern
wither balms of realist birds present in his cage.
Formaldehyde troughs rid us of coarse pinches
Whether thirst alighted dull span she speeds
from thirst from his sight, towards tremors of showers
History's seams on each disturbance, each free shot bower,
melancholy's fiat, steady before swerves mutter
blister withdrawals, fragment this furtive mirth
sprung on caskets, beaten shared rushes.
Rafts over showers and sweet the coming on
pleases the apple top, the blossom's realisation,
Of grateful evening mild, but no more quiet
more like repetition and tumours.
The bird man sells his songs and sore throat,
until juiced in horror or debt.
Screeds engender a hastened, startled brain;
what the Burglar could prevent, his sleep explains and gives courage,
but neither breath on the mirror, where he intends
a deliberate innocence, walks over the ice
with calm and early song, nor a shattered glass
as if its crystals brokered his energy for numbness.
For this frightful set of connections remain done,
a trommeled selection.The Moorman switches
a listening device, without scent or damp.

If the Moorman worries about
independence of his feelings from his will
this is not evident.
To have remember'd
not to taste that fruit crippling freedom
in which he possessed himself in the
experience of his embodiment precisely
because it entailed the feelings of possession
of his own body, or its reflection,
so that what consciousness
becomes for him
basis for a fusion of synchronic two-way interactions
between periphery and inside.
A shopping list that included imaginary goods
Stopped short by in disbelief faced with
concepts of nonlocality, to the Moorman a pantopy
where all objects, that have once
interacted, are still connected,
where the present trapped,

but not sustained, stems from
an abandonment of truth in a realist drain condition
and the first response replodes a strain gauge,
an independent crowd-out to survive,
what the Moorman called, the rather dirty work.
A storm hung over the High Road as I wheeled
my bike up the walkway for repair.

The Moorman cuts ice, makes
a rigorous distinction between the individual
as a natural specimen and the concept
of individuality with the status
of an ideological-semiotic superstructure.

Waddle

1.

I focus on a bridge form
as it moves
releases pinches releases
pylons lift in sunlight from grassland
catch sky base a range of cloud shapes
cirrus interrupted by striations
A figure embraces and unfolds in rhythm
it could be a bird, trapped to the ground
attempts to free from this instructs its
unseen other in operation beyond view
Gender unspecific but questions are raised
regard for freedom
About situation
between edges of perception, now
reaches between strata:
a state of uplift:
a new freedom.
This celebrates an increase in existents
a multiple self, enhances embrace.

2.

In simulated light surveillance I lift
heat coil and appear alienated
up from a bird screech marked by wing beats
Listen up, an overhead
pours a neon spread pathway
shut against an actual road
serpentine from animal wander
felt pushed in the back lost footing,
stammered, loose metal bushes burn
exactness and expectation. Dice clenched, apparency,
return in to light shafts
recorded in blind stripes or
exhausted definition in measured speed
Somehow, it's difficult to know,
I prove my shell metal mossed wrath
vivify flight indoctrination
through hector lime hash robbery's guise.

Ponderous eruption
shakes London
Named in laws of interaction
break them
Named jubilance and speak of joy and worry,
a net released and tightened, a sparrow chick
simulates flight in fledged flurry
on gutter edge
capital's main street the Banker
sharpens his steel it skins a chance replaced
his finesse. Can you imagine his loss
shaken. The Banker chances with
his speculation
"free to arrest transcendence" stolen in conscience,
cell wrapped and
unwrapped stingray
Beaver's ontology
condemned to be free
without value judgements
authenticities.

3.

Who the I is confuses the narrative
tossed in translation
eroded her language like a kid
with a trick
this common individual
the inert limit
of freedom
In keeping with my intention
maintenance of close relations
between ideal and real measurements
now a collective observation
in which decoherence occurs. For as long
as the struggle lasts, always
to others that the very contingency
of events and the qualified freedom
of individuals express the conflict itself
always possible to put an end to it
a sort of comportment necessary
an individual pleroma, imagined
virtuality, normative and catalytic,
gratuitous play, ascetic

expressions of sadness, joy, love
in very limited particulars

4.

always the historic and circumstantial
result of conditions outside
the domain of knowledge
to get away from it
and destroy it where
freedom includes
the decision
to be miserable.
The Banker
studies complicated
by extreme variation
in substitution rates
between sites the
consequence of parallel mutations
difficulties in estimations of
genetic distance
Constantly before the reader
an accidentality of any
surface stricture
chosen as realisation
of underlying thought
told spelled tould
to rhyme with would.

5.

the discrepancy a prediction error
demonstrated by observation
that learning is blocked
a dreadful state of misery
may overtake the
in uncertain hope of annihilation
simple temporal contiguity
between stimulus and reinforcer
Presentations of surprise generate
positive prediction errors
encoded neuronal messages modify

synaptic connection in snares
of reason, absoluteness and knowledge
the decision to be
in misery
made by someone else.

Watusi

In Memoriam
Barry MacSweeney and Doug Oliver

5.i

We are dying in April showers
falsehood of sweet options
The geneticist joins us for lunch
The garden is rosy
I can smell metal
lift from the bleach dew
surrounded in bitterness
even though I am the spinner, whose
music willing did mask
with spacetime talk, in rested weeds
odorant one
a new breed of men and
women spend their measured
meal counting
between one and two in the afternoon
36 people walked
past the bus stop.

4.i

Tired of walking marks
the reader reaches dizziness
energy and position exchange values
experience distinguished from information
an international convention to return a stolen
mesh of organic and abstract
economic products
commodity and
peddled possessions
wandered at random,
debated as an order,
"in a congealed state"
the imagined petrified
"substitutable", in Fit
theory, a personal relation to things,

1.i

The Inspector lifted her glass emptied it,
I simply wanted to label the axons, it was only,
The Geneticist ordered more cocktails,
coincidental that cell bodies become involved.
Weren't you using a modified gene trap?
When I trapped my first gene I used a
placental alkaline phosphatase, produced
I was very taken by the recognition,
a bicistronic[1] transcript from the enhancer
two encoded proteins.
Using these traps you can identify
gene functions in the brain.

1.ii

You have to accept an element of risk.
Well, in the process of introducing transgenic markers
the genes began to mutate. Obviously you
balance uncertainty with a confidence curve.
You can compare this to economic conditions
The vague fear of the unknown doesn't help.
knowledge of recombinant DNA has put the scares about,
broader social problems,

1.iii

taboo and classification systems proposed by the Anthropologist
transformed into biological pollution.
The Inspector checked her watch,You can calculate
the risks within acceptable margins of error.
This need to experience
the ideas of a work as they exist in the work
ever-prepared to apply a systematic interpretation

1.iv

the tropology of the argument
in a locality under authority
The good outnumbered and everything for sale

love truth justice
stripped naked in courtesy and beauty
afraid and released from mere dependence
on speculation, Truth finally
not simple but tied to reward
Conscience's insistence upon complexity
The seat of impetuosity organised
in familiar grooves of self-interest,
given this opportunity, preys upon itself.

4.ii

released as criminal offence
through spurious adaptation to realistic needs
denotated as "thing"—
without truth
dominated with colour
without locality
an expansive illusion isomorphic with cosmos
persuaded that we can't make a difference
attached to things
the sheer quantity of the specific
due to an inside
antagonist to the self
dream cabinet, opposing diodes
revolving in a box.

5.ii

When taste brings death
and the wall is smashed
genetically modified or simply cloned
a sinking music on a sacred top
spins inspiration like is was truth
united
with reed of burlap
how the head long and birth
rosy in dawn shop
delays the float
the oracle of a narrator's
smear-guided flight
indicator synaloepha[2]

followed by a draught
This compromise and talk down
beckons wrath. She begins to
question this. Her balm starts switching

6.i

Offended by reliance on measurement
a contrast of quantum-field and symmetry
unification at a scale too large to study
held beneath pigmented tension
I was not in the garden
but heard a thrush cracking snail shells
the constant beat larger than the time of flight
a question of locality discussed in phase space
in face of contradictions resulting from measurement
without influence of orientation some
mechanical predictions impossible to mimic
by realistic street occasions
grains sinking to the base of a coffee

2.i

The International Human Genome Sequencing Consortium used a hierarchical mapping and sequencing strategy to construct the working draft of the human genome. This clone-based approach involves generating an overlapping series of clones that covers the entire genome. Each clone 'fingerprinted' on the basis of the pattern of fragments generated by restriction enzyme digestion. Clones selected for shotgun sequencing and the whole genome sequence reconstructed by map-guided assembly of overlapping clone sequences.
At the time of the pilot phase the sequencing efforts were renewed to develop clone-based maps covering specific regions of the genome.
To construct these regional maps, we screened artificial chromosome clones for sequence-tagged site markers,

2.iii

Techno-inauthenticity signals
orgiastic return encourages
indifference boredom the demonic

levels irreplaceable response of self
reliance localised misunderstands
individual as a role, not a person
persona, not existence
one speechless carriage
filled with sounds of departure

2.iv

goodness given
"dissymmetry of the gift that is also death"
subjects receivers as law
another kind of death
irreplaceability confined
from the site of death
calls to responsibility
"No one can die . . . . . in my place."

2.ii

fingerprinted the positive clones, integrated them into the existing maps, and selected the largest, intact clones with minimal overlap for sequencing.
In three years, to keep pace with the ramping up of the sequencing effort, the ongoing efforts to construct the whole-genome bacterial artificial chromosome map were increased approximately tenfold. This map allowed the integration of a range of data, including fluorescence *in situ* hybridisation cytogenetic clone localisations, landmark data, obtained by polymerase chain reaction and hybridisation screening, clones from other libraries with associated map data, and working draft and finished clone sequence and associated electronic polymerase chain reaction landmarks.
Together, the human genome clone map and the anchored sequence map provide synergistic resources for future analysis.

6.ii

glued to internal consciousness—visible
photons in selected in breath cascades
multiply-connected visible light
from birefringent[3] crystal balls

predict two output channels and an adjustable
orientation, a scheme in which settings are changed
during flight, and consequent locality partly realised
in practice instead replace each polariser
with a system involving a random periodic switch
to significantly violate distance and levels of confidence
influences faster than thought allowing separate
parts of the free will become entangled
deeply felt physical existence somewhat a non-local
aloneness and without tangible proof.

5.iii

gate of a stair well
near do well
create share bell flick from dimmer switch
breaks the lead a pitch
of a night top
of the stair's falls ebb
shock at a stare gate
of the light trap
flicker in brain sight
green yellow to blue light
orange lilac to red
damson shed
ripens juice in the heat
                                        reddens sheet
"Stop it!"
The Painter turns to the others

5.iv

In morning pink striations lift
proceed and dew us
in a switch from dream
levitated and warm breath
on trees in window and a stream
flicker of light and wings
in distance call sounds amazed
as she rested from love in array
looked on the *Primavera* dawn
and on the opposite wall

surfing towards flowerfall
lifts head to speech
"What's going on?" she asks
Shared boldness admonishes her,
disrupts ascesis[4] and
diegesic[5] representation encased in
a third-person narrative

3.i

A general virtualisation
without conscience sustains
the aesthetic of disappearance
a science of truth removal
without momenergy's particularity
an endless back-fed
telescoped advice in acceleration.
Abuse deemed absent without
universal gravity's pursuit of limit-performance.
Loss of local time cancels
any reality of distance
a substitution that mobilises
destruction of cultures and geography,
a local exterior to all
in situ, precisely localised.

3.ii

In accumulated wealth
in speed its concentration
reduces distances from temporal compressions
to tele-surveillance spread
a soft stupor enumerated in
victims of reversal
a noisier foolishness where
flowers bloom among radioactive fire engines
kinetosis[6] for traveller-voyeurs
in preparation for instant transmission—weightlessness
—I can no longer walk
back on my feet at high speed
I can't hug or see light my
embrace and eyesight devour each other.

4.iii

Substitutability persists relates
distance and enlivened order
Materials and how he thought them
inexplicably intertangled
in place through connection
his ecological niche
liberated from single location

4.iv

promotes a social set-up the
site hovering over a range of edges
bundled kinesthetic situation
in fields of perceptions solved
altogether through walking
more important than locality a
punctuated equilibrium
records this onto film.

3.iii

A process of substitution placed
affect in self-consuming gunfire
a discourse from definity[7] of place
acquired rationalisms
of knowledge and ratio
without bend frozen process
typology of before renewed
in representation scattered over
visible surfactant unfolds
on mortuary ground
exclusion of existential relation to
what this becomes through saying it

3.iv

then scansion contrasted to paratactic
delight not surprise hence
a calculus of possible coordinates

analyses situation
miniaturised complexity fudged,
it is enough to fix the image
as paradigm, reiteration that it
happened, a gesture of setting aside
rifted lapse of an ecstasy
without identity
hidden inside a system
invincible summation.

5.v

Now enforce a far unfitter rasp,
For clones burn to change my open needs,
and rave out of nights and
Gentleman's Relish paraded sleep
in long silence
too smashed, the sacred regiment
to raise the ground in leaves of
dull tongue
fetter the wars and loves moralised
as song
rendered inexcusable
in prolepsis[8]
the warning signs
and flesh yield
pulls as they clone
to spark through song
our tendered pants
out throws the cited mode.

Winging Step

Initial engagement recorded risk in London commerce
a recognition of damage perhaps simply fragmentation
dimensions recorded in exhaust gas and tiredness
given shape in air moved
the narrative takes rein specifies location on a road
encounter with a second tarmacker
abrupted into syntax and narrative journey simultaneous with
natural phenomena juxtaposed rail tracks crabs of colour.
A following engagement named discipline and context
then specific quest and spacetime
linked back into initial risk and at a county boundary
traps and ideas of eternity or
the movement of a müller over glass
and in a garden focussed
followed by a return to the second engagement.
A new initiative locks in with specific semiotics
chains onto a shift of meaning
notes troat artificiality
and its natural semantic parallel
crossed with further record of damage
in rationalised details.
Again initiative clocks in as imaginative
memory of self in the image
trapped in London commerce
with a sense of helplessness.

A momentary sheen from complexity unfastens
relieves a pressure
undermines history
intertraced with added memory.
Rhetoric held in deluded appearance of natural images
the possible absence of representational tropes
superimposed orders, the riflemen cross the border
permits multiplication of represented object
implies a series riflemen cross the border.
An enveloping sheen, gossamer egg
a paranomasis braided to
mimesis and metaphor
a diachronic pattern of narrative discourse
usurped by radicals injected by machines
Another record of explosion or gun fire

as if randomly spotted
across a graph of moving trail lines
in a witness box, on a geiger check, by the self.
The Painter skate boards a range of chemistry boxes
posts a range of letters.

Tendency to perceive connected regions
uniform image properties
different from the neutron trap
luminance, colour, texture,
motion and disparity
stops responses
adapts, but retinal blood not
perceived sees what she expects
experience on the basis of edge information
lost focus, reception dependence
shape largely invariant over similarity transformations
underlie internal representation
conscious perception of texture segregation
requires attention
suggests expectation
as an important component of inattention's blindness.
From the middle of the enclosure
clipped hedges and a fountain
air craft and sirens dependent
on personal meaningfulness of extra stimulus
a kind of attentional blink
perceived viewpoint remains
non-conscious process to the level
of memory.

The trapping region fills
with isotropically pure helium
in a cupronickel tube. A cold
beam passes through a series of
teflon windows, collimated
by a boron carbide ring, and
into the trapping region gets absorbed
by a beam stop. The trapping field
created by an assembly
of superconducting magnets continue to be
confined by quadruple racetrack constructions.

Switches from one object to another
incur additional cost
do not attribute to distance
a number of disconnected spatial regions
at the sametime attention split
among multiple objects
at different levels of her visual system.
A direct association cluster
printed colour word and sound of colour name
between colour itself and the naming
A logic of relation
between brain and consciousness
a supervenience in which conscious events
require corresponding neural activity
without relational structures she does not
experience different colours as more closely related
than shapes. Her expression of red
could be completely different from
the Burglar's attention to corresponding
internal experiences that arise from
viewing the same modified plant forms
"We were up," the mobile noted,
"I don't study objects but the relations
between them."The emergent complexed
neurons firing as low as 35 hertz
and as high as 75 correlate their
brain activity of visual consciousness.

More material than the Painter can possibly
cope with each moment she
visualises a recalcitrant fact
rises out of confrontation with this
to break it up and
make a further effort again
and again several until something
not in the surface looks
somehow in imaginative grasp
consciousness immersed in activity
that she may not wake up from
to reinvent herself enters
the room knowing she is away
in another country a different trap
attempts to keep innocence
to avoid dilution of the world

noticing what no one else has paid attention to
as surprising as a new species of lizard
incoherent experience caught in coherence
conveys new sensation of proportion or connection
early in the morning
incessant burning
200 sketches blazing in preparation
for anyone to warm from
integrated to its background
in revulsion for what she did before
a geometrical diagram
richness and sadness transformed into
subtlety and joy.

It gets easy to manipulate
the parameters used in sequence
interpreted without knowhow.
Resistance reflected in music
the exploitation of already existents
a defiance, profound horror of society
signs of irrational exuberance
strong growth in money supply
a rise investment share
widening current account deficit
personal sector plunging
into deficit
all indicators flashing red
soft landings never seem
in reach a combination
of further rises in interest
rates falling dollar
the left hand revolves around
irregular ostinato defies
sense of pulse the right
plays increases quirky
figuration above this
switch between quite different
materials meaning generated
by juxtaposition dissolves occurs
instead of a cut
material developed off-camera
well-equipped *ingenios*
investment before completion ready
for operation at least eighty or

a hundred men at once set
up a mill *trapiche* to crush
canes pressed sweet syrup after
extraction from *cunyayya* lever press
turned a steady wheel around
old chain pumps the artifice
of oppression. In tobacco terms
a *cachimba* becomes *cachimbo*
contempt for a humble plant
puffing smoke-stack set against
need to buy slaves, experts and
skills for mills, boils, refinery,
capital to *manificar* the sugar
money enough to induce
departure from a history of death.

Ripped apart stars and gas suck
simply adds up the masses dead
quasars in neighbourhood calculates
energy equivalent of mass
from formula multiplies
efficiency factor do the
sums, the total energy
radiated by quasars
turns larger than accounts.
Recurrent intense headaches
visual and gastrointes
tinal disturbances characterises
attack conversations between
friends reveal friendly follows
different patterns a one-at-a
time overlaps speed avoids
hedge against personal issues
shared matched conversational
floor incompleteness paid up
dream of single formality
the untenable meta-narrative
incompleteness result absolutely
undecidable infinity surpass
powers of finesse a new
consciousness.Tame and medicine
pursued the melot bites off his testicles
throws them in front of the hunters
escapes reforms bites and is

unclean. This badger in rocky places
scrapes and digs
against spines against deceits
and robberies torn inside
cage-traps baited and caught on the border
between Ross and Hereford
the pro-cull zone caught and shot,
A comparison of left edges on
autoradiograph image
and corresponding gel
computer-assisted drawing
represents match section
on filter paper with gel.
On the basis of blot results
one *badger*, four *hare*
sites, three *hind* sites,
nine *hedgehog* sites present in
human genomic DNA
amplification product.
Spatial organisation develops
targeted sampling uses
standard immunostaining,
fluorescence microscopy and
digital image analysis to
scrutinise cell surface
molecule expression performed
on intact monolayer and results
in cellular intensity
distributes reflect spatial
heterogeneity in adhesion
molecule expression returns
rifle to his holster lights a fag.

The image obtained upon scan
inverted to give a more normal
looking image, the nucleotides
appeared as dark bands on a
light ground.The Rifleman
set the upper and lower limits.
Proximity to most intense inverted
band against intensity background.
Image then exported to other
manipulation the badger on its
hind legs revealing its loss of genitals

for printing and labelling.
Phosphor storage erasing screen
by visible light in a linear
fashion, with adequate erasure
needing five minutes.
Visualisation of amplification
a finger print profile and rough
measure for the specifics of complexity
where a higher degree of speed
is supported by a rise in asset prices
and an equity correction likely to
give a larger economic impact
starts to beat the drum too early
for world fiscal stimulus
do not believe a hard landing
is inevitable a shelf of plans
ready for temporary fiscal going
beyond automatic stabilisers.
Sugar at 470 showed 9.1 increase.
Real and abstract form inwardly
equal. No definable difference
between emotional significance of
a chord and the formal relationship
of the chord to other notes in the work
the dissonance and symbolism related
and do not mean or signify each other.
Easy to manipulate the parameters
used in sequence interruption
without knowhow of programming
the production of diagrams
show distribution of change,
hydrophobic, hydrophilic, antigenic,
propensity to form
different types of structure
along the sequence.

The original building design
in the shape of an X to
maximise natural light.
A reliance on physical infrastructure
food not found in a cafeteria
subsidised prices and electronic
cohesion. Many small buildings
for smaller groups to encounter

co-workers in daily routine.
Virtually all offices the same
furnishings and dimensions such
that struggles were sitting and
thinking that included hierarchy
a *Biosphere 2* self-sufficiency
instead of a health club or child-care
four weeks paid leave, business and
life built upon successful mediocracy
and how to get the most out of ordinary folks.

Unused mental band width a waste
set against genetic maps posted on ceiling
massively parallel until the
good programmer sought to work
with others in the same field
capacity on a thesis of
n minus one in a situation
of growth to underline message
that we cannot understand
the coordinates of quantum escape
breath and gravity.
The human body, bridge and tree
all alike in constant struggle
for balance between unceased
attack and defence of gravity
a condition of nondisappearance
as a whole toward the Earth
centre supplemented by a condition
of balance of each part of the
structure of interaction forces.
Action on the human structure
weight as a force keeps them
on the surface digging and many
a hard bump holds individual
parts as the head sits and ribs hang
the pelvis is braced. A knowhow
of weights transferred one to the other.
Feel the sharp tuberosites the
ischia in relation to the end of the
spine and thigh points.
The animal faces the rifle in a
deep-seated growl or hiss which
serves to lower its centre of gravity

frees its structures for active
forward movement.The sound
of "sssss" continued and valued
in slow and lazy hiss
without break employs
deep throat and body-wall
muscles lengthens the thoracic
cavity and ribs become closed
inward and downward and the
circumferential border of
the diaphragm with them.
Sugar 401 down 3 per cent.
The central nervous system
vulnerable to ischaemia
downregulated by endogenous
mechanisms in hibernation
resist hypoxic attacks in
a sleep organised to celebrate winter.

Democracy could only be made
in phased spacetime.
The Rifleman raises his sights
promotes a mysticism of fixed time
where the shilling in your head and the
two bob in your pocket never meet.
The experience on robbery controls
hope in a self-conscious anthropo
morphism without analysis the
badger confronts the rifle in a cage
as the chemistry destroys grey cells
turns them cadmium orange and red in
a black explosion, an organised
disassembly in the garden of love
tomb-stones where flowers should
in black gounds the riflemen
walk their rounds
binding with briars
Blake's joys and desires
vomiting poison.
The marksman's reflex
undergoes learning when
there is persistent retinal slip.
Flocculus signals the brain stem with
feedback visual motion

neurons announce learning need
feedback of image target velocity
minus eye velocity provides
negative signals to allow adjustment
as the Rifleman tracks target.
A copy of the motor signal
the efference-copy information
goes from the brain stem to
the cerebellum. During target
acquisition this signal builds up
maintains a positive feedback memory
as the slip velocity goes to zero.

The Rifleman continues to track,
stable vestibulo-ocular flex
achieved by adjusts feed forward
inputs to the cerebellum cancel
the positive feedback copy
syntax and semantics overlap.
The introduction in 1990
of phagemid vectors in combination
with wild-type helperphage made it
possible to construct a hybrid destroyer.
Shot-gun cloning displays of
ligand-binding domains of prokaryotic
receptors approach 100% correct clones
without any prior knowledge of the receptor.

Wobble

1.

Helicopter streetscreech lawnrain
a city obscured by a nation
Image of city   a source of value
one in front of the other, crowd-out, a process of grouping
Aboriginal authorities pulled from ancestral dead
native land, mother tongue
Stretching beneath pressed care breeds to authentic critique.
Theatres of strain invigorate furriers.
A facility to draw a laced tied cummerbund.
I started to remember, to respect, the miserable
"Were you dreaming just now?"
Commitment to justice and then the earthly
Occipital lobes register vision reload pattern
Erkenntnis opposes self-preservation, factures distress in burns.
Twelve pumpkin seeds a day to stave off prostate cancer
A mind's violence to landscape through appropriating a correspondence
a sherbet meander   entrained aesthesia
luminance, colour, texture, motion, disparity
". . . wring their barriers in bursts of fear or rage."
Art operated against nature and for reason
composed of an extremely large number of degrees of freedom
Love of land and language
replace love of fellow citizens
tunnel shrieks in confusion.
To be young, healthy and employable
was a kind of paradise
Purple incendiary disgust of vision.
Production in stable trap an energy capture system
mistaken tropes intend sector preventions
A whole sponsored energy-expending ergotropic triangle
a bodily self, a dream self, a self in deep sleep
looking in pan of a water
even now the body is blind.

2.

Freedom now the shoddy his kind.
locking-in pain offers shorter
self-organisation become structural development
driven algorithms cut across both search and consistency
shaken topos bends vector permissions
on the agreement that RNA and protein evolved together.
Perpetual sensory discussion of vision. First principle
that torture is organised violence.
trammels reek in consciousness.
Traces of land beneath damage
inscribe the citizens' garden
Both the tilt energy and the barrier at zero-tilt vary on site.
Sight apprehends materials and partly precludes where we are.
And all to spare to spill that spend shall another.
experience of shape and colour on the basis of edge
assertive leapiness in contained aestivation
Sells a post-obit to a moneylender named Starling.
Used Chinese radish to remove accumulated fatty deposits.
But words also function as vectors manifest in turns.
The balance quite delicate, a tendency to jump levels of energy
Commissure to junction and bent nerve ends
sleep's new combinations of hormones and messengers
"I started to dismember, to dissect, the visual experience
grouped into isolated bundles
inner aspects of a hand without fingers
conceptual sensations distortion of vision
nieve hand, smothers sung
original priorities pulled from sestinal said
from image and edge map to grouping and parsing
Imagine the pity a false economy
a pity scorched by predation
Above figure of Amitabh Buddha sound of drillvibration.

3.

Hormones shift treeleaves in rustlewind
spit scored by snails
Management slipping   a coarse ergonomics
where expectation contributes to inattentional blindness
impinged periodicities scrawled for obsessional plaid
nerve habit smudges strung
out stretches from band width lingers
perpetual installations reporting decision
gouged onto isochores and burnt
You have to deal with visual frequency.
a jolt of panic in the face of peril
Commodity functions spent verve rends
focal discharge into anterior temporal lobe access to the amygdala
Free from cratylic delusions.
Cholesterol and bile acid bound to excreted oat fibres
Waits 9 years after notice to develop 360 acres of the lands.
Alertness-sleepiness continuum as a function of sleep debt
unperceived direction to the level of meaning
Singest with vois memorial in the shade
There can be no truly credible semblance
In the absence of coherence, degeneracy lifted.
mowed the lawn, spiked the ground, killed the foxes
plantains lifted between concrete
tropolises a break in consciousness. Second principle
Positive intervention through attention and sustained support
Perpetual sensory discussion of vision
Progressive cooling out-of equilibrium in kinetic traps.
scriven algebra cuts x,y underneath Descartes' portrait
blue calls forth orange, purple reaches for yellow, green follows red
insidious void, arid and a trap
protected by the glass
Descried notation estimates trauma.

4.

Smeared rotation levitates schema
projected through transparency
inside to avoid acrid anatropy, a state of arousal lifted
by norepinephrine, dopamine and amino acids in mid-brain
The urgent exercise of freedom to destroy representations of freedom.
Holistic compromise to optimise continuous operation.
An ability to draw embraced by everyone. Third principle:
The creation of a containing environment for survivors.
"Getting a breath of fresh air" leads to authentic technique.
an ingestion of mucilages from the seeds of ribwort
rolled out on the grass, breathed in, cicatrised
Flux becomes a proper basis to describe the dynamics.
casts doubt on my ability to competence and constructive ability
Cleaned off with water and with porous sponges.
illumination produced similar hue and saturation values on the edge
Conscious of environment, a millisecond later totally blind
"Lay weaving on the tissue of my dream"
his head on a pillow of mung bean husks to reduce heat
epistemology cleansed of aberrant reference
acetylcholine pivots the quantity and qualities of consciousness
Community brunches pentimento swerve sheds
homeostatic sleep's independence from the bio-clock
the task of disentangling different pigments of violet
chalked out by gouache or blurred by linseed oil
persistent performance disporting derision
the fragility of memory about the unbearable
Fourth and Fifth principles: to reawaken inner strengths; and
and give testimony in a place where memories are thought important.
blue edges of a shadow from a shutter on a yellow wall
Behave Yourself, in a constant sense of emergency a
spliff scored by sales of newsdata
a small moth hits the light bulb descends vertically.

Woodpecker

1.

Some humbler attendant of my understanding
the rate at which we rotate limits
to a series of set values and not continuous range
the pleasant gratifications of a luxurious city
a Placeness different from embracing weather
Spacetime's tool to breed method in air
a particular place a certain inward effect
differentiates representation by likeness from chance
Vexed chores display tragacanth shrub of vine tomatoes
the sublimation of passion, a narrow skylight
positioned above the easel, extends the width of the studio
a breeze throated in wealth. Richmond.

A tiger leaps the wall to catch a water-rail
a long-scattered score of broken processes
sentiment free of instinctive report units
this asceticism of the negative
enthusiasm I felt that day its origin in the future
the harmony of mutually divergent things
            that kind of muddle
constructed out of experience in the presence of place
a lability of long-term memory at
each recall modified and reconsolidated
tears filled me a suppuration all the long day
my heart full of a tremulous inner spacetime
a friendship derived from instant intimacy
announce a fall regained to trick stammering bereavement
Some humbler attendant of my understanding
negative spacetime as potential meeting within me
envenomed traces from rays that strike
Stalked agreement to share careerman's site
marked on local maps with a purplish blotch
the lineaments of the body express a diversity of passion
Shift the toadstool showers stenched with spores.

2.

She entered a fluorescent, timed air
shot with gene-coated gold particles
knowing in transition does not to abide
held by ligare in the cut ring of the plasmid
sporzando duties
amid roots in the cork sway
liberating subjectivity from lack of culture
abstraction as a method, landscape experience as source

rails and wires gleamed like so many traps
the possibility that we might be organised in
hitherto unsuspected avenues of gravity
Join'd to the prattle of the purling rills

An itinerary of procedures in the form of recipe
the scents of an Eden's mulberry
hair upon the Horses the Leaves upon the Trees.
the real visible and tangible promotes the problem of consciousness
that each of us constructs projects it into a further construction
Precarious descent of Roehampton Lane
experience a fund for spacetime's properties
nervous excitement in which idle speculation chases

devices discreetly play white noise mask window
vibrations picked by laser-based eaves dropper scans
Fraught by twinges in position
torn against a random pleiotropic effect
the gravitational pull of oblivion
Bright pink walls, *The Haywain*
arousing spleen to administer vapour
on circuit through viable purchasers
a care frayed to pen
A pleasing land of drowsy-head
in strident disbelief read
photocopy of an antique map.

3.

It is a question of changing the horizon itself
the fish gene did not work in the tomato
until a promoter with a flag was included
a street in Italy set against a plastic frog
emulsion of tubercular bean sprout phage
to stake out shifts between gas and solid
registered by the sounds of burning acids
the whole process of gene expression

Anxiety for knowing, for the beautiful and good
promotes a confusion of time without space
Glistens in a waste of regeneration
This far suffering concealment
dispelled wonders from a constructed posterity
polished copper, glass, chrome, plasticised wood
and the Stones and Gravel upon the road
station to station in a wireless embrace
a false consciousness of timid objects
The time chosen early morning before Sunrise
transcribed into a single-stranded molecule
simulation energised with poly-adenylation

horizontal bands of wood chrome buttons
The smooth returning flow of epanalepsis and epanodos
Rent in perturbance and re-sorted clones
A fall fastened and penned
Drawn in fragility and combustible
A warning
In each quiver of line each breakage
the copiousness of merismus within merismus
Pour fleece and fronds
Storm in fragility and combustible to
a gather clocked and screened
marble aggregates table tops and floor

4.

In a quest for chasing and haranguing the self
on a map in suspended animation
            that kind of fudge
north of an exclusion zone, “the night bar”
Does it really matter what we die of ?
passaged in snow ash bleats beyond strain
contours intertwined, sometimes through each other
an inscribed wall of plaster hung on the surface
The factual concealment and configured purism
enthusiasm I felt that day
infra-sound of the trochaic conundrum
deplored this sheen of taste
become active in the “quiet” DNA
An enclosure inside the enclosure beginning to burst
Taste, a myriad intruding nose and eyes
rotating with continual range
Bent into the risk of a scud before wind
Simulates permission to cross concrete and gravel
shifting views of the same location
exquisite posing of similarity against variety
in a poignantly negative reprise
Acoustic torch a message without signs
Lace rimes fool to feed mesmerise care
Anamorphic shoes tread gas where
the soul remains unnumbered unmeasured
she knows influx without worry if its lead
a broken mirage in toasted air
distinct, indivisible preoccupations
analysis of new samples of weight
studs in boot base confirm marked out space
turquoise, maroon, cream wall blanks
a still-life, a chrome and neon ‘R’
in the midst of the town, the feeling of being self-sufficient.

X-Buckle

Born a designer from inarticulate creativity
Intimate connections to imaginative life
The ephemeral and intangible of the spoken
Screeches on complexity as if obstructive
A precision of relationships that counted
Preparation coupled to working in particular ways
A contingency on narrative trap his balance the blue
weight of blossom on sunken catalpa
Fresh and unexpected simplicity without serif

The school does not belittle this specialist
messenger unconditioned by considerations of spacetime inscription on rock face garden wall
Necessities for craft insufficient for art
A matter of instants straight after saturated blue

Drawing a way of thinking, a form of thought
Made conscious through art
Sediments crushed between tar and feet
Visual aspects of weight and movement
spring against the left to right reading roles
Emotion, imagination and cognition within recollections

"Extirpation of mere printers' errors"
A new insincerity, a new variety of bad taste

Subdivisions sprung to tension boundaries.

Controlled by the images of things
attendant rights formulated by each individual work
leaded through an intuitive logic of oppositions

These permanent conference situations
A complete self-consciousness in a process of dissing
"interrupting voice's addition to continuous narrative

"conjoining preformed elements and adjusting boundaries
Not entirely ephemeral or material
etched cedar awash in rainfall
Visual forces across passive horizontals
Immediacy of sensations through a sense of sight.

Reality is the earth
detached with a cap of invisibility,
Edges of page or frame
the place where brain and universe meet
Meditation as rhetorical process and product
Made complete by arguing civic being and identity
Orthopractice for the invention of meditation
By unlocked powerful lines which zigzag.

demand each moment in a longer process plans for a future
Almost no idea of what things really look like
gravity of newsprint on granite steps
Subdivisions benefit different units
A great bell clapper swung in slow arcs
Gathers connects to meditating upon
The constructing of ideas rather than having them
contemptuous first beams of the Sun, seen above Horizon
Invention, disposition, style, memory, delivery

to go "synchronically and contextually showing the boundaries".
entomic scatter and irretention   Two distinct beauties
reflections undisturbed mirrorpool
Thought, creativity and economics addressed in freedom
engagement of spacefelt attentions
Balance between ease and order
A line indicated by a sudden bend
bunched type placed on blank sheets
marks of touch in a flystorm

Change begins in the way we think
The rhythm of a line
full round of clappers in a bell funnel
The necessity of complexities' grid
Rhetorical excesses and unbridled violence
held-back eloquent speech *ex tempore*
Resistance to movement
A creation of textual pattern

From left and top a sequence.

Torn documents announce liberty, fraternity, equity
Experience inertia's resistance
hands in geological time spread
Hone the aesthetic aspects

Blue pitched against the narrative skin
Proportionate change in spatial alignment
Timed between elements the vehicle for syntax

How much longer will people continue to believe
Dullness and melancholia in relation to colour
To analyse the stretch of situation—
Form, weight, size, texture and direction
In a storage of diverse materials
As one Age falls another rises
Repeated again and in Animals Vegetables Minerals
Charged against its background
Optimum solution effective on its own

Raw and chaotic to the point of melting
In relation to the inclination to the edge of a plane
Vertigo sentence prolonged anticipation
Refines, loops back, myriad demands
community you have to deal with visual frequency.
Regard and joy characterise aesthetic judgement
A synergy required to develop and realise idea.

"Strictly nonlinear frames of reference"
Melting in terms of love
energy unlocked and articulated

Communicating through the body.
The distance at which enchantment begins
Thought become physical feeling
"I hear the ruin of all spacetime all shattered glass"
contractile structure evaluates design intertwines with emotion

breath held in teethpain latchwork
Succeeds when consciousness returns by an ecstasy
Fountain spills in sound of nightfires   the difficulty
Not only creating the concept you have seen, but
How they do their work and from their faces understand.

Yanayallow

"a combination of the use of language and the subject"

1.

discontinuity in narrative method
observed polyphonic structure

the controlled manipulation of entanglement
experiments involve quantum control of charged
atoms confined in a trap and vacuum
manipulated by laser pulses
'horizontal' line of action persistently tested
against vertical co-ordinates
superimposed upon source agitated in design a variety of
processes calls
into question linguistic procedures,
contrasts in formal terms with what preceded the principles
of an individual
through examinations
of various selves

special correlation in the composite quantum systems
retains entanglement's constituent parts

to gain preparations anticipates themes images abandons apparent
gains of selfhood through
writing it in processual interaction and distance
in oscillations of difficulty,
emblems of self-contradictory
confusion over the rubble
beneath new,
"but it's not exactly where I am

2.

shifting weight from protagonist
and history to loss of direction or need on many
buses, extinguished faculties set against her

★

body a misconstrued value responded to

★

a controlled logic gate between a pair of quantum bits
precise state-preparation and readout, high-quality memory
already reliable, taken for granted ion-trap technology
misfortune as asserted dignity to avoid
despair the impact of changed experience
associated with narrative challenges an

★

image of self traveller through eternity moral
and intellectual

★

The method is to apply an oscillating force to the unbalanced
trapped ion pair
"and they oscillate slightly towards and away from each other
dignity despair at what he
might become poetic procedures to intense
scrutiny his own life against images of what himself becomes
never actually a
private matter, disturbance and disproportion
single phases in the larger structure of plans and plots
beyond levels of text,
"upon the sad and serious discourse"

★

3.

impact of images or suddenness
to reverse annihilation
when the ions are prepared in a superposition of
states, the net effect is to entangle them, because the
final quantum phase of each depends on the other

★

imaginative intensities of momenta adumbrated
renewal of pain
where repetition indicates outline in process of construction,
painful patterns of repetition,
half-perceived regularity
in image against confusion,

★

while the force is acting to and fro the energy
of the positions are different from half the energy of the state
"I speak only what it appeares to us without doors,
the image of a tree made emblem
for stability and deceit, civilisation and courtesy,

inner significance judged
from a vision
of penitents in premonition of paradise,
grasped absence and presence, a promise of health
a phase gate logically equivalent to the 'controlled NOT'
renewed pain named solace

"till better cause be declared, and I am confident"

★

4.

or an attempt at evasion in suicide,
each step of bread through the conditions of history
that I should clasp myself a little while

in speech lock
and unlock so gently how to
deal with shape
the quantum logic operation determined purely
by area of the loop traced in position-momentum
space, and not by its shape

the status and trust in language
ineffable tropos of Paradise

a performative and implicit critique of narrative
peaches in gravity
thought trapped personality
in archaic coherence

"shifts of gravity in solemn patterns"
from scientific expression
disentangled from its enclosure its part realised
cross-referenced images
made part emblem
then roadrun tears of things
a violation
on which the Technologist depends
constrained to defend himself
a screened disappointed intelligence

"I fear me barbarous, or rather scarce to be exampled

★

5.

among any Barbarians"
or such slip fluid loss of common voice
the quantum state of the ion pair is translated around a
loop in position-momentum space, as the relative
phase between the ion and laser oscillations changes
a deliberate decision to
unexampled composition
in gravitational variety
a dismissal of direct access to neurons
deprived of olfactional preference
the oscillated force generated
by a pair of counter-propagated beams
directed at the ions,

★

style affected by critique of truth

★

the responses to affirmation

★

raises what poetry does

★

raw sense made meaning
a mechanism to enable isolation

"Celebration of restraint
an exuberant growth of frontal and
temporal lobes provides
self-consciousness
activities dissolve reform change in relation to entrap
others stretch forth to change any proposal of a
self known by action the roars of reception
blend the intricate a cupped ear affordance

momentary ploy from the brain through the
body
how patterns intention towards an external lead
to assimilation of meaning formed strengthened
weakened or deleted through learning.

"that a paid army should for no other cause, thus subdue

6.

the supreme power that sett them up,
machine-tooled extricable values chooses health
preference to originality irritable peaching after fat and treason
care interrupts himself

★

a fabric of interlocked
observed measured imaging
non-linear brain dynamics

superposition of currents enables dendrites to
integrate their input
a western trapeze
engined by recentered thought onto

singularity of being a drive
to actualise all the power of possible intellection
archaic modernity crunched into
a multiple choc bar a new consciousness
of dignity and viciousness

wrapped in perfections and homohomo
transcendence become immanence become,
intensive appropriation of the multitude into
irreversible damage in which peace
becomes miserable humiliation escape
from death or prevention of aesthetic values
critique of truthfulness,
aesthetic moments different from intelligence
weight of engagement
to prevent unity

discard disinterestedness in favour of action.

constructed a list of less than a hundred

relief from fought-for imprecision
productive manifestations of nakedness
changes itself in accord
with consequences of the seen
destabilises cortices the
pattern of neural actions.

this lately renowned for the most civil and best ordered
in the world, and by us here smug at home
the most conscientious

Notes and Resources

1. Gravity

The following notes derive from a scan of the preface and twelve *Gravity* poems cross-referenced into the bibliography. The poems were made directly or indirectly relative to the first fifteen pages in William Blake's notebook, numbered by Erdman N1 to N15 (with the exclusion of those three solely attributed to drawings by Robert Blake [N3, N5 & N7]).

The Preface: Cage and Skilling.
African Boog: Martin's drawings to undermine any metrical completeness; Lotringer (in san serif face); Jakobson and Mayakovsky (in italics); Reid and Einstein (with inverted commas); Conrad, Ladzekpo, Tipper.
African Twist: Joris (in italics); *The Nation* (i) (in san serif face); Williams and *The Nation* (ii) (with inverted commas); Hofmann.
Around the World: calculations relating sub-atomic masses to; Brecht and Flaubert (in italics); Millers word list (in san serif face); MacDiarmid and Williams (with inverted commas); Crick, Dickens, Leacock, Leavis, *Protect and Survive*.
Atkins Stomp: Pound (with inverted commas); Miller's word list (in san serif face); George (in italics); *Investors Chronicle, Hansard,* Janson, Mandelbröt, Sedgwick.
Ballin' the Jack: Johnson, Link, Nutrition, *Protect and Survive*, Tankas, Waddington; a Chinese film titled *Two Sisters* (in italics).
Banda: Angry, Besharse, Beuys 1973, Einstein, Frescobaldi, Gris, Gorz, Jakobson, Jones, Messiaen, Misner, Meyers, Nicholson, Palmer, Reid.
Bel Air: Adorno, Diogenes (*Lives* and in Blunt), Eliot, Fanon, Gorz, Grinstein, Hammitzsch, Hofmann, Nietzsche, Leacock, Maritain, Misner, Moulton, Russell, Sweeney, Zeeman 1977, Zeldovich.
Birdland: Halliburton, Kristeva, Mallarmé, Reid.
Black Bottom: Mayan (with inverted commas); Beuys 1982, Char, Faye, Góngora, Klopstock, Ravel, Renders, Schwartz, Waddington, Wordsworth, Zeeman 1960.
Boogaloo: Albers, Arak, Close, Edwards, Hilton, Teper, Varèse.
Boogie Break: Garrison, Greimas, Glover, Grinstein, Hutter, Jameson, Knight, Kristeva, Lewis, Moulton, Onsager, Walls, Whalley, Zeeman 1979.
Boogie Stomp: Boublik, Calculus, Clusin, Dahlen, Keilmann, Neisser, Nunn, Olson, Poirier, Ritterbush, Salemme, Wilson.

Bibliography for *Brixton Fractals*:

Theodor W. Adorno. 'Theses Against Occultism' and 'The Stars Down to Earth', in *Telos*, 1974.
Josef Albers. *Interaction of Color*, Yale, 1963.
The Angry Brigade. Bombing of the American Express Building, street newspaper stand announcement, London, 1983.
Anthony Arak. 'Sexual selection by male-male competition in natterjack toad choruses', Cambridge, 1983.
Joseph C. Besharse and Michael Iuvone. 'Circadian clock in *Xenopus* eye controlling

retinal serotonin N-acetyltransferase', Atlanta, 1983.
Joseph Beuys exhibition at Anthony D'Offay Gallery, 1982.
Beuys. *Some artists, for example Joseph Beuys multiples, drawings, videotapes,* California (including conversations), 1973.
William Blake. *The Notebooks of William Blake* (facsimile), edited by David V. Erdman, Oxford, 1973: N97.
Anthony Blunt. *The Paintings of Nicolas Poussin, A Critical Catalogue*, London, 1966.
Blunt. *Nicholas Poussin*, London, 1967.
J.H. Boublik with M.J. Quinn, J.A. Clements, A.C. Herington, K.N. Wynne, and J.W. Funder 'Coffee contains potent opiate receptor binding activity', *Nature*, 1983.
Bertolt Brecht. American Poems 1941–47 and Last Poems 1953–56 in *Poems Part Three*, translations by Anderson, Bridgwater, Bowman, and Willett, London, 1976.
John Cage. *Themes and Variations*, New York, 1982.
The Open University. *Calculus of Fields, An Introduction to Calculus*, 1979.
René Char. *Feuillets d'Hypnos*, Paris, 1946.
Frank Close. 'Chromodynamics', *Nature* 1983.
William T. Clusin. 'Caffeine induces a transient inward current in cultured cardiac cells', *Nature*, 1983.
Joseph Conrad. *The Shadow-Line*, London, 1917.
Francis Crick and Graeme Mitchison. 'The function of dream sleep', Nature, 1983.
F.A. Dahlen. 'Simulation shows wobble period neither multiple nor variable', Princeton, 1983.
Charles Dickens, *Hard Times*, quoted in Hayman.
Diogenes Laertius. *Lives of Eminent Philosophers*, translation R.D. Hicks, London, 1925.
C.T.J. Dodson and T. Poston. *Tensor Geometry*, London, 1977.
C. Edwards. 'Glue balls', *Physical Review Letters*, 1983.
Albert Einstein. *Einstein, A Centenary Volume*, edited by A.P. French, London, 1979.
T.S. Eliot. *Four Quartets*, London, 1944 (1974 edition). See also Gardner.
Frantz Fanon. *A Dying Colonialism*, translation Chevalier, London, 1965.
Jean Pierre Faye. *Analogues*, Paris, 1964.
Paul Feyerabend. *Against Method*, London, 1975.
Gustave Flaubert. *Bouvard and Pecuchet*, translation Earp and Stonier, London, 1954.
Girolamo Frescobaldi. Organ music, BBC Radio 3: sudden mood changes; unprepared dissonances; rhythmic restlessness; jerky motifs, 1983.
Helen Gardner. *The Composition of Four Quartets*, London, 1978.
David L. Garrison with Stephen F. Ackley and Kurt R. Burk. 'A physical mechanism for establishing algal populations in frazil ice', Santa Cruz and New Hampshire, 1983.
Stefan George, 'Der hügel wowir wandeln'; 'Komm in den totgesagten'; and 'Wir shreiten auf und ab in reicher'.
James J. Gibson. *The Ecological Approach to Visual Perception*, Boston, 1979.
Malcolm Glover. 'Phase conjugate mirrors', Laser Division, Didcot, 1984.
Luis de Góngora. *Polyphemus and Galatea,* translation Cunningham, Edinburgh,1977.
André Gorz. *Farewell to the Working Class*, translation Sonenscher, London, 1982.
A.J. Greimas. 'Elements of Narrative Grammar', *Diacritics*, 1977.
G. Grinstein and John Toner. 'Abundant phase transitions', New York. See Moulton, &c., 1983.

Juan Gris' paintings in *The Essential Cubists* show at the Tate, 1983.
David Halliburton. *Poetic Thinking, An Approach to Heidegger*, Chicago, 1981: includes fragments translated from *Erläuterungen zu Hölderlins Dichtung*, Frankfurt, 1971.
Horst Hammitzsch. *Zen in the Art of the Tea Ceremony*, translation Lemesurier, London, 1979.
Hansard, 30th June 1983, Oral Answers, Rooker, Thatcher &c. Ronald Hayman. F.R. Leavis, a biography, London, 1976.
Roger Hilton. *Night Letters and selected drawings*, Newlyn, 1980.
Hans Hofmann. *Search for the Real*, 1948, MIT, 1968.
Kolumban Hutter. *Theoretical Glaciology*, London, 1983.
Investors Chronicle, July 1983, account of Thatcher and Leigh-Pemberton at lunch before his appointment as Governor of the Bank of England.
Roman Jakobson. *Verbal Communications*, San Francisco: includes fragments from Glinka, Kirsanov and Voznesensky, 1977.
Frederic Jameson. *The Political Unconscious*, London, 1981.
H.W. Janson and Dora Jane Janson. Description of Roman wall painting from Villa of Livia at Primaporta in *A History of Art*, London, 1977.
Diane Johnson reviews books on wildernesses, *New York Review of Books*, 1978.
David Jones. *Use & Sign*, Golgonooza Press, 1975.
Pierre Joris. A private letter to the author from Togo, 1983.
F. Keilmann and D.B. Kell. 'Non-linear systems: Coherent excitation in biology', Stuttgart and Aberystwyth, 1983.
Friedrich Klopstock (1811) *The Messiah* (1748–1800), translation Collyer and Meeke, London.
Charles A. Knight with Arthur L. DeVries and Larry D. Oolman. 'Fish antifreeze protein and the freezing and recrystallization of ice', Boulder and Illinois, 1984.
Julia Kristeva. *Desire in Language*, translation Gora, Jardine and Roudiez, New York, 1980.
C.K. Ladzekpo, interviewed by Melody Sumner and Sheila Davies, *Ear/West*, 1982.
Edwin H. Land. *The Retinex Theory of Color Vision*, San Francisco, 1977.
Eleanor Burke Leacock. *Myths of Male Dominance*, London, 1981.
Leavis, see Hayman.
Wyndham Lewis. *Enemy of the Stars* (facsimile of *Blast* 1 (1914), Santa Barbara, 1981.
Winston O. Link. Exhibition at The Photographers Gallery, London, 1983.
Sylvere Lotringer (ed) *German Issue of semiotext(e)*, New York: work from Lotringer, Paul Virilio, Heiner Müller, Jean Baudrillard, Helke Sander, Martin Heidegger, Joseph Beuys, Michel Foucault, &c., 1982.
Hugh MacDiarmid. 'The Goal of All the Arts' in *The Complete Poems*, London, 1978.
Stéphane Mallarmé see Kristeva.
Benoit B. Mandelbröt. *Fractals: Form, Chance, and Dimension*, San Francisco, 1977: includes discussion of Sierpinski's work.
Jacques Maritain. *Creative Intuition in Art and Poetry*, London, 1953/54.
Kenneth Martin. *Chance and Order*, drawings by Martin, Waddington Gallery, London, 1973.
Vladimir Mayakovsky. *How are Verses Made?* translation Hyde, London, 1970.
Mayan prayer, see Varèse.
Olivier Messiaen. Sleeve notes to *The Awakening of the Birds* and *Catalogue of Birds*, Neumann recording, 1967.

Jeffrey Meyers. *The Enemy, A biography of Wyndham Lewis*, London, 1980.
Richard Miller. Made in Togo, *Strange Faeces,* 1974.
John Milton, *Paradise Lost* (1974) edited by Alastair Fowler, London.
Charles W., Misner with Kip S. Thorne and John Archibald Wheeler (1973) *Gravitation*, San Francisco.
D.E. Moulton with A.H. Moudden, A.H. Wilson and J.D. Axe. 'Abundant phase transitions', *Physical Review Letters*, 1983.
The Nation, 1982 : (i) article by Peter H. Stone, December 25th, on re-employment of retired CIA field operatives; (ii) article by Giff Johnson, December 11th, on situation of inhabitants of Palau where the USA are siting a military base with nuclear equipment.
National Advisory Committee on Nutrition Education, commissioned by government and subsequently refused publication. Article in *Nature*, 1983, by member of committee.
Ulric Neisser. 'Memory Observed: Remembering in Natural Contexts', San Francisco, 1982.
Ben Nicholson. Exhibition at Kettles Yard, Cambridge, 1983.
Friedrich Nietzsche. *Thus Spake Zarathustra,* translation Hollingdale, London, 1961.
Nietzsche's Return, special issue of *semiotext(e)*: work from Bataille, Cage, Deleuze, Foucault, Lyotard, 1978.
David Norton and Lawrence Stark. *Eye Movements and Visual Perception*, San Francisco, 1971.
B.J. Nunn and D.A. Baylor. 'Visual transduction in retinal rods of the monkey *Macia fascicularis*', Stanford, 1982.
Charles Olson and Ezra Pound, *An Encounter at St. Elizabeths,* edited by Catherine Seelye, New York, 1975.
Lars Onsager with Eytan Domany and A.H. Wilson. 'Special solutions of the Ising-lattice problem in 3 dimensions', Stanford, 1984.
Samuel Palmer. *A Vision Recaptured: The Complete Etchings and The Paintings for Milton and Virgil* (facsimile), Trianon, 1978.
J.P. Poirier. 'Rheology of ices: a key to the tectonics of the ice moons of Jupiter and Saturn', Paris, 1982.
Nicos Poulantzas. *Fascism and Dictatorship,* translation White, London, 1974.
Ezra Pound. *The Pisan Cantos LXXIV–LXXXIV*, 1948, New Directions, 1970.
Pound. *Ezra Pound Speaking, Radio Speeches of World War II*: (2, 5, 111, 104 & 1), edited by Leonard W. Dobb, Connecticut, 1978.
Protect and Survive, H.M.S.O. 1982.
Maurice Ravel (1906). 'The Peacock', 'The Cricket', 'The Swan', 'The Kingfisher', and 'The Guinea-Fowl', by Jules Renards, used in Ravel's *Histoires naturelles.*
Constance Reid. *Hilbert*, a biography of the mathematician David Hilbert, London, 1970.
Elsie Renders. 'The gait of Hipparion sp. from fossil footprints in Laetoli, Tanzani', Utrecht, 1984.
Frank H.T. Rhodes. 'Gradualism, Punctuated equilibrium and the Origin of Species', Cornell, 1983.
Paul Ricoeur. *Freedom and Nature: The Voluntary and the Involuntary,* translation Kohák, Northwestern, 1966.
Philip C. Ritterbush. 'Dürer and geometry: Symmetry in an enigma', *Nature*, 1983.
Muriel Rukeyser. *Willard Gibbs*, New York, 1942.

Bertrand Russell. *History of Western Philosophy*, chapters regarding Rousseau and Voltaire, London, 1957.
F.R. Salemme. 'Cooperative motion and hydrogen exchange stability in protein beta-sheets', New Haven, 1982.
Jeffrey H. Schwartz. 'The evolutionary relationships of man and orang-utans', Pittsburgh, 1984.
Peter Sedgwick. *Psycho Politics*, London, 1982.
John Skilling. 'The maximum entropy method', Cambridge, 1984.
Pat Sweeney interviews the makers of *Carry Greenham Home*, Beeban Kidron and Amanda Richardson, handout at Cinema Action, 1984.
Tankas in the Gulbenkian Museum, Durham.
M. Teper and K. Einsweiler. *European Physical Security Conference*, Brighton, 1983.
René Thom. *Structural Stability and Morphogenesis*, translation Fowler, Massachusetts, 1975.
D'Arcy Wentworth Thompson. *On Growth and Form*, Cambridge, 1961.
J.C. Tipper. 'Rates of sedimentation, and stratigraphical completeness', *Nature*, 1983.
Edgar Varèse. *Ecuatorial*, including Mayan prayer translated in programme note, Royal Festival Hall, 1984. The performance included Jeanne Loriod and Cynthia Miller playing Ondes Martenots.
C.H. Waddington (ed.). *Towards a Theoretical Biology*: Vol. 1 *Prolegomena*; Vol. 3 *Drafts*; and Vol. 4 *Essays*, Edinburgh and Chicago, 1968, 1970, 1972. Includes work from Waddington, Lewis Wolpert and Christopher Zeeman.
D.F. Walls. 'Squeezed states of light, Hamilton', New Zealand, 1983.
E. Whalley and J. Poirier. 'Ices in the Solar System', Ottawa and Paris, 1984.
H. Whitney. 'On singularities of mappings of Euclidean spaces I. Mappings of the plane into the plane', *Ann. Math.* 2, 1955.
William Carlos Williams. *Autobiography*, New York, 1951.
Kenneth Wilson. Various discussions of his application of particle fields theory to analytical solutions of thermodynamic lattice problems and phase shifts, e.g. *Nature*, 1982.
Herman A. Witkin. *The Perception of the Upright*, San Francisco, 1959.
William Wordsworth (1827) Sonnet XLIV.
E.C. Zeeman. 'A Geometrical Model of Ideologies in Transformations', included in *Mathematical Approaches to Cultural Change*, 1979.
Zeeman. *Catastrophe Theory, Selected Papers 1972–77*, Massachusetts, 1977.
Zeeman. *Unknotting Sphere in Five Dimensions, Bulletin of the American Mathematical Society*, 1960.
Ya. B. Zeldovich, J. Einasto and S.F. Shandarin. 'Giant voids in the Universe', *Nature*, 1982.

Dispossession & Cure

Dirty Dog: Virginia Woolf (1931) *The Waves*.
The art referred to is exhibited at Knightsbridge Crown Court.

Accounts

An article, now lost, giving a floral chemical analysis of perfumes used by heads of state.
C.T.J. Dodson and T. Poston (1977) *Tensor Geometry, The Geometric Viewpoint and its uses*, London and Belmont, California.

Convalescence
Richard Bauman, *Verbal Art as Performance.*
Ruth Benedict, *Patterns of Culture.*
John Bellany in conversation on television, March 1989.
Jack Bilbo (1945) *Pablo Picasso: Thirty Important Paintings from 1904 to 1943*, London.
William Blake. *Notebook*, Erdman, 1973, N36–N39.
Elizabeth Barrett Browning, edited by Elizabeth Berridge (1974) 'A Curse for a Nation', 1856, and from her Diary beginning 4th June 1831.
W. Kates Burton, G.F. White (1978) *The Environment as Hazard.*
Cyril Connolly, Comment, *Horizon*, January 1940.
Jacopo Coppi, *Invention of Gun Powder*, one of the painting in the Studiolo of Francesco I de' Medici in the Palazzo Vecchio, Florence, c.1568-75.
Marguerite Duras (1985) *Le Douleur.*
Nigel Franks (1989) *The Swarms of Complexity,* reported by Matt Nicholson.
Stephen Spender (1989) *Waiting for the bombers.*
Adrian Stokes (1959) *Art and Science, A Study of Alberti, Piero della Francesca, and Giorgione*, London.
Thomas Traherne, 'On News', 'Desire', 'Nature', and 'Innocence'.
Journal of the Warburg and Courtauld Institutes, Volume 44, 1981.
Marcus Weisen (1987) 'Oxford unseen', *The British Journal of Visual Impairment*, Volume 1.

Work Consciousness Commodity: Three Kinds of Perception
Simone de Beauvoir (1984) *Adieux*, translation Patrick O'Brian, New York.
Phil Drabble (1969) *Badgers at my window,* London.
Allen Fisher. Chapter discussing the work of Joseph Beuys, 1985-86, in *Imperfect Fit, Aesthetic function, facture and reception*, 2016.
Peter Hardy, *A Lifetime of Badgers*, Newton Abbot, London.
Richard Hayman (1986) *Writing Against, A Biography of Sartre*, London.
Frederick Jameson (1961) *Sartre: The Origins of a Style*, New Haven.
Richard Perry (1978) *Wildlife in Britain and Ireland*, London.
Sartre by Himself (1978) translation Richard Seaver, New York.

Dispossession and Cure
Peter Brook interviewed in *Time*, 1991.
Filippo Brunelleschi, The Pazzi Chapel.
Ted Cohen and Paul Guyer (eds.)(1982) *Essays in Kant's Aesthetics*, Chicago and London.
Dante, *The Divine Comedy, Paradiso*, the end of Canto 33.
Gilles Deleuze (1963, 1984) *Kant's Critical Philosophy, The Doctrine of the Faculties*, translation Hugh Tomlinson and Barbara Habberjam, Minneapolis.
Domenico di Michel, fresco in S.Maria Fiore.
The Riddles from The Exeter Book, no.15, translation John Porter, Market Drayton, 1978.
E.H. Gombrich (1979) *The Sense of Order, A study on the psychology of decorative art*, London.
Jasper Johns (1973) interviewed in *Art News*, March.
Immanuel Kant (1960) *Observations on the Feeling of the Beautiful and Sublime,*

translation John T. Goldthwait, California.
Immanuel Kant (1928, 1952) *Critique of (Aesthetic) Judgement*, translation James Creed Meredith.
Benoit B. Mandelbröt (1977) *FRACTALS, Form, Chance, and Dimension*, San Francisco.
Martin Pawley (1990) *Eva Jiricna, Design in Exile*, London.
Joseph Paxton, Design for the Crystal Palace, 1851, redesigned for Sydenham Hill, 1852.
George Rhee, Las Cruces, New Mexico, reported measurement of the disputed Hubble constant, *Nature* 21.3.91.
Jean-Paul Sartre (1976) *Critique of Dialectical Reason*, Vol.1, *Theory of Practical Ensembles*, translation Alan Sheridan Smith, London.
Cyril Stanley Smith (1981) *A Search for Structure, Selected Essays on Science, Art and History,* MIT, Cambridge, Mass.
Springboard of Bristol, the stairs at Josephs in London, 1988, designed for Eva Jiricna.
Stratagene, 1991, Cambridge, Details on 'in style' cloning and designer genes.

The cover for *Fizz* included an eighteen century engraving by R.Scott proposed as the 'Exterior of the Ark' which is juxtaposed to Allen Fisher's photograph of the mill at Lugg Meadows, Hereford. The frontispiece included the following:
'Do not in your relations with your left-hand neighbour what annoys you if done at your right, nor in your relations to your right-hand neighbour what annoys you if done at your left. This is called having the compass and T-square of process.' Tseng's comments on Confucius' *Ta Hsio, The Great Digest*, Ezra Pound's 1928 translation.

2. Entanglement and Leans

Introduction to *Entanglement*

C. H. Bennett and S. J. Wiesner, 'Communication via one- and two-particle operators on Einstein- Podolsky-Rosen states', *Physical Review Letters*, 69 (1992), 2881-84.
C. H. Bennett et al., 'Purification of noisy entanglement and faithful teleportation via noisy channels', *Physical Review Letters*, 76 (1996), 722-25.
H. Bennett et al., 'Teleporting an unknown quantum state via dual classical and Einstein-Podolsky-Rosen channels', *Physical Review Letters,* 83 (1993), 3081-84.
Deitsch et al., 'Quantum privacy amplification and the security of quantum cryptography over noisy channels', *Physical Review Letters*, 77 (1996), 2818-21.
Ekert, 'Quantum cryptography based on Bell's theorem', *Physical Review Letters*, 67 (1991), 661-63.
Gottesman and I. L. Chuang, 'Demonstrating the viability of universal quantum computation using teleportation and single-qubit operations', *Nature* 402, 1999, 390-93.

Fish Jet

The poems in the group *Fish Jet* use a four co-ordinate structure. This structure scans visually as a folding cylinder marked in Fibonacci ratios which have been made asymmetrical by curvature and movement. The initial Cartesian co-ordinates of this scan are a rationalist physics of force and consciousness damaged by the philosophical ideas of Giambattista Vico and cross-cut with a history of the 1640s civil war viewed by a townsman remote from London.

In 'Jersey Bounce' these co-ordinates are intercepted by both the cultural studies of Paul Virilio and the non-Aristotelian work of Alfred Korzybski. In 'Fish' these co-ordinates are intercepted both by relativistic anthropology and commentaries on various conceptions of Beauty and judgement. In 'Fish' the bundle of narratives balances on discussions of gravity, levity and consciousness in the seventeenth-century works of Robert Hooke, Giovanni Alfonso Borelli, Gilles Personne de Roberval, Rene Descartes, John Locke and Isaac Newton. 'Jet' uses the structures of 'Fish' and 'Jersey Bounce' and adds ideas from twentieth century views on the seventeenth century work of Baruch Spinoza (particularly the 1968 work of Gilles Deleuze) and ideas transformed from the works of Richard Dawkins, Roger Penrose and Brandon Taylor.

In addition to those writers and scientists, texts by the following were used as the basis of derivations: Sir Thomas Browne, Christopher Hill, Thomas Hobbes, Edward Hyde, Ben Jonson, C. S. Lewis, John Locke, Sir Isaac Newton, Edmund Spenser, Rev. John Webb.

Now's the Time

Samuel Beckett, translations from Francisco de Terrazas, Fernan Gonzalez de Eslava, Bernardo de Balbuena and Juan Ruiz de Alarcon from his *Anthology of Mexican Poetry* (selected by Octavio Paz), London, 1959.
William Blake. *Notebook*, Erdman, 1973.
Peter Coveney and Roger Highfield, *The Arrow of Time,* London, 1990.
Francis Fukuyama, *The End of History and the Last Man*, London, 1992.
Erich Harth, *Dawn of a Millennium: Beyond Evolution and Culture*, London, 1990.
E. J. Hobsbawm, *Primitive Rebels*, London, 1971.
Peter and Ann MacTaggart, *Practical Gilding*, Chard, Somerset, 1984.
Ajit Mookerjee, *Yoga Art*, London, 1975.
Eric Mottram, *Estuaries: Poems 1989-91,* Twickenham, 1992.
Pearl, an anonymous 14th-century middle-English poem, in the Cawley and Anderson edition, London, 1962.
Andrew Porter's notes to the Vegh Quartet's recordings of Bartok's string quartets.

Two of the works alluded to in 'Jitterbug' are Joseph Beuys' sculpture *End of the Twentieth Century,* now in the Tate Gallery, London, and Marcel Duchamp's sculpture *The Bride Stripped Bare by Her Bachelors, Even* (often referred to as *The Great Glass*), now in Philadelphia [and Richard Hamilton's copy in the Tate].

Mummer's Strut

William Blake. *Notebook*, Erdman, 1973: N61.
Serge Bramly, *Leonardo: The Artist and the Man*, 1988, translation Sian Reynolds, London, 1992.
Cicero, *De Optimo Genere Oratorum, Topica*, translation H. M. Hubbell, London and Cambridge, Mass., 1976.
Kurt Cobain, fragments from his lyric sung for the Nirvana *Bleach* collection,1989.
William Cowper, 'Ode to Peace'.
Dante Alighieri, *The Divine Comedy*, Dent translation, 1909.

G. W F. Hegel, *Aesthetics: Lectures on Fine Art,* volume two, translation T. M. Knox, Oxford,1975.
Hugo von Hofmannsthal, *Buch der Freunde, Tagebuch-Aufzeikhnungen*, 1929.
Anthony Kenny, *The Legacy of Wittgenstein*, Oxford, 1984.
Peter Kropotkin, *The Conquest of Bread*, 1913.
The Notebooks of Leonardo da Vinci, 1988, reprinted 1992.
Helmuth Plessner, *Laughing and Crying: A Study of the Limits of Human Behavior*, translation Jane Spencer Churchill and Marjorie Grene, Northwestern University Press, Evanston, 1970.
Pliny, *Natural History*, volume nine, book XXXV, translation H. Rackham, Cambridge, Mass., 1968.
C. Quatremere de Quincy, *An Essay on the Nature, the End, and the Means if Imitation in the Fine Arts*, translation J. C. Kent, 1837; facsimile reprint, London, 1979.
Gottfried Semper, *The Four Elements if Architecture and Other Writings*, translation H. F. Mallgrave and W. Herrmann, Cambridge and New York, 1989.
Heinrich Tessenow, *House-Building and Such Things*, translation Wilfred Wang, London, 1989.
Eugène-Emmanuel Viollet-le-Duc, *Lectures on Architecture*, two volumes, translation Benjamin Bucknall, New York, 1987.
Vitruvius, *On Architecture*, volume one, book one, translation Frank Granger, London and Cambridge, Mass., 1983.

Pecking

Michel Foucault (1991), *Remarks on Marx, Conversations with Duccio Trombadori*, translation R. James Goldstein and James Cascaito, New York: Semiotext(e).
Ludwig H. Heydenreich,(1974), *Leonardo. The Last Supper*, London: Allen Lane.
Denise Riley (2000), *The Words of Selves. Identification, Solidarity, Irony*, Stanford: Stanford University Press.

Philly Dog

A. V. Arkhangelski and L. S. Pontrygin, eds. *General Topology 1: Basic Concepts and Constructions, Dimension Theory,* Springer-Verlag, 1990.
Rita J. Balice-Gordon and Jeff W. Lichtman, 'Long-term synapse loss induced by focal blockade of postsynaptic receptors', *Nature*, 1994.
Sir Thomas Browne, The Garden of Cyrus or The Quincunciall, Lozenqe, or Net-Work Plantations if the Ancients, Artificially, Naturally, Mystically Considered, 1658.
Aime Cesaire, 'Interlude', from *Solar Throat Slashed*, translation Clayton Eshleman and Annette Smith, 1983.
Charles Darwin, *The Origin of Species by Means of Natural Selection or The Preservation of Favoured Races in the Struggle For Life*, 1859.
Gilles Deleuze and Felix Guattari, *A Thousand Plateaus,* translation Brian Massumi, Minnesota, 1987.
J. Heinze, G. R. Mangun, W Burchert, H. Hinrichs, M. Scholz, T. F.Miinte, M. Scholz, A. Gos, M. Scherg, S. Johannes, H. Hundeshagen, M. S. Gazzaniga and S. A. Hillyard, 'Combined spatial and temporal imagining of brain activity during visual selective attention in humans', *Nature*, 1994.
Fazillskander, 'Memory of a School Lesson', in *Post-War Russian Poetry*, edited by Daniel Weissbort, 1974.

Anthony F. Michael, Nicholas R. Bata, Ken O. Buessler, Craig A. Carlson and Anthony H. Knap, 'Carbon-cycle imbalances in the Sargasso Sea', *Nature*, 1994.
Paul Ricoeur, *Time and Narrative*, volume one, Chicago, 1984.
James A. Spudich, 'How molecular motors work (What is the molecular basis of cell movementand changes in cell shape?)', *Nature*, 1994.
C. H. Waddington, *Tools for Thought*, St. Albans, 1977.
Douglas A. Weins, Jeffrey J. McGuire, Patrick J. Shore, Michael G. Befvis, Kitione Draunidalo, Gajendra Prasad and Saimone P. Helu. 'A deep earthquake aftershock sequence and implications for the rupture mechanism of deep earthquakes', *Nature*, 1994.
John Wieners, preface to *Cultural Affairs in Boston, Poetry and Prose 1956-1985*, 1988.
S. Yun, P. T. P. Ho and K. Y. Lo, 'A high-resolution image of atomic hydrogen in M81 group of galaxies', *Nature*, 1994.

Title page quotations for *Philly Dog* by Eric Mottram are from:
William Burroughs: *The Algebra of Need*, London, 1977.
'The American Imagination of Synthesis: Studies in American Culture in the Twentieth Century' (unpublished course notes given to the author in the early 1970s).
Introduction to *The Scripture of the Golden Eternity*, by Jack Kerouac, Totem/Corinth, New York, 1970.
'Pound, Olson, and *The Secret of the Golden Flower*', *Chapman*, 1972.

Pimp Walk
In addition to William Shakespeare's *King Lear*, 1608/1623, the text uses:
Carl B. Boyer, *A History of Mathematics*, 1968.
Serge Chermayeff and Alexander Tzonis, *Shape of Community, Realisation of Human Potential,* 1971.
John Clare, 'The Badger'.
Gilles Deleuze and Felix Guattari, *What is Philosophy?* 1991, translation 1994.
David Ruelle, *Chance and Chaos*, 1991.
William Shakespeare, *The Tragedie of Titus Andronicus*, 1594.

Epsilonics (delta-and-epsilon proofs) replace the heuristic devices and intuitive views promoted by traditionalist mathematics and poetics with critical precision. Karl Weierstrass and H. E. Heine, in the late 19th century, introduced a cold and precise limit of a function without suggestion of flowing entities generating magnitudes of higher dimensions, and without recourse to moving points or lines, or dropping of infinitely small quantities.

Pirate's Walk
T. W. Adorno, *Aesthetic Theory*, 1970.
Biotechnics journals, January-March 1995.
Jeanne Calment, on the radio, at 120 years old.
Fossing, V. A. Gallardo, R. N. Glud, J. K. Gundersen, J. Kuver, N. B. Ramseing, A. Testke, B. Thamdrup and O. Ulloa, 'Concentration and transport of nitrate by the mat-forming sulphur bacterium Thioploca', *Nature*, 1995.
Jin Xing after a sex change in April 1995.

Kenji Miyazawa, 'The Thief', c. 1920.
Miriam Rothschild (using discoveries made by Wendell Crew) described the worm *Halipequs* and its parasitic life cycle involving four different hosts, BBC television, 1995.
Jalaluddin Rumi, *Diviani Shamsi Tabriz*, 13th century.
Oliver Sacks, *Migraine, Understanding a Common Disorder*, revised edition 1985.
John Searle, *The Rediscovery of Mind*, MIT, 1992.
O. L. Wong, A. Chernjavsky, S. J. Smith and C. J. Shatz, 'Early functional neural networks in the developing retina', *Nature*, 1995.

Electricity from Sizewell B nuclear power station was connected to the National Grid in January 1995.

Pulling Up and Quasi Queen

Louis Althusser, *For Marx,* London, 1977.
Althusser with Etienne Balibar, eds. *Reading Capital*, London, 1970.
John Blofeld, 'Yogic Experience with Mescaline', *Psychedelic Review* 7, 1966.
Y. T. Chen and Alan Cook, *Gravitational Experiments in the Laboratory,* Cambridge, 1993.
Benedetto Croce, *Historical Materialism and the Economics of Karl Marx*, London, 1996.
P. J. Harvey interviewed, *Q* magazine, 1995.
G. W. F. Hegel, *Hegel's Logic*, translation W Wallace, Oxford, 1975.
Hegel, introduction to *Lectures on the Philosophy of World History,* translation H. B. Nisbet, Cambridge, 1975.
Hegel, *The Phenomenology of Spirit,* translation A. V. Miller, Oxford, 1977.
Hegel, *The Philosophy of Mind*, translation A. V. Miller, Oxford, 1971.
Hegel, *The Philosophy of Right,* translation T. M. Knox, Oxford, 1970.
Hegel, *The Science of Logic,* translation A. V. Miller, London, 1969.
Robert Heller, *The Naked Manager For the Nineties*, Little Brown, 1995.
Immanuel Kant, *Critique of Judgement*, translation J. H. Bernard, New York, 1951.
Georg Lukacs, *History and Class Consciousness*, translation R. Livingstone, Cambridge, Mass., 1971.
David Macey, *The Lives of Foucault*, London, 1993.
Herbert Marcuse, *Reason and Revolution*, Boston, Mass., 1960.
Karl Marx, *Capital: A Critique Political Economy*, ed. Friedrich Engels, translation Samuel Moore and Edward Aveling, 1954 (1983).
Marx and Engels, *Selected Correspondence: 1846-1895*, New York, 1965.
Marx Engels Werke, Dietz Verlag, Berlin, 1961-66, translation and selected by Allen Wood in *Karl Marx: The Argument of the Philosophers*, RK&P, 1981 (particularly *Anti-Duhring, Grundrisse, Dialectics of Nature* and *Theories of Surplus Value*).
Novabiochem, 'Combinatorial Chemistry', 1995.
Prasanna de Silva, H. Q. Himal Gunaratne and Colin P. McCoy, 'A molecular photoionic AND gate based on fluorescent signalling', *Nature* 368, 1993.
Tiltinen, J. Sinkkonen, K. Reinikainen, K.Alho, J. Lavikainen and R. Naatanen, 'Selective attention enhancers, the auditory 40-Hz transient response in humans', *Nature* 364, 1993.
Raphael Tsu, letter to *Nature* 364, 1993.

Ring Shout
Kenneth L. Alvin, *The Observer's Book of Lichens*, illustrated by Claire Dalby and K. A. Kershaw, London, 1977.
Walter Benjamin, *Selected Writings, Volume 1: 1913-26*, edited by Marcus Bullock and Michael W Jennings, Harvard, 1997.
William Blake. *Notebook*, Erdman, 1973.
Momme Brodersen, *Walter Beniamin.A Biography,* 1997.
Nicholas Campion, *The Great Year: Astrology, Millenarianism and History in the Western Tradition*, Penguin, 1994.
Chin Chiang, Ying Litingtung, Eric Lee, Keith E. Young, Jeffrey L. Corden, Heiner Westphal and Philip A. Beachy, 'Cyclopia and defective axial patterning in mice lacking Sonic hedgehog gene function', *Nature* 383, 1996.
Patricia S. Church land and Terrence J. Sejnowski, *The Computational Brain,* Cambridge, Mass.,1992.
The Epicurus Reader: Selected Writings and Testimonia, edited and translated by Brad Inwood and L. P. Gerson, Indianapolis, 1994.
Albert Goldbetter, *Biochemical Oscillations and Cellular Rhythms: The Molecular Basesof Periodic and Chaotic Behaviour*, Cambridge, 1996.
Cornelia Hesse-Honegger, *After Chernobyl,* touring exhibition at The Hancock Museum, Newcastle-upon-Tyne; Oxford University Museum; Tullie House Museum, Carlisle; July 1996-January 1997.
Jill Johnston, *Jasper Johns, Privileged Information*, London and New York, 1996.
Rosalind E. Krauss, *The Optical Unconscious*, Cambridge, Mass., 1993.
Jack R. Laundon, *Lichens*, Aylesbury, 1986.
Andre Malraux, *Man's Estate*, 1933, translated as *Storm in Shanghai,* Alastair MacDonald, London, 1938.
Shirley Manson interview, *The Times*, 30th November, 1996.
Paige Mitchell, letter to Hugh Barton, 13th February, 1997.
S. J. Mojzsis, G. Arrhenius, K. D. McKeegan, T. M. Harrison, A. P. Nutman, and C. R. L. Friend, 'Evidence for life on Earth before 3,800 million years ago', *Nature* 384, 1996.
Rudolf A. Raff, *The Shape of Life: Genes, Development, and the Evolution of Animal Form*, Chicago, 1996.
Damian Thompson, *The End ofTime: Faith and Fear in the Shadow of the Millennium*, London, 1996.
Keith Vaughan , *Journals 1939-1977*, London, 1983.
Lawrence Walker's recall of service with a tank regiment in Iraq,
John Wargo, *Our Children's Toxic Legacy: How Science and Law Fail to Protect Us From Pesticides*, Yale, 1996.
A. Whitbread, *Herefordshire Inventory of Ancient Woodlands (Provisional),* Nature Conservancy Council, August 1986.
Alfred North Whitehead, *Process and Reality, An Essay in Cosmology*, New York and London, 1929.
Emile Zola, *The Beast in Man*, translation Alec Brown, London, 1956.

Slop
Francis Bacon (1601). *Essays*, with annotations by Richard Whately, London, 1876.
M. Bajcsy, A.S. Zibrow and M.D. Lukin. 'Stationary pulses of light in an atomic

medium', *Nature*, 426, 2003.
William Blake. *Notebook*, Erdman, 1973: N97.
Mark Bowden. 'It all depends on what you mean by torture', *The Atlantic Monthly*, 2002.
Neil Jorgense. *A Guide to New England's Landscape*, Chester, Connecticut, 1977.
Y. R.C. Kato, Myers, A.C. Gossard and D. D. Awschalom. 'Coherent spin manipulation without magnetic fields in strained semiconductors', *Nature*, 427, 2004.
Edmund Spenser (1596). Two Cantos of Mutabilitie in *Faerie Queene*, Book VII, London.

Slow Drag
Alciati (1531). *Emblematum liber.*
S. Aumaitre, S. Fauve, S. McNamara and P. Poggi. European *Physics* J.B. 19, 449–460 and *Nature*, 424, 2001.
William Blake. *Notebook*, Erdman, 1973: N96.
B.B. Blinov, D.L. Moehring, L.-M. Duan and C. Monroe. 'Observation of entanglement between a single trapped atom and a single photon', *Nature*, 428, 2004.
Jirí Fajkus, Kvet, a Koppová and Zuzana Kunická. 'Dual-color real-time telomeric repeat amplification protocol' in *BioTechniques*, 35, 2003: 912–914.
A.V. Gaponov-Grekhov and M.I. Rabinovich. *Nonlinearities in Action Oscillations Chaos Order Fractals*, Berlin, Heidelberg and New York, &c.: Springer-Verlag, 1992.
Michael Hudson. *Super Imperialism. The Origin and Fundamentals of U.S. World Domination*, London &c.: Pluto Press, 2003.
Helge Kragh. *Quantum Generations*, Princeton, New Jersey: Princeton.University Press, 1999.
Thomas Munro. T*oward Science in Aesthetics, Selected Essays*, Indianapolis, New York and Kansas City: Bobbs-Merrill, 1956.
Gerhard Richter. *Gerhard Richter—Atlas*, edited by Iwana Blazwick and Janna Graham, London: Whitechapel, 2003.
Shelley (1816 and 1817). 'Hymn to Intellectual Beauty' and 'Loan and Cythna or The Golden City' in Neville Rogers. *The Complete Poetical Works of Percy Bysshe Shelley*, Vol. II, Oxford: The Clarendon Press, OUP, 1975.

Snake Hips
Giorgio Agamden. *Homo Sacer. Sovereign Power and Bare Life*, Stanford, 1998.
Catherine Clément. *Syncope. The Philosophy of Rapture*, Minneapolis, 1994.
Andrea Dworkin. *Intercourse*, London, 1987.
Ernst Fehr and Bettina Rockenbach. 'Detrimental effects of sanctions on human altruism', *Nature*, 422, 2004.
Interview with Sylvie Guillem, September 2004.
Emmanuel Levinas. *Time and the Other*, Pittsbugh, 1987.
Mary Lydon, Lawrence R. Schehr et al. *Jean-François Lyotard: Time and Judgement*, Yale French Studies, 1999.
Alain Robbe-Grillet, *Topology of a Phantom City*, London, 1978.

Sojourns
The Big Issue 238, 23-29 June 1997, 'Glastonbury, Should the fence come down?'

Matthew Mitchell and Mordechai Segev, 'Self-trapping of incoherent white light', *Nature* 387, 1997.
Gillian Rudd, *Managing Language in Piers Plowman*, D. S. Brewer, Cambridge, 1994.

Diayostelium discoideum is a social amoeba which in preamble to morphogenesis consists of a gathering together of widely dispersed individual cells, mediated by their periodic relaying of a chemotactic signal from a pacemaker cell. (Discussed by Arthur T. Winfree, *The Geometry of Biological Time*, 1980.)

Spinor

Diana Kormos Buchwald. 'Into the unknown', review of Richard Panek, *The Invisible Century: Einstein, Freud, and the Search for Hidden Universes*, *Nature*, 430, 2004.
Mayer Hillman. *How We Can Save the Planet*, London, Penguin, 2004.
Jochen Mannhart and Darrell G. Schlom. 'The value of seeing nothing', *Nature*, 430, 2004.
David A. Muller, Naoyuki Nakagawa, Akira Ohtomo, John L. Grazul and Harold Y. Hwang. 'Atomic-scale imaging of nanoengineered oxygen vacancy profiles in SrTiO3', *Nature*, 430, 2004.
James M. Murphy, David M.H. Sexton, David N Barnett, Gareth S. Jones, Mark J. Webb, Matthew Collins and David A. Stainforth. 'Quantification of modelling uncertainties in a large ensemble of climate change simulations', *Nature*, 430, 2004.
Alain Robbe-Grillet. *The Immortal One*, translation A. M. Sheridan Smith, London: Calder & Boyars, 1971.

Stamping Sequence

D.R. Bellwood, T.P. Hughes, C. Folke and M. Nyström. 'Confronting the coral reef crisis', *Nature*, 429, 2004.
'Trisha Brown in conversation with Yvonne Rainer', New York: *Bomb: artists, writers, actors, directors*, Fall, 1993.
John Milton (1644). *Areopagitica*.

Stroll

Theodor W. Adorno. *Aesthetic Theory*, newly translated by Robert Hullot-Kentor, London, 1997.
Isabel Armstrong. *The Radical Aesthetic*, Oxford, 2000.
Neil Belton. *The Good Listener. Helen Bamber: A Life Against Cruelty*, London, 1998.
Catherine Clément (1994) *Syncope. The Philosophy of Rapture*, translation Sally O'Driscoll and Deirdre M. Mahoney, Minneapolis.
Rolf Crook, Abi C. Graham, Chareles G. Smith, Ian Farrer, Harvey E. Beere and David A. Ritchie. 'Erasable electrostatic lithography for quantum components' *Nature*, 424, 2003.
Antonio Damasio. *The Feeling of What Happens. Body, Emotion and the Making of Consciousness*, London, 2000.
Michael Hardt and Antonio Negri. *Empire*, Harvard, 2000.
Martin Heidegger. *The Metaphysical Foundations of Logic*, translation Michael Heim, Indiana, 1992.
Hilary Lawson. *Closure, A Story of Everything*, London and New York, 1992.
Tom Lutz. Crying, *The Natural and Cultural History of Tears*, New York, 1999.

Bridget Riley. *The Eye's Mind: Bridget Riley, Collected Writings 1965–1999*, edited by Robert Kudielka, London, 1999.
Denise Riley. 'On Julia Ball's Paintings' in Rachel Fleming-Mulford and Jeremy Mulford (eds.). *Out of Light. The Work of Julia Ball*, Bristol: Falling Wall Press, 2002.
Meyer Schapiro. *Theory and Philosophy of Art: Style, Artist, and Society, Selected Papers*, New York, 1994.
Amartya Sen. *Rationality and Freedom*, Cambridge, Mass., and London, 2002.
Susan Sontag. 'The fragile alliance', *The Guardian*, 18.10.03.
James A.Theobald, Beil S. Oxtoby, Michael A. Phillips, Neil R. Champness and Peter H. Beton. 'Controlling molecular deposition and layer structure with supramolecular surface assemblies' *Nature*,424, 2003.
V.N. Volosinov (1929). *Marxism and the Philosophy of Language*, translation Matejka, Ladislav and Titunik, New York, 1973.

Watusi
Ascesis: practice of self-discipline.
Birefringent: doubly refracting.
Cistron: section of chromosome which controls protein structure.
Definity: neologism from infinity proposed as defined and/or contained.
Dieqesic: narration of the facts.
Kinetosis: motion sickness.
Prolepsis: rhetorical figure of anticipation.
Synaloepha: melting of a final vowel or diphthong into initial vowel or diphthong of next word.

Winging Step
The printed visual presentation for 'Winging Step' included a graphic view of 53 clustered gene duplications between the 16 chromosomes of burglar. Each chromosome was represented by a bold horizontal line. All chromosomes were aligned according to the centromere, shown as a vertical line. Gene clusters were represented by the stolen tones. A cluster is detected if, within a window of 25kb, at least 5 blocks of coding DNA (block size 500 nucleotides) are duplicated in a synthetic way. Tys and both telomeres were filtered out because these sequences are known to be highly repetitive.

Wobble
The *occipital lobes* are at the back part of the human brain.
wring their barriers ...: Gerald Manley Hopkins, 'The Caged Skylark' (1877).
And all to spare ...: William Langland, *Piers Plowman* (c. 1379).
aestivation, summer retreat
commissures, bands of nerve-substance which connect parts of the brain
nieve, clenched hand, fist
Amitabha Buddha, the sculpture on the British Museum west stairs.
isochore, a curve representing variation under conditions of constant volume.
Free from cratylic delusions: Paul de Man, *Aesthetic Ideology* (1996).
Singest with vois memorial ...: Geoffrey Chaucer.
scriven, written by pen
anatropy, a turned back ovule attached to a funicle, which thus becomes a ridge on the ovule

norepinephrine and dopamine, amine neurotransmitters involved in focused attention
cicatrised, forming scar tissue in process of healing
Lay weaving on the tissue ...: S. T. Coleridge, 'Stanzas Addressed to a Lady on Her Recovery with Unblemished Looks, from a Severe Attack of Pain' (1827).
acetylcholine, amine neurotransmitter which generates tract from septum to hippocampus and to cerebral cortex, involved in sustained memory and learning.

Woodpecker

H.C. (Cornelius) Agrippa, 'De incertitudine et vanitate scientarium et artium', 1530, in Jurgis Baltrusaitis, *Anamorphic Art*, 1969, translation W J. Strachan, Cambridge, 1976.
Hart Crane, *Complete Poems if Hart Crane*, ed. Marc Simon, New York, 2000.
Elizabeth Cropper and Charles Dempsey, *Nicholas Poussin. Friendship and the Love of Painting*, New Jersey, 1996.
Alastair Fowler, introduction to John Milton, *Paradise Lost*, second edition, London, 1998.
Luce Irigaray, *I Love to You: Sketch of a Possible Felicity.* in *History*, translation Alison Martin, London, 1996.
Edvard Lieber, *Willem De Kooning: Reflections in the Studio*, New York, 2000.
John O'Mahony, *'Reports from the world's only radioactive nature reserve'*, London, 1999.
Plato, *Cratylus*, translation B. Jowett, Oxford, 1875.
Jules Romains, *The Body's Rapture*, translation John Rodker, Oxford, 1932.
Ricarda A. Steinbrecher, 'What is Genetic Engineering?' in *The Gene Files*, London: Women's Environmental Network, 2000.
Chris Stephens, Peter Lanyon: *At the Edge if Landscape*, London, 2000.
James Thomson, *The Castle if Indolence*, 1748.
Max Velman, *Understanding Consciousness*, London, 2000.

Plasmids are small rings of DNA with a limited number of genes. They are relatively small, separated from chromosomes and thus quickly replicable and are easy to manipulate and study.
Pleiotropic effects are unpredictable side effects consequent of genetic engineering.
Poly- adenylation: the process in which, following the transcription of information to RNA, an addition is made to the tail in the form of a string of up to 200 'A' type nucleotides initiated by a poly 'A' Signal located towards the end of the gene.
PCR (polymerase chain reaction) is a technique for rapidly producing many copies of a fragment of DNA for diagnostic or research purposes.
Polymerases are enzymes that catalyse the synthesis of a polymer, especially the synthesis of DNA or RNA.
Polymers are naturally occurring or synthetic compounds, such as starch or Perspex , that have large molecules made up of many relatively simple repeated units.

Afterword
Leans is the condition experienced by jet pilots as they leave the Earth's gravity.

Acknowledgments

Brixton Fractals was first published by Aloes Books, London, 1985 and republished by Tsunami, Vancouver, 1999. Thanks are due Michael Barnholden, Nate Dorward, and Deanna Ferguson. All of the poems in *Brixton Fractals* appeared before those publications, sometimes in earlier drafts. Thanks for support go to Ric and Ann Caddel, Ken Edwards, Dick Ellis, Clayton Eshleman, Geoffrey Godbert, Pierre Joris, Peter Middleton, Eric Mottram, Sylvia Paskin, Jay Ramsay, Jerome Rothenberg and Tim Woods for their support. Other earlier books include *African Boog,* Ta'wil Books, London 1983; *Banda*, Spanner/Open Field, London, 1983; *Boogie Break*, Torque Editions, Southampton 1985.

Breadboard was first published by Spanner, Hereford, 1994. Most of the poems in *Breadboard* appeared before that publication. Thanks for their support go to Tony Baker, Marzia Balzani, Hanne Bramness, Chris Broadribb, Adrian Clarke, Tim Fletcher, Ulli Freer, Pierre Joris, Steven Pereira, Tom Raworth, Spencer Selby, Robert Sheppard, Stephen Want, and Shamoon Zamir. *Buzzards and Bees* was published as a book by Spanner, 1986 and republished by microbrigade, London, 1987.

Civic Crime was first published by Sound & Language, Lowestoft, 1995. Thanks are due to cris cheek and Sianed Jones. Most of the poems in *Civic Crime* appeared before that publication. Thanks for their support go to Cydney Chadwick, Tim Coppard, John Cornall, John Cussans, Ken Edwards, Steve Lewis, D.S. Marriott, Geoff Mowam, David Rhodes, and Pat Smith. *Camel Walk* first appeared as a *Spanner* broadsheet, Hereford, 1988.

Dispossession & Cure was first published by Reality Street Editions, London and Saxmundham, Suffolk, 1994. Thanks are due to Ken Edwards and Wendy Mulford. Most of the poems in *Dispossession & Cure* appeared before that publication. Thanks for support go to Marzia Balzani, Hanne Bramness, Cydney Chadwick, Andrew Duncan, Andrew Lawson, Anthony Mellors, Lawrence Upton, Stephen Want and Shamoon Zamir. Earlier books include: *Convalescence*, Wiwaxia, London, 1992; *Work Consciousness Commodity: Three Kinds of Perception*, Spanner 1989 and revised Spanner 1990; *Horse and Hubble*, RWC, Surrey, 1992.

Fizz was first published by Spanner, Hereford, 1994. Many of the poems in *Fizz* appeared before that publication. Thanks go to Jeremy Hilton, Pierre Joris, Peter Manson, Rod Mengham, Robin Purves, Peter Riley, and Alaric Sumner. *Jerk* appeared as a broadsheet, Ta'wil Books & Documents, Encinitas, California, 1991.

Now's the Time was first published by form books, London, 1995. Thanks for his support to Harry Gilonis.

Most of the poems in *Disaster Bag* and *Tools or Traps & Damage* were published in the 1990s in a variety of journals and magazines. Thanks for their support go to Adrian Clarke, Andrew Duncan, Ulli Freer, Robert Hampson, Nicholas Johnson, Peter Quartermain, Peterjon Skelt and Lawrence Upton.

'Itch' was published in *One for jimmy*, 1992, edited by Matthew Sweeney. 'Jerk' was first published as a broadsheet by Ta'wil Books & Documents, Encinitas. Thanks for his support to Pierre Joris. 'Mambo' was published in the Picador anthology *Conductors of Chaos* in 1996. Thanks for his support to Iain Sinclair.

Philly Dog first appeared as a Spanner chapbook in 1995.

Pulling Up and Quasi Queen first appeared as an issue of *Spanner* in 1996. Parts of this work were published before this edition. For having first shown parts of this work, thanks are due to Miles Champion, Richard Caddel and Peter Middleton.

Fish Jet was first published by Torque Press, Southampton and Aberystwyth, 1995. Thanks for their support are due to Peter Middleton and Tim Woods. Parts of the text were published earlier in *Angel Exhaust* and *Parataxis*. Thanks for their support go to Adrian Clarke, Andrew Duncan and Drew Milne. Thanks also to musician Lol Coxhill, who intercepted the first reading from the work at the joint Sub Voicive reading and *Eonta* launch at Compendium Books, 1991.

Ring Shout first appeared as an Equipage chapbook in 2000. Thanks for his support are due to Rod Mengham. Parts of this work were published before this edition in *Crayon*, 1997, New York. Thanks for their support are due to Andrew Levy and Bob Harrison.

'Running in Place', 'Scronch', 'Shag', 'Shango' and 'Shika' first appeared in the chapbook *Sojourns*, published by Wild Honey Press in 2000. Thanks for his support are due to Randolph Healy.

All the poems in *Sledge Trap* appeared in earlier publications. 'Skate' first appeared in *The Gig*. Thanks are due to Nate Dorward for his support. 'Shorty George' first appeared in *Sulfur*. Thanks are due to Clayton Eshleman for his support. 'Tensor' was first published online in the *Alterran Poetry Assemblage* and subsequently in *Fire*, Oxfordshire. Thanks are due to David Dowker and Jeremy Hilton.

'Vole' was first published in *Neon Highway*. 'Volespin' was first published in *The Gig*. Thanks are due to Alice Lenkiewicz and Nate Dorward for their support. *Vole Volespin* appeared as a Spanner chapbook in 2002 and in a performance published as a Root & Branch videotape by Paige Mitchell in 2003.

'Waddle' was first published in 2001 as part of an exchange with Karen Mac Cormack online at *Philly talks*. Thanks are due to Louis Cabri and Aaron Levy.

Watusi first appeared in 2001 as a Spanner chapbook. Thanks are due to Peter Riley and Wendy Mulford, who included part of the poem in *A Meeting for Douglas Oliver*, published in 2002 by infernal methods, Street Editions and Poetical Histories.

Winging Step first appeared in text form on the *Jacket* web journal, 2000. Thanks are dueto John Tranter. A special visual-text edition was subsequently published by Spanner, 2000.

‘Wobble’ first appeared in linear text form in *Poetry Salzburg Review*. Thanks are due to the editor, Wolfgang Gortschacher.

Woodpecker first appeared as a Spanner chapbook in 2001.

‘X-Buckle" first appeared in *Fulcrum*. Thanks are due to the editors, Philip Nikolayev and Katia Kapovich. The work is also featured in the video *Vole Volespin*.
‘Watusi’, ‘Tensor’ and ‘Ring Shout’ appear on the audio CD *Gravity Shapes* published by Stem, 2004. Thanks are due to Rob Holloway.

Stroll & Strut Step first appeared as a book with three *Meditation Studies* published by Spanner, 2004.

‘Olbolo’ first appeared on *Argotist*.
‘Oleke’ in *Pilot*.
‘Papa Doc Walk’ in *Spanner*.
‘Pasmala’ in *The Gig*.
‘Shuffle’ in a *Subvoicive* programme.
‘Slop’ on the *Great Works* site.
‘Slow Drag’ in *On Literature and Science. Essays, Reflections, Provocations*, edited by Philip Coleman, Four Courts Press, Dublin, 2007.
Sway Back as an edition of *Tolling Elves* with a graphic by John Wall.
Part of ‘Swim’ in *Rentner*.
‘Trucking’ on *Aterran*.
‘Turkey Trot’ on *Lollipo*.
‘Twist’ in *Queen Street Quarterly*, Toronto.
‘Twisted Camel’ on *PORES*.
‘Underbelly Jump’ in *Quid*.
‘Yanayallow’ in *The Paper*, Sheffield.

Thanks are due to Matthew Chambers, Philip Coleman, Nate Dorward, Thomas Evans, Bill Griffiths, David and Christine Kennedy, Peter Philpott, Robert Sheppard, Will Rowe, Keston Sutherland and Andrea Brady, Lawrence Upton, Adam Laurence and the Rentner Collective, Karen Mac Cormack, Jeffrey Side and Suzanne Zelazo.

Stroll & Strut Step and all the poems from ‘Oleke’ to ‘Yanayallow’ appeared in *Leans, Gravity as a consequence of shape, volume 3*, published by Salt Publishing, Cambridge, 2007, reprinted in 2013. Thanks to Chris and Jennifer Hamilton-Emery.

Author's Note

All of the poems that constitute *Gravity as a consequence of shape* are collected in this volume. They were all collected, along with the texts and poems from *Ideas of the culture dreamed of*, in three volumes:
Gravity (2004)(published by Salt Publishing, Cambridge, UK and Applecross, Western Australia);
Entanglement (2004)(published by The Gig, Willowdale, Canada);
Leans (2007 and 2013)(published by Salt Publishing, Cambridge, UK).
My grateful thanks to Chris and Jennifer Hamilton-Emery and to Nate Dorward for their extended work on these volumes.

The texts from *Ideas of the culture dreamed of now* appear as a separate publication.

For his continued support over many years and for his attention and work on *Gravity as a consequence of shape*, my extended and grateful thanks to Ken Edwards.
All of the work in this book owes considerable thanks to Paige Mitchell, my co-worker in the studio, garden and streets.

REALITY STREET titles in print

Poetry series

Kelvin Corcoran: *Lyric Lyric* (1993)
Maggie O'Sullivan: *In the House of the Shaman* (1993)
Fanny Howe: *O'Clock* (1995)
Maggie O'Sullivan (ed.): *Out of Everywhere* (1996)
Cris Cheek/Sianed Jones: *Songs From Navigation* (1997)
Lisa Robertson: *Debbie: An Epic* (1997)
Maurice Scully: *Steps* (1997)
Denise Riley: *Selected Poems* (2000)
Lisa Robertson: *The Weather* (2001)
Lawrence Upton: *Wire Sculptures* (2003)
Ken Edwards: *eight + six* (2003)
Redell Olsen: *Secure Portable Space* (2004)
Peter Riley: *Excavations* (2004)
Allen Fisher: *Place* (2005)
Tony Baker: *In Transit* (2005)
Jeff Hilson: *stretchers* (2006)
Maurice Scully: *Sonata* (2006)
Maggie O'Sullivan: *Body of Work* (2006)
Sarah Riggs: *chain of minuscule decisions in the form of a feeling* (2007)
Carol Watts: *Wrack* (2007)
Jeff Hilson (ed.): *The Reality Street Book of Sonnets* (2008)
Peter Jaeger: *Rapid Eye Movement* (2009)
Wendy Mulford: *The Land Between* (2009)
Allan K Horwitz/Ken Edwards (ed.): *Botsotso* (2009)
Bill Griffiths: *Collected Earlier Poems* (2010)
Fanny Howe: *Emergence* (2010)
Jim Goar: *Seoul Bus Poems* (2010)
James Davies: *Plants* (2011)
Carol Watts: *Occasionals* (2011)
Paul Brown: *A Cabin in the Mountains* (2012)
Maggie O'Sullivan: *Waterfalls* (2012)
Peter Hughes: *Allotment Architecture* (2013)
Andrea Brady: *Cut From the Rushes* (2013)
Bill Griffiths: *Collected Poems & Sequences* (2014)
Peter Hughes: *Quite Frankly* (2015)
Emily Critchley (ed.): *Out of Everywhere 2* (2015)
Bill Griffiths: *Collected Poems Volume 3* (2016)

Narrative series

Ken Edwards: *Futures* (1998, reprinted 2010)
John Hall: *Apricot Pages* (2005)
David Miller: *The Dorothy and Benno Stories* (2005)
Douglas Oliver: *Whisper 'Louise'* (2005)
Paul Griffiths: *let me tell you* (2008)
John Gilmore: *Head of a Man* (2011)
Richard Makin: *Dwelling* (2011)
Leopold Haas: *The Raft* (2011)
Johan de Wit: *Gero Nimo* (2011)
David Miller (ed.): *The Alchemist's Mind* (2012)
Sean Pemberton: *White* (2012)
Ken Edwards: *Down With Beauty* (2013)
Philip Terry: *tapestry* (2013)
Lou Rowan: *Alphabet of Love Serial* (2015)

For updates on titles in print, a listing of out-of-print titles, and to order Reality Street books, please go to www.realitystreet.co.uk. *For any other enquiries, email* info@realitystreet.co.uk *or write to the address on the reverse of the title page.*

Reality Street has depended since 1998 for its existence on the Reality Street Supporters scheme. We are grateful to all Reality Street Supporters over the years.

Visit our website at: **www.realitystreet.co.uk**

Reality Street Supporters who have sponsored this book:

Nigel Alderman
Joanne Ashcroft
Alan Baker
Peter Bamfield
Tina Bass
Chris Beckett
Charles Bernstein
C D Blanton
John Bloomberg-Rissman
Jasper Brinton
Manuel Brito
Peter Brown
Clive Bush
Duncan Campbell
Matthew Carbery
John Cayley
Cris Cheek
Stephen Clews
Simon Collings
Clare Connors
Ian Davidson
David Dowker
Laurie Duggan
Rachel DuPlessis
Carrie Etter
Clive Fencott
Jim Goar & Sang-yeon Lee
Paul Griffiths
Chris Gutkind
Catherine Hales
John Hall
Jeff Hilson
Peter Hodgkiss
Rob Holloway
Peter Hughes
Michael Hunt
Keith Jebb
Pierre Joris
Linda Kemp
Lisa Kiew
Joshua Kotin
Steve Lake
Chris Lord
Michael Mann
JCC Mays
James McDonald
Ian Mcewen
Maggie O'Sullivan
Richard Parker
Gareth Prior
Tom Quale
Josh Robinson
Samuel Rogers
Lou Rowan
Robert Sheppard
Iain Sinclair
Jason Skeet
Yasmin & Peterjon Skelt
Valerie Soar
Harrison Sullivan
Andrew Taylor
Michael Tencer
Philip Terry
Scott Thurston
Keith Tuma
Lawrence Upton
Stephen Want
Sam Ward
Carol Watts
Michael Whitworth
John Wilkinson
Tyrone Williams
Lissa Wolsak
Anonymous x 1

www.ingramcontent.com/pod-product-compliance
Lightning Source LLC
Chambersburg PA
CBHW030815190426
43197CB00036B/478

* 9 7 8 1 8 7 4 4 0 0 7 2 1 *